THE CHALLENGE
OF THE
AMERICAN
REVOLUTION

OTHER BOOKS BY EDMUND S. MORGAN

*The Puritan Family: Religion and Domestic Relations
in Seventeenth-Century New England*

*Virginians at Home: Family Life
in the Eighteenth Century*

*The Stamp Act Crisis: Prologue to Revolution
(with Helen M. Morgan)*

The Birth of the Republic

The Puritan Dilemma: The Story of John Winthrop

The Gentle Puritan: A Life of Ezra Stiles

Visible Saints: The History of a Puritan Idea

Roger Williams: The Church and the State

So What about History?

*American Slavery—American Freedom:
The Ordeal of Colonial Virginia*

EDITED WORKS

*Prologue to Revolution: Sources and Documents
on the Stamp Act Crisis*

*The Diary of Michael Wigglesworth: The Conscience
of a Puritan*

Puritan Political Ideas

*The Founding of Massachusetts: Historians
and the Sources*

*The American Revolution: Two Centuries
of Interpretation*

THE
CHALLENGE
OF THE
AMERICAN
REVOLUTION

by Edmund S. Morgan

W · W · NORTON & COMPANY

New York · London

W. W. Norton & Company, Inc., 500 Fifth Avenue, New York, N.Y. 10110
W. W. Norton & Company Ltd., 37 Great Russell Street, London WC1B 3NU

Published simultaneously in Canada by
Penguin Books Canada Ltd,
2801 John Street, Markham, Ontario L3R 1B4.

Printed in the United States of America.

First published in the Norton Library 1978.

LIBRARY OF CONGRESS CATALOGING IN PUBLICATION DATA

Morgan, Edmund Sears.
    The challenge of the American Revolution.

    Includes bibliographical references and index.
    1. United States—History—Revolution, 1775–
1783—Collected works.   I. Title.
E208.M86 1976   973.3   76–19381

"The American Revolution Considered as an Intellectual Movement"
was first published in A. M. Schlesinger, Jr., and Morton White, eds.,
Paths of American Thought (Boston, 1963), 11–33, and is reprinted here
with the permission of the publisher, Houghton Mifflin Co.

"Slavery and Freedom: The American Paradox," was delivered as the
presidential address of the Organization of American Historians at
Washington, D.C., April 6, 1972, and was first published in the *Journal
of American History*, LIX (June, 1972), 5–29. It is reprinted here with
permission.

7 8 9 0

ISBN 0-393-00876-2

For Helen

CONTENTS

INTRODUCTION

EVERY nation needs a history. Without the collective memory embodied in history a people would lose their collective identity in the same way that an individual suffering from amnesia loses his personal identity. But collective memory, like the memory of an individual, is apt to be faulty: it suppresses some events and reshapes others, and because it fades with the passage of time it often needs refreshing.

In the collective memory of Americans the Revolution has occupied a key place, and the fervent ceremonies attending the bicentennial are only one sign of the need we feel as a nation to keep the memory of the Revolution fresh. We want reassurance that the Founding Fathers are *our* fathers. We look to them for a posthumous blessing and perhaps a posthumous admonition, to keep us straight on course or pull us back from paths we should not have taken.

Ironically, neither the Revolution nor any other part of our past can be so reassuring for a historian. His business precludes it. Spending his days with documents, he generally comes to know more about the past than he does about the present and more than most people in the past knew about their present.

He studies not only events that have been preserved in the collective memory but those that have been left out, either because they are disconcerting or because they were known at their occurrence only to a select few, who buried the record of them in pages that only historians have cared to read. The historian even assembles information (such as statistics) previously unknown to anyone. He accordingly becomes so aware of complexities and uncertainties that the past seldom reassures him of anything. Instead it becomes a part of the endless puzzle of human behavior, to be studied and savored and, if possible, understood for its own sake.

Because he becomes so immersed in the past, the historian's understanding of it is not usually shaped by any conscious desire to explain the present. And yet the influence of the present upon him is strong, albeit so subtle that he may not be aware of it. Historians, like other men and women in search of anything, tend to see what they expect to see and to find what they set out to find. Their expectations may be dictated in part by what other historians, who have been over the ground before, tell them is there. But different historians have found different things in the same records, and often the same historian will find new things when he retraces his own steps over the same ground at a later time. The differences may come simply from keener perception or from taking a closer look, but they are also affected, consciously or unconsciously, by the time and place in which the historian lives and by the people who live there with him. Though he may study the past for its own sake, simply to know what really happened, he usually wants to report his discoveries, and he hopes to instruct and inform not only other historians but the people among whom he lives. He wants to improve the collective memory. If only to gain an audience he will try (not always successfully) to answer the questions that his non-professional contemporaries are likely to ask.

A historian's understanding of the Revolution may thus reflect, however remotely, the needs of his time, which may differ from the needs of earlier times and differ also from year to year within his own lifespan. He will not attempt directly to draw lessons from the past for the present, since he does know that the past is an uncertain teacher and that, contrary to popular assumption, history does not repeat itself. By the same token, he will try not to read the present into the past. But his own progress in understanding may grow out of trying to answer the different questions about the past that are prompted by the successive problems and perceptions of his own changing present.

The essays in this volume represent one historian's progress over the past thirty years in trying to understand the American Revolution. I hope that they may strike a responsive chord among those who have shared the problems and perceptions of those years and that they may suggest some new perspectives on the Revolutionary experience, the experience that remains at the center of our national identity. If they leave the reader with less certainty about that experience, I hope they will also leave him with a greater sense of its richness and complexity and that they will address some of the questions he may already be asking. The Revolution will continue to challenge our understanding as long as we remain a nation. In thinking about it, we think about what kind of a people we are.

April 19, 1976   E. S. M.

THE CHALLENGE
OF THE
AMERICAN
REVOLUTION

CHAPTER I

COLONIAL IDEAS OF
PARLIAMENTARY
POWER, 1764-1766

❖❖❖❖❖❖❖❖❖❖❖❖❖❖❖❖❖❖❖❖❖❖❖

*I first began to think about the Revolution because I had to.
As a novice assistant professor at Brown University, I was
scheduled to teach the subject in a general survey of American
colonial history. My research as a graduate student had been
confined to the period before the Revolution—what we colonial historians think of as the first half of American history—
but I knew nothing about the Revolution beyond what I
remembered from a course I had taken in college.*

*Those were the days when most American historians were
still following the footsteps of Charles Beard, looking for the
basic and inevitable economic motives that lay beneath the
window dressing of constitutional argument, patriotic rhetoric,
and political theory. The one thing I could remember clearly
about the colonists' objections to British taxation, with which
the story of the Revolution usually begins, was that the colonists did not really mean what they said. What they wanted
was to avoid being taxed, and they had improvised one set of
high-sounding principles after another to block the efforts of
the British Parliament to make them pay. When Parliament
passed the Stamp Act, imposing a duty on legal and other*

documents, the colonists invented a distinction between external taxes, which were allowable, and internal taxes, which were not. When Parliament obliged them by repealing the Stamp Act and giving them some external taxes in the Townshend duties, they decided that Parliament could tax only for the regulation of trade, not for revenue. When Parliament repealed most of the Townshend duties but then passed the Coercive Acts to punish Massachusetts for the Boston Tea Party, the colonists decided that Parliament had no authority over them at all, that their only connection with England lay in their loyalty to the king. And they finally repudiated that too in the Declaration of Independence.

It seemed important, in teaching the history of the American Revolution, to demonstrate this progression (or retreat) of the colonists from one untenable intellectual position to another until they finally brought themselves to independence. And since historians like to recur constantly to the original sources, I set about looking for characteristic examples of each position, beginning with the distinction between internal and external taxes. I turned first to the collection of documents through which I had myself been shown the progression ten years before in college. To my surprise, the document which was supposed to convey this distinction, an excerpt from Daniel Dulany's Considerations on the Propriety of Imposing Taxes in the British Colonies, was curiously unsatisfactory for the purpose. The distinction which I had been taught to see in it was not made with anything like the clarity I remembered. Indeed, as I pored over the words, the distinction did not seem to be there at all. I would have to find another passage. This was, after all, only an excerpt, a few pages long, from a pamphlet that ran to fifty-five pages. I would go to the original and find a better example.

It was only after I had failed to find a better example in that pamphlet and in several others of the same period that I began to think about the Revolution. It was gradually borne in upon me that what I had been taught about the progression of colonial arguments might conceivably not be so. After two years of reading every statement of the colonial position I could *find, I* knew *it was not so. The article that follows was my first attempt to show what I was now sure* was *so, an attempt to state what objections the colonists did in fact make to Parliamentary taxation.*

If the article had been wholly successful, there would be no point in reprinting it here. But although many historians have been convinced by it, others either have not been convinced or else have not seriously considered the evidence it offers. I accordingly offer it up again, for I have not seen a refutation of it that addresses the evidence it presents. And as it represents my first thinking about the Revolution, it forms the starting point for the train of thought that runs through the subsequent pages of this book. *

THE distinction between internal and external taxes, said Charles Townshend, was "ridiculous in everybody's opinion except the Americans'."[1] The House of Commons was disposed to agree. Members had declared at the time of the Stamp Act that the distinction was meaningless. Some thought that the Americans were fools for espousing such sophistry; others thought that they were knaves, who would seize any pretext to avoid paying for their own protection. And knaves the Americans certainly appeared to be when they objected to the Townshend duties almost as vehemently as they had to the Stamp Act. The colonists in fact seemed to be hypocrites, who capered from one pious notion of their rights to another. Their conduct was shameful and their efforts to justify it even more so. First they quibbled about external taxes and internal taxes. When this distinction failed them, they talked about taxes for regulating trade as against taxes for revenue. Before long they were denying that Parliament had any authority to tax

* The paper, in a shortened version, was read at a meeting of the American Historical Association at Cleveland on Dec. 28, 1947, and was first published in the *William and Mary Quarterly*, 3rd ser., V (July, 1948), 311–42.

[1] Quoted in J. C. Miller, *Sam Adams: Pioneer in Propaganda* (Boston, 1936), 115.

them, and finally they concluded that they were simply not subject to Parliament at all. The frivolous way in which they skipped from one of these views to the next was sufficient evidence that they had no real devotion to any principle except that of keeping their pockets full.[2]

The modern historian, who has thrown off the mantle of patriotism and Whigism for the more sober garments of impartiality, has tended to accept the Tory analysis of American resistance to taxation. He does not always cast doubt on the sincerity of the successive theories of American constitutional rights, but he agrees with Charles Townshend that it was the Americans who distinguished between internal and external taxes, that they abandoned this distinction for another, which likewise proved untenable, and so on until they reached the Declaration of Independence. Thus in the book which examines the American theories most closely, Doctor Randolph G. Adams' *Political Ideas of the American Revolution*,[3] the American advance toward independence is broken down into three stages:

In the first, the colonies admitted the right of Parliament to levy customs duties (external taxes), but denied the right of Parliament to levy excise taxes (internal taxes) upon them. In the second, the colonies conceded the right of Parliament to regulate the trade of the Empire, and hence exercise a legislative authority over the unrepresented colonies, but denied the right of Parliament to levy taxes of

---

[2] See William Knox, *The Controversy between Great-Britain and her Colonies Reviewed* (London, 1769), 34–35: "When the repeal of the stamp-act was their object, a distinction was set up between internal and external taxes; they pretended not to dispute the right of parliament to impose external taxes, or port duties, upon the Colonies, whatever were the purposes of parliament in laying them on, or however productive of revenue they might be . . . but when parliament seemed to adopt the distinction, and waiving for the present the exercise of its right to impose internal taxes, imposed certain duties on merchandizes imported into the Colonies, . . . the distinction between internal and external taxes is rejected by the colony advocates, and a new one devised between taxes for *the regulation of trade,* and taxes for the *purpose of revenue.*"

[3] New York, 1939 (second edition).

any kind whatever, internal or external. In the third stage of the controversy, the colonies admitted the right of Parliament to act as a quasi-imperial superintending power over them and over all the dominions, but denied that Parliament had any legislative authority over the colonies as a general proposition, on the ground that the colonies were not represented in Parliament.[4]

The first two stages of American Revolutionary thinking, as defined by Doctor Adams, have received less attention and are consequently less well understood than the last stage.[5] My purpose is to examine the colonial ideas of Parliamentary power in the period covered by Doctor Adams' first stage, the period of the Stamp Act crisis.

I

It will be remembered that the Stamp Act was under discussion in the colonies from the spring of 1764 to the spring of 1766. Although it was in force for less than four months before its repeal in February, 1766, the colonists had begun to consider it as soon as they received news of the resolution passed by Parliament on March 10, 1764, the resolution which declared, "That, towards further defraying the said Expences, it may be proper to charge certain Stamp Duties in the said

[4] P. 69. For similar views by other historians, see C. P. Nettels, *The Roots of American Civilization* (New York, 1940), 634–35; C. L. Becker, *The Declaration of Independence* (New York, 1922, 1942), 80–134; H. J. Eckenrode, *The Revolution in Virginia* (Boston and New York, 1916), 28.

[5] Since this essay was written, the political ideas of the colonists have been subjected to much closer scrutiny, but the notion persists, though sometimes in diluted form, that they admitted the constitutionality of external taxes while denying that of internal taxes. See, for example, L. H. Gipson, *The Coming of the Revolution, 1763–1775* (New York, 1954), 76–78; *The British Empire before the American Revolution*, vol. X, *The Triumphant Empire: Thunder-Clouds Gather in the West, 1763–1766* (New York, 1961), 236–40, 258–59, 285; Bernard Bailyn, *Ideological Origins of the American Revolution* (Cambridge, Mass., 1967), 209–15.

Colonies and Plantations."[6] The resolution was one of a series which George Grenville had introduced as the basis of his budget for the ensuing year. The others furnished the substance of the Revenue Act of 1764, the so-called Sugar Act, which became a law two months later. But the resolution for a stamp tax was phrased so as to indicate that no action would be taken on it until the next session, though its ultimate passage was almost a certainty.[7] The colonists were thus presented with two measures which threatened their prosperity and which consequently obliged them to think about the relation which they bore to the body which threatened them. They had to consider the Sugar Act, in which Parliament made use of trade regulations to raise money and which in itself would have been sufficient to set discerning minds at work on the question of Parliamentary taxation. At the same time they had to consider the Stamp Act, an act which would directly affect almost every person in the colonies. Of the two, the Stamp Act appeared to most colonists to be the more dangerous, but in formulating their ideas of Parliamentary power they could not afford to neglect either measure; they had to decide in what way their rights were affected both by the internal taxes of the Stamp Act and by the external taxes of the Sugar Act.

Under the pressure of these two acts colonial ideas reached a remarkable maturity during the period under discussion. In some regions and among some persons the theory of complete colonial autonomy was enunciated. For example a meeting of citizens at New London, Connecticut, on December 10, 1765, adopted resolutions which rehearsed the principles of government by consent, specified that the Stamp Act was a violation

[6] *Journals of the House of Commons,* XXIX, 935.

[7] Grenville warned the colonial agents that he would bring in a bill for a stamp tax at the next session of Parliament. See the letter from Jasper Mauduit to Massachusetts, May 26, 1764 (Massachusetts Archives, XXII, 375); the letter from Charles Garth to South Carolina, June 5, 1764 (*English Historical Review,* LIV, 646–48); and the account by William Knox, agent for Georgia, in *The Claim of the Colonies to an Exemption from Internal Taxes Imposed by Authority of Parliament Examined* (London, 1765), 31–35.

of those principles, and finally declared, "That it is the Duty of every Person in the Colonies to oppose by every lawful Means, the Execution of those Acts imposed on them—and if they can in no other way be relieved to reassume their natural Rights, and the Authority the Laws of Nature and of God have vested them with."[8] If there was any confusion in the minds of the colonists as to how to go about reassuming natural rights, newspaper writers were ready with detailed discussions of the technique of revolution.[9] Short of this, other writers expounded the theory which later found more classic expression in the writings of John Adams and James Wilson, the theory that is assumed in the Declaration of Independence, that the colonies owe allegiance only to the king and are not bound in any way by acts of Parliament.[10]

But in the effort to arrive at what may be called the official colonial position during this period, one cannot rely on newspapers and pamphlets nor on the resolutions adopted by informal gatherings of small groups, for these may represent the views of factions or the idiosyncrasies of a single man. Fortunately it is not necessary to depend upon such partial statements, for in every colony except Georgia and North Carolina the formally elected representatives of the people produced some official statement of belief. Five of the colonies which later revolted drew up statements in 1764 while the Stamp Act was pending; nine colonies, including all of the first five, did the same in 1765 after the Act was passed; and in the same years at the Stamp Act Congress, nine colonies combined in a declaration which was formally approved by a tenth. These statements, in the form of resolutions, petitions, memorials,

---

8 *Boston Post-Boy and Advertiser,* Dec. 16, 1765.

9 See, for example, *Boston Gazette,* Dec. 2, 1765.

10 *Maryland Gazette,* May 30, 1765; *Providence Gazette,* May 11, 1765; *Boston Gazette,* Feb. 24, March 3, March 17, 1766. Governor Bernard reported to the Lords of Trade, Nov. 30, 1765, that the Massachusetts politicians were claiming that the colonies "have no Superiors upon Earth but the King, and him only in the Person of the Governor, or according to the terms of the Charter." Bernard Papers, IV, 203, Harvard College Library.

and remonstrances, are the safest index of colonial opinion about Parliamentary power. They were carefully phrased by the regularly elected representatives of the voting population and adopted, in many cases unanimously, after deliberation and debate.

In these formal statements it is scarcely possible to discern a trace of the ideas which the Americans are supposed to have adopted during the period under discussion. Almost universally the documents deny the authority of Parliament to tax the colonies at all. Nowhere is there a clear admission of the right of Parliament to levy external taxes rather than internal, and only in three cases does such a right seem to be implied. In at least one of these three, the implication which may be suggested by a partial reading is denied by a full consideration of the document and the circumstances under which it was produced.

II

As might be expected, the statements drawn up in 1764 while the Stamp Act was pending were generally not as explicit as those prepared a year later, when the Act had been passed and the colonists had had more time to think over its implications. The clearest of the early statements was that made by the New York Assembly in three petitions, to the King, the Lords, and the Commons, on October 18, 1764. These petitions, in objecting to both the Sugar Act and the proposed Stamp Act, claimed that the colonists should be exempt "from the Burthen of all Taxes not granted by themselves." Far from singling out internal taxes, the New York Assembly stated pointedly:

. . . since all Impositions, whether they be internal Taxes, or Duties paid, for what we consume, equally diminish the Estates upon which they are charged; what avails it to any People, by which of them they are impoverished? . . . the whole wealth of a country may be as effectually drawn off, by the Exaction of Duties, as by any other Tax upon their Estates.

In accordance with this principle New York admitted the authority of Parliament to regulate the trade of the empire for the good of the mother country, but insisted that

. . . a Freedom to drive all Kinds of Traffick in a Subordination to, and not inconsistent with, the *British* Trade; and an Exemption from all Duties in such a Course of Commerce, is humbly claimed by the Colonies, as the most essential of all the Rights to which they are intitled, as Colonists from, and connected, in the common Bond of Liberty, with the uninslaved Sons of *Great Britain*.[11]

The statement made by Virginia in 1764 was almost as plain as that of New York. The Virginia Council and House of Burgesses in a petition to the King, a memorial to the House of Lords, and a remonstrance to the Commons, claimed an exemption from all Parliamentary taxation. To the King they asserted their "Right of being governed by such laws, respecting their internal Polity and Taxation,[12] as are derived from their own Consent"; to the Lords they stated their right as British subjects to be exempt from all taxes, "but such as are laid on them by their own Consent, or by those who are legally appointed to represent them"; to the Commons they remonstrated "that laws imposing taxes on the people ought not to be made without the consent of representatives chosen by themselves," and added that they could not discern "by what Distinction they can be deprived of that sacred birthright and most valuable inheritance, by their Fellow Subjects, nor with what Propriety they can be taxed or affected in their estates by the Parliament, wherein they are not, and indeed cannot, constitutionally be represented."[13]

[11] *Journal of the Votes and Proceedings of the General Assembly of the Colony of New York. Began the 8th Day of November, 1743; and Ended the 23d of December, 1765* (New York, 1766), II, 769–79.

[12] For the question whether or not the adjective "internal" modifies "taxation" as well as "polity" see the discussion below of the same phrase in the Virginia Resolves of 1765.

[13] *Journals of the House of Burgesses of Virginia 1761–1765* (Richmond, 1907), liv–lvii.

Rhode Island, Connecticut, and Massachusetts took a less precise view of their rights in 1764 than did New York and Virginia, although Massachusetts and Connecticut, at least, cleared up the uncertainty of their position in the following year. In Rhode Island the General Assembly deputed Governor Stephen Hopkins to write a statement of the colony's rights and in addition sent a petition to the King, dated November 29, 1764. Both Governor Hopkins' pamphlet and the petition ignored the constitutional question raised by the Sugar Act, the question of external taxes; they argued against the act simply as a trade regulation which would have ruinous economic consequences. Since none of the colonies at this time denied Parliament's right to regulate colonial trade, Rhode Island, in considering the Sugar Act simply as such a regulation, made no attempt to deny Parliament's right to enact it. Against the proposed Stamp Act Hopkins and the Assembly did raise the question of right. This proposal, if carried into execution, would be "a manifest violation of their just and long enjoyed rights. For it must be confessed by all men, that they who are taxed at pleasure by others, cannot possibly have any property, can have nothing to be called their own; they who have no property can have no freedom, but are indeed reduced to the most abject slavery." The petition to the King recited the same objections and concluded with a request

that our trade may be restored to its former condition, and no further limited, restrained and burdened, than becomes necessary for the general good of all your Majesty's subjects; that the courts of vice admiralty may not be vested with more extensive powers in the colonies than are given them by law in Great Britain; that the colonists may not be taxed but by the consent of their own representatives, as Your Majesty's other free subjects are.[14]

Thus Rhode Island sidestepped the question of external taxes by ignoring the declared intent of the Sugar Act to raise a revenue. She took a stand upon constitutional grounds only against the proposed Stamp Act, only, in other words, against

14 James R. Bartlett, ed., *Records of the Colony of Rhode Island and Providence Plantations* (Providence, 1861), VI, 414–27.

internal taxes. Yet she did not quite admit Parliament's right to levy external taxes, because she considered the Sugar Act, erroneously to be sure, as a regulation of trade and not as a tax. Her position on external taxes was ambiguous: she didn't say yes and she didn't say no.

Connecticut in 1764 was guilty of the same ambiguity. Connecticut's statement took the form of a pamphlet drawn up by a committee, consisting of Governor Fitch, Ebenezer Silliman, George Wyllys and Jared Ingersoll, deputed by the General Assembly, "to collect and set in the most advantageous light all such arguments and objections as may justly and reasonably [be] advanced against creating and collecting a revenue in America, more particularly in this Colony, and especially against effecting the same by Stamp Duties &c."[15] This committee, of which Governor Fitch was the working member, produced a pamphlet entitled *Reasons why the British Colonies in America should not be charged with Internal Taxes, by Authority of Parliament.*[16] The pamphlet came as close as any American statement to admitting the right of Parliament to levy external taxes. Like the Rhode Island statement, it confined its constitutional objections to internal taxes and failed to consider the problem, raised by the Sugar Act, of whether Parliament could make use of trade regulations as a source of revenue. Instead, it assumed that Parliament would act for the good of the whole in its regulation of trade. "If Restrictions on Navigation, Commerce, or other external Regulations only are established," it said, "the internal Government, Powers of taxing for its Support, an Exemption from being taxed without Consent, and other Immunities, which legally belong to the Subjects of each Colony . . . will be and continue in the Substance of them whole and entire."[17] This was a rather naïve view of the situation, but it did not necessarily commit the colony to a constitutional acceptance of external taxes.

[15] C. J. Hoadly, ed., *Public Records of the Colony of Connecticut* (Hartford, 1881), XII, 256.
[16] New Haven, 1764. Reprinted in Hoadly, XII, 651–71.
[17] *Ibid.*, 661.

The address of Massachusetts to the House of Commons, dated November 3, 1764, like the pamphlets issued by Rhode Island and Connecticut in this year, was not entirely clear on the question of external taxes. Massachusetts affirmed that the American colonists "have always judged by their representatives both of the way and manner, in which internal taxes should be raised within their respective governments, and of the ability of the inhabitants to pay them." The address concluded with the request that "the privileges of the colonies, relative to their internal taxes, which they have so long enjoyed, may still be continued to them."[18] By specifiying internal taxes, the address seemed to imply that the inhabitants of Massachusetts did not object to the idea of an external tax imposed by Parliament. This implication was fortified by the rest of the document, which objected to the Sugar Act on economic rather than constitutional grounds as a measure which would ruin the trade of the colony.

Before this address is interpreted as an implied assent to external taxes the circumstances of its origin must be considered. The General Court adopted the address only because the Council refused to concur in a much more inclusive assertion of rights, originally passed by the lower house. In this version the House affirmed that "we look *upon those Duties as a Tax* [i.e., the duties imposed by the Sugar Act], and which we humbly apprehend ought not to be laid without the Representatives of the People affected by them."[19] The abandonment of this earlier version was regarded in Massachusetts as a victory for the Council under the leadership of Lieutenant Governor Hutchinson, and the House, even though it acquiesced in the new address, did not consider it a proper statement of colonial rights.[20] Accordingly, when they sent it to

18 Alden Bradford, ed., *Massachusetts State Papers. Speeches of the Governors of Massachusetts from 1765 to 1775 etc.* (Boston, 1818), 21–23.

19 Massachusetts Archives, XXII, 414.

20 See the letters by Governor Bernard, Nov. 17 and 18, 1764, to the Earl of Halifax, to John Pownall, and to Richard Jackson, relating the success of the Council in toning down the petition. Bernard Papers, II, 181–87, 189, 260–64.

their agent in London for presentation, they warned him that it did not represent the views of the House. "The House of Representatives," they said

were clearly for making an ample and full declaration of the exclusive Right of the People of the Colonies to tax themselves and that they ought not to be deprived of a right they had so long enjoyed and which they held by Birth and by Charter; but they could not prevail with the Councill, tho they made several Tryalls, to be more explicit than they have been in the Petition sent you . . . You will therefore collect the sentiments of the Representative Body of People rather from what they have heretofore sent you than from the present Address.[21]

What the House of Representatives had heretofore sent the agent included a long letter instructing him in the doctrine of natural rights and an explicit statement that any attempt by Parliament to tax colonial trade would be "contrary to a fundamentall Principall of our constitution vizt. That all Taxes ought to originate with the people."[22] The House had also approved and sent to the agent a pamphlet written by one of their members, James Otis, entitled *The Rights of the British Colonies asserted and proved.*[23] In this pamphlet Otis had argued against Parliament's right to tax the colonies and had stated in the most unequivocal manner that "there is no foundation for the distinction some make in England, between an internal and an external tax on the colonies."[24] It would

21 *Collections of the Massachusetts Historical Society,* LXXIV, 170–71.
22 *Ibid.,* 39–54, 145–46.
23 Boston, 1764. See *Journal of the Honourable House of Representatives of His Majesty's Province of the Massachusetts-Bay in New-England, Begun and held at Concord, in the county of Middlesex, on Wednesday the Thirtieth Day of May, Annoque Domini, 1764* (Boston, 1764), 66, 77.
24 P. 42. Strangely enough these were also the private views of Lieutenant Governor Hutchinson, who was principally responsible for suppressing the original address of the House. In a piece which he wrote in June or July, 1764, but never published, he argued against the Stamp Act on precisely the same line which was later followed by the House. He pointed out that the Sugar Act had been passed, not for the regulation of trade, but "for the sake of the money arising from the Duties," and that the

hardly seem proper, then, to draw from the Massachusetts Address the inference that the people of the colonies accepted the right of Parliament to levy external as opposed to internal taxes.

III

At the end of the year 1764, when the five initial colonial statements were all on the books, the colonial position was still a little obscure. New York and Virginia had been plain enough, but Rhode Island, Connecticut, and Massachusetts, while denying Parliament's right to levy a stamp tax, had evaded the question of external taxes. By the close of the following year all signs of hesitation had disappeared. The Stamp Act produced an all but unanimous reaction: Parliament had no right to tax the colonies.

The first declaration of rights to be made after passage of the Act was the famous set of resolves which Patrick Henry introduced into the Virginia House of Burgesses on May 30, 1765. As recorded in the Journals of the House of Burgesses, there were four of these resolves which passed the House. The first two asserted the right of the inhabitants of Virginia to all the privileges of Englishmen. The third declared "that the Taxation of the People by themselves, or by Persons chosen to represent them" was a "distinguishing Characteristick of *British* Freedom, without which the ancient Constitution can-

---

privileges of the people were no less affected by it than they were by an internal tax. (Massachusetts Archives, XXVI, 90–96.) Moreover, on Nov. 9, 1764, just after he had succeeded in getting the Massachusetts Address toned down, Hutchinson wrote to Ebenezer Silliman in Connecticut, criticizing the Connecticut pamphlet for neglecting to object against external taxes. He told Silliman, who was a member of the Connecticut Committee which drew up the pamphlet, that "the fallacy of the argument lies here it is your supposing duties upon trade to be imposed for the sake of regulating trade, whereas the Professed design of the duties by the late Act is to raise a revenue." (Massachusetts Archives, XXVI, 117–18.) Why Hutchinson should have objected to these views when they came from the Massachusetts House of Representatives is not apparent.

not exist." The fourth stated that the inhabitants of Virginia had always enjoyed and had never forfeited or yielded up "the inestimable Right of being governed by such Laws, respecting their internal Polity and Taxation, as are derived from their own Consent."[25]

Henry had proposed three more resolutions which either failed of passage or later were expunged from the records. The first of these merely repeated what the others had already implied, namely, that the General Assembly of Virginia, in its representative capacity, had "the only exclusive right and power to lay taxes and imposts upon the inhabitants of this colony." The second, more radical, stated "That his Majesty's liege people, the inhabitants of this colony, are not bound to yield obedience to any law or ordinance whatever, designed to impose any taxation whatsoever upon them, other than the laws or ordinances of the General Assembly aforesaid." The last provided that anyone who denied the Aessembly's exclusive power of taxation should be considered an enemy of the colony.[26]

The Virginia Resolves, even without the inclusion of Henry's three additional clauses, constituted a clear denial of Parliament's right to tax. The only phrase which could be interpreted as distinguishing between internal and external

[25] *Journals of the House of Burgesses of Virginia 1761–1765*, 360.

[26] *Ibid.*, lxvii. When the Resolves were printed in the newspapers, the three unsuccessful resolves were included along with the others as though they had been passed. The Resolves, so far as the incomplete newspaper records enable us to tell, were first printed in the *Newport Mercury* on June 24, 1765, and copied in the Boston papers from the version given there. The text printed in the papers, besides including the three unsuccessful resolves, omitted one of those actually passed (the third) and considerably abridged the others. The abridgment did not seriously alter the meaning of the resolves, but the wording was sufficiently changed to suggest that the newspaper text was obtained from an unofficial source, probably from some member of the assembly who had been present when the Resolves were passed. Possibly the source was Henry himself, for the newspaper version, except in its omission of resolution number 3, closely approximates a copy of the Resolves which is endorsed on the back in Henry's handwriting. See *Journals of the House of Burgesses*, frontispiece and lxv.

taxes was the phrase in the fourth resolution "internal polity and taxation." Here it was possible to read the adjective "internal" to modify "taxation" as well as "polity." That such a reading would have been incorrect is suggested by the fact that in the version of the Resolves which was printed in the newspapers this phrase was changed to read "taxation and internal police."[27] Furthermore this was also the wording in a copy of the Resolves endorsed on the back in Patrick Henry's handwriting.[28]

The Virginia Resolves served as a model for similar declarations in most of the other colonies. Rhode Island, where the Virginia Resolves were first published, was the first to copy them. In September, 1765, the Rhode Island General Assembly passed six resolutions, three of which were adapted from those passed by the Virginia House of Burgesses, two from Henry's unsuccessful resolutions (which had been printed in the newspapers without any indication that they had failed to pass), and one original resolution which, in effect, called upon officers of government to pay no attention to the Stamp Act.[29] On the question of Parliamentary authority the Rhode Island statements, being copied from those of Virginia, were no less definite: the General Assembly of the colony had always enjoyed control over "taxation and internal police" and possessed "the only exclusive right to lay taxes and imposts upon the inhabitants of this colony."[30] Rhode Island in fact went farther than the Virginia Burgesses had been willing to go and farther than any other colony went in the next eight or nine years, by calling for direct disobedience to Parliament. She passed the measure which Virginia had rejected and declared that her inhabitants need not submit to a Parliamentary tax. Yet in so doing Rhode Island added a qualification which makes her position on the question of external taxes open to

27 *Newport Mercury,* June 24, 1765; *Boston Post-Boy and Advertiser,* July 1, 1765; *Boston Gazette,* July 1, 1765; *Georgia Gazette,* Sept. 5, 1765.

28 *Journals of the House of Burgesses of Virginia, 1761–1765,* frontispiece and lxv.

29 Bartlett, *Records of the Colony of Rhode Island,* VI, 451–52.

30 *Ibid.,* 452.

suspicion. In the fifth Rhode Island resolution it was stated that the inhabitants of the colony were "not bound to yield obedience to any law or ordinance designed to impose any internal taxation whatsoever upon them, other than the laws or ordinances of the General Assembly, aforesaid."[31] In Henry's version the word "internal" had not occurred. Rhode Island by inserting it implied that her citizens could disobey an act of Parliament imposing internal taxes but not one imposing external taxes. It should be noted that this distinction did not appear in the assertion of right contained in the preceding resolutions, where the authority of Parliament to tax the colony was denied without qualification. It was only in the summons to rebellion that the Rhode Island Assembly felt obliged to draw back a little. Though their caution on this score was boldness when compared to the stand of the other colonies, which confined themselves to declarations of right, nevertheless the appearance of the word "internal" makes one wonder whether there may not have been a moderate faction in the assembly which would have allowed Parliament a right over external taxes. If there was such a faction, it was not able to insert its views into the resolutions which defined the rights of the colony but only into the one which proposed open rebellion. Moreover, a few weeks later, on November 6, 1765, Rhode Island's popularly elected governor, Samuel Ward, wrote to General Conway that the colonists were oppressed, because "duties and taxes" were laid upon them without their knowledge or consent.[32]

If the Rhode Island Resolves of 1765 still left some room for doubt on the question of external taxes, the same was not true of the other colonial statements of that year. The Maryland Assembly, on September 28, passed unanimously resolutions denying Parliament's right to tax, in which the only use of the word "internal" was in the familiar phrase "Taxes, and internal Polity."[33] Meanwhile Pennsylvania, on September 21,

---

31 *Ibid.*
32 *Ibid.*, 473.
33 *Maryland Gazette*, Oct. 3, 1765.

had drawn up its own set of Resolves, to much the same effect. The first draft of these resolves, written by John Dickinson, included one clause objecting specifically to internal taxes,[34] but in the version finally adopted by the assembly there was no mention of the word "internal." The crucial item read: "Resolved therefore, N.C.D. That the taxation of the people of this province, by any other persons whatsoever than such their representatives in assembly, is UNCONSTITUTIONAL, and subversive of their most valuable rights."[35]

Massachusetts, because of the recess of her assembly, did not take action until October, though the newspapers began to agitate for a more spirited statement of rights as soon as they received news of the Virginia Resolves.[36] Accordingly when the assembly was called together in October, it produced a set of resolutions which defined the rights of British subjects and concluded, "that all acts, made by any power whatever, other than the General Assembly of this province, imposing taxes on the inhabitants, are infringements of our inherent and unalienable rights, as men and British subjects; and render void the most valuable declarations of our charter."[37] The Connecticut Assembly likewise cleared up the ambiguity of its earlier statement by a set of resolves modeled partly on those of Virginia and affirming that an act for raising money in the colonies "by duties or taxes" was beyond the authority of Parliament. Connecticut, like Maryland and Rhode Island, in-

---

[34] Charles J. Stillé, *The Life and Times of John Dickinson, 1732–1808* (Philadelphia, 1891), 339–40.

[35] J. Almon, ed., *A Collection of interesting, authentic papers, relative to the dispute between Great Britain and America* (London, 1777), 20–21.

[36] See, for example, the *Boston Gazette* of July 8, 1765: "The People of Virginia have spoke very sensibly, and the frozen Politicians of a more northern Government say they have spoke Treason: Their spirited Resolves do indeed serve as a perfect Contrast for a certain, tame, pusillanimous, daub'd, insipid Thing, delicately touch'd up and call'd an Address; which was lately sent from this Side the Water, to please the Taste of the Tools of Corruption on the other." The reference, of course, was to the Massachusetts Address of 1764.

[37] Bradford, *Massachusetts State Papers,* 50–51.

cluded an item copied after the fourth of the Virginia Resolves, in which once again the questionable phrase was
rendered as "taxing and internal police."[38]

South Carolina, on November 29, 1765, denied Parliament's
right to tax, in a set of eighteen resolves copied from the
declarations of the Stamp Act Congress[39] (see below). New York
could scarcely state the colonial position more explicitly than
she had done the year before, but nevertheless on December
11, 1765, she adopted three more petitions to King, Lords, and
Commons, restating the case with the same clarity.[40] New
Jersey in the meantime had adopted eleven resolutions copied
principally from those of the Stamp Act Congress, with nothing said about internal taxes;[41] and New Hampshire, which
did not participate in the Congress, had given formal approval
to all the resolutions and petitions of that body.[42]

The Stamp Act Congress had met in New York during
October, attended by delegates from Massachusetts, Rhode
Island, Connecticut, New York, New Jersey, Pennsylvania,
Delaware, Maryland, and South Carolina. These delegates had
produced a set of resolutions and three petitions, to the King,
the Lords, and the Commons, all denying the authority of
Parliament to tax the colonies.[43] Here as in the other formal
colonial statements of this year there is no distinction made
between internal and external taxes. The Stamp Act Congress
has frequently been treated by historians as a rather conservative body of men, possibly because it acknowledged "all due
subordination" to Parliament. But as conservatives at the time

[38] Hoadly, *Public Records of the Colony of Connecticut*, 421–25.

[39] John Drayton, *Memoirs of the American Revolution* (Charleston, S.C., 1821), I, 39–41.

[40] *Journals of the Votes and Proceedings of the General Assembly of the Colony of New York 1743–1765*, II, 795–802.

[41] *New Jersey Archives*, 1st ser. (Paterson, 1902), XXIV, 683–84.

[42] Nathaniel Bouton, ed., *Documents and Records Relating to the Province of New Hampshire* (Nashua, 1873), VII, 92.

[43] Hezekiah Niles, *Principles and Acts of the Revolution* (Baltimore, 1822), 457–60.

recognized, this phrase was an empty one unless you stated what subordination was due. It is true that the conservatives, in Massachusetts at least, had hoped to gain control of the Stamp Act Congress.[44] They actually succeeded in securing Timothy Ruggles as one of the Massachusetts delegates, and Governor Bernard wrote at least one letter to Ruggles before the convention urging him to secure submission to the Stamp Act pending its probable repeal.[45] Ruggles remained faithfully conservative, but the true character of the Congress is sufficiently indicated by the fact that, as a conservative, he refused to sign the Resolutions it adopted and was later reprimanded for his refusal by the not-so-conservative Massachusetts House of Representatives.[46] The Stamp Act Congress, in other words, was no less "radical" than the colonial assemblies which sent delegates to it. Though it acknowledged due subordination to Parliament, it denied without qualification the right of Parliament to tax the colonies.

In sum, during the period of the Stamp Act crisis, fifteen formal statements of colonial rights had been issued. Of these only the three early statements by Rhode Island, Connecticut, and Massachusetts could be interpreted as implying an assent to the constitutionality of external taxes. The statement by Massachusetts was clearly not representative of official opinion,

[44] Governor Bernard wrote to the Lords of Trade on July 8, 1765, that in Massachusetts, where the proposal for the congress initiated, "It was impossible to oppose this measure to any good purpose and therefore the friends of government took the lead in it and have kept it in their hands, in pursuance of which, of the Committee appointed by this House to meet the other Committees at New York on 1st of October next, two of the three are fast friends to government prudent and discreet men such as I am assured will never consent to any undutiful or improper application to the Government of Great Britain." (Sparks Manuscripts 43: British Manuscripts, IV, Harvard College Library).

[45] Bernard Papers, IV, 72. The letter is dated Sept. 28, 1765.

[46] Boston Gazette, Feb. 17, 1766. The membership of the Stamp Act Congress has been analyzed in an unpublished paper by Mr. David S. Lovejoy, in which it is indicated that of the twenty-seven members only two are known to have become Tories at the time of the Revolution.

and both the Massachusetts and the Connecticut statements
were clarified the following year by resolutions which unequiv-
ocally rejected the authority of Parliament to tax the colonies
at all.

IV

The question suggested by all these declarations of right is:
what did the Americans mean when they admitted due subordination to Parliament and at the same time denied Parliament's right to tax them? What subordination was due? If
they did not distinguish between internal and external taxes,
but denied all authority to tax, what authority did they leave
to Parliament?

The answer is given clearly enough in the documents: the colonists allowed the right of Parliament to legislate for the whole
empire in any way that concerned the common interests of all
the members of the empire (as yet they made no claim that the
colonial assemblies were entirely coordinate with Parliament
in legislative authority), but they denied that Parliament's
legislative authority extended either to the internal polity of
the colonies or to taxation. Not all the colonies insisted on
exclusive control of internal polity, for Parliament at this time
was not attempting to interfere in this department. The issue
of the day was taxation, and what the colonies insisted on most
vigorously was that Parliament's supreme legislative authority
did not include the right to tax. Taxation and legisation, they
said, were separate functions and historically had always been
treated as such. Legislation was a function of sovereignty; and
as the soverign body of the empire, Parliament had absolute
legislative authority. Under this authority Parliament was entirely justified in regulating the trade and commerce of the
empire. There was, in other words, nothing unconstitutional
about the Acts of Trade and Navigation. But taxes were something else. Taxes were the "free gift" of the people who paid
them, and as such could be levied only by a body which repre-

sented the people. As far as Great Britain was concerned, the House of Commons was a representative body and could therefore tax the people of Great Britain; but since the colonists were not, and from their local circumstances could not be, represented in Parliament, they could not be taxed by Parliament. The only body with a constitutional right to tax them was a colonial assembly, in which the people upon whom the tax would fall would be represented. Thus the Connecticut Assembly in October, 1765, resolved,

That, in the opinion of this House, an act for raising money by duties or taxes differs from other acts of legislation, in that it is always considered as a free gift of the people made by their legal and elected representatives; and that we cannot conceive that the people of Great Britain, or their representatives, have right to dispose of our property.[47]

According to this distinction the power to levy taxes even in Great Britain was limited to the House of Commons, the representative part of Parliament. The petition from the General Assembly of New York to the House of Commons, December 11, 1765, while expressing "all due submission to the supreme Authority of the *British* Legislature," affirmed

That all parliamentary Aids in *Great-Britain,* are the free Gifts of the People by their Representatives, consented to by the Lords, and accepted by the Crown, and therefore every Act imposing them, essentially differs from every other Statute, having the Force of a Law in no other Respect than the Manner thereby prescribed for levying the Gift.

That agreeable to this Distinction, the House of Commons has always contended for and enjoyed the constitutional Right of originating all Money Bills, as well in Aid of the Crown, as for other Purposes.

That all Supplies to the Crown being in their Nature free Gifts, it would, as we humbly conceive, be unconstitutional for the People of *Great-Britain,* by their Representatives in Parliament, to dispose

[47] *Public Records of the Colony of Connecticut,* XII, 423.

of the Property of Millions of his Majesty's Subjects, who are not, and cannot be there represented.[48]

It was this distinction which the members of the Stamp Act Congress had in mind when they acknowledged "due subordination" to Parliament, for they asked in their petition to the House of Commons,

Whether there be not a material Distinction in Reason and sound Policy, at least, between the necessary Exercise of Parliamentary Jurisdiction in general Acts, for the Amendment of the Common Law, and the Regulation of Trade and Commerce through the whole Empire, and the Exercise of that Jurisdiction by imposing Taxes on the Colonies.[49]

V

Most members of Parliament would have answered this query with a flat denial that the power of taxation could be distinguished from that of legislation. Taxation, they would have said, was inseparable from sovereignty. But there were some members willing to speak in favor of the colonial view. The question arose in debate over the Declaratory Act, which accompanied repeal of the Stamp Act and which announced the legislative authority of Parliament over the colonies "in all cases whatsoever." Colonel Isaac Barré, a veteran of the French and Indian War and a staunch defender of colonial rights, moved to strike the phrase, "in all cases whatsoever." His motion was intended to exclude Parliament's authority to tax the colonies, and in the debate that followed, Barré and William Pitt the elder argued for the motion in much the same terms as were used in the colonial statements. Visitors were not admitted to Parliament during this session, so that few ac-

---

[48] *Journal of the Votes and Proceedings of the General Assembly of the Colony of New York 1743–1765*, II, 800.

[49] *Proceedings of the Congress at New York* (Annapolis, 1766), 23. The reprint of the proceedings in Niles, *Principles and Acts of the Revolution*, is inaccurate at this point.

counts of the debate have been preserved, but according to Charles Garth, member for Devizes borough, Wiltshire, and agent for several of the southern colonies, the speakers for Barré's motion contended: "That the Principles of Taxation as distinguished from Legislation were as distinct Principles and Powers as any two Propositions under the Sun." The speakers cited the precedents of the counties palatine of Chester and Durham which had been subject to Parliament's legislative authority but had not been taxed until they were represented. The clergy, it was pointed out, taxed themselves separately but did not have separate legislative power. Another indication that the two functions were separate was that taxes were the free gift of the Commons, and tax bills could not be considered by the Lords or the King until the Commons had made a grant. Other bills remained in the Upper House for the King's signature, but tax bills were sent back to the Commons, whose speaker presented them to the King as the free gift of the Commons. All this, it was said, showed that Parliament might legislate as the supreme authority of the realm but that it taxed only in its representative capacity. Since the colonies were not represented in Parliament, they could not constitutionally be taxed by Parliament.[50] In the House of Lords, Lord Camden argued the case to the same effect.[51]

In spite of these arguments Parliament decided by an overwhelming majority[52] to include the words "in all cases whatsoever," and thereby, as far as Parliament was concerned, it was concluded that taxation and legislation were not separate functions and that Parliament's authority over the colonies included the right to tax. But strangely enough the Declaratory Act did not include any explicit statement of the right to tax, so that the colonists could not have recognized that Parliament

50 Garth's account is in *Maryland Historical Magazine*, VI, 287–305. Another account is in *American Historical Review*, XVII, 565–74.

51 *Archives of Maryland* (Baltimore, 1895), XIV, 267–68.

52 *Maryland Historical Magazine*, VI, 300; *Archives of Maryland*, XIV, 280; Sir John Fortescue, ed., *The Correspondence of King George the Third* (London, 1927), I, 254.

was denying their position. What the act said was that the King in Parliament had "full power and authority to make laws and statutes of sufficient force and validity to bind the colonies and people of *America*, subjects of the crown of *Great Britain*, in all cases whatsoever."[53] Though the members of Parliament knew that the words "in all cases whatsoever" meant in cases of taxation, there is nothing in the act itself to give the words that meaning. Nor was the ambiguity entirely accidental. When the act was being drawn up, Charles Yorke, the attorney general, suggested that the crucial phrase should read "as well in cases of Taxation, as in all other cases whatsoever." But when he submitted this suggestion to Rockingham, who was then prime minister, Rockingham thought it impolitic to make any mention of the word "taxation." "I think I may say," he wrote to Yorke, "that it is our firm Resolution in the House of Lords—I mean among ourselves—that that word must be resisted."[54] Thus the omission of any mention of taxation was deliberate. By supporting the act as it stood, with the resounding but ambiguous phrase "in all cases whatsoever," the Rockingham government could gain support in Parliament by encouraging the members to beat the drum of Parliamentary power—behind closed doors—without giving offense to the colonies.

The colonies can hardly be blamed then for not getting the point of the Declaratory Act. They had not generally been informed of the debate which had taken place over the words "in all cases whatsoever,"[55] and since the Act was accompanied by the repeal of Parliament's most conspicuous attempt to tax them, they might very well interpret it as a simple as-

[53] Danby Pickering, ed., *The Statutes at Large* (Cambridge, England, 1767), XXVII, 20.

[54] British Museum Additional Manuscripts 35430, ff.37–38 (Rockingham's letter). The exchange of correspondence between Yorke and Rockingham is printed in part in George Thomas, Earl of Albemarle, *Memoirs of the Marquis of Rockingham* (London, 1852), I, 285–88. The date of Yorke's letter is not given. Rockingham's letter is dated Jan. 25, 1766

[55] So far as I have been able to discover, Garth's account was the only one sent to the colonies, and it was not published at the time.

sertion of legislative authority with no necessary implication of a right to tax. They knew that the Declaratory Act was a copy of the earlier statute of 6 George I regarding Ireland. And they knew also that in spite of this statute Ireland had not been taxed by Parliament. The Massachusetts Assembly even before passage of the Stamp Act had argued from the example of Ireland that the colonies might be dependent on England without allowing England a right to tax them.[56] After passage of the Declaratory Act the Massachusetts agent in London, Richard Jackson, encouraged Massachusetts to believe that the same reasoning was still valid, for he wrote to Governor Bernard that the act would probably affect the colonies as little "as the Power we claim in Ireland, the manner of exercising which you are acquainted with."[57] The same view was expressed by Daniel Dulany of Maryland in a letter to General Conway. According to Dulany the Declaratory Act could not imply a power to tax, because if it did, then the act of 6 George I must give authority to tax Ireland, and such authority had never been claimed or exercised.[58] Thus the fact, so often remarked by historians, that the colonists took little notice of the Declaratory Act does not mean that the colonists were indifferent to the question of principle. They simply did not recognize the Act as a challenge to their views. They could acquiesce in it with a clear conscience and without inconsistency, unaware that ther interpretation differed radically from that held in Parliament.[59]

[56] Massachusetts Archives, XXII, 415. The argument is made in the petition to the King passed by the House of Representatives on Oct. 22, 1764, and non-concurred by the Council.

[57] *Ibid.*, f.458. The letter is dated March 3, 1766.

[58] Sparks Manuscripts 44, bundle 7, ff.10–11. The letter is not dated.

[59] George Grenville wrote that the Americans were justified in rejoicing at the repeal of the Stamp Act "especially if they understand by it, as they justly may, notwithstanding the Declaratory Bill passed at the same time, that they are thereby exempted for ever from being taxed by Great Britain for the public support even of themselves." William J. Smith, ed., *The Grenville Papers* (London, 1853), III, 250.

VI

Unfortunately this misunderstanding on the part of the Americans was matched by a similar misunderstanding on the part of many people in England with regard to the colonial position. We have seen that the American protests against the Stamp Act did not distinguish between internal and external taxes but denied that Parliament had any right to tax the colonies. Yet some Englishmen, at least, thought that the American protests were directed only against internal taxes. The American misunderstanding of the Declaratory Act is explicable by the vagueness of the Act itself, the absence of any official interpretation of it, and the fact that the Parliamentary debate on it had been closed to the public. But the colonial statements had all been communicated to the British government by the beginning of the year 1766, before Parliament began to consider repeal of the Stamp Act. Why then did Englishmen suppose that the Americans distinguished between internal and external taxes?

Of course not all Englishmen did suppose so; those who took the trouble to read the colonial statements knew better. But apparently many Englishmen, including members of Parliament, did not take that trouble. It should be remembered that the colonial petitions were never formally considered by Parliament. Those sent before passage of the Stamp Act were thrown out because of the procedural rule against receiving petitions on money bills. Those sent for repeal of the Act were excluded for other procedural reasons and because they called the authority of Parliament into question. Thus although the contents of the statements could doubtless have been learned by anyone who wished to discover them, they were never given a regular hearing in Parliament.[60]

In the absence of any direct acquaintance with the colonial statements the average member of Parliament must have gained his impressions from one of two sources; either from

[60] *Collections of the Connecticut Historical Society,* XVIII, 332-35; *Maryland Historical Magazine,* VI, 282-88.

the multitude of pamphlets dealing with the Stamp Act or from speeches in Parliament. It is possible but not probable that the authors of pamphlets against the Stamp Act were responsible for creating the impression that the Americans did not object to external taxes. We have already observed an ambiguity in the two pamphlets by Stephen Hopkins and Thomas Fitch which received the approval of Rhode Island and Connecticut respectively in 1764. Both these pamphlets used the phrase "internal taxes" in such a way as to suggest that external taxes might be constitutionally acceptable, though neither Hopkins nor Fitch explicitly said as much. Two other pamphlets, which enjoyed a wide circulation though not a formal legislative approval, also used the words "internal taxes" in a way which may have helped to bring about a misunderstanding of the American position. Richard Bland in *An Inquiry into the Rights of the British Colonies*[61] demonstrated that the colonists could not constitutionally be subjected to an internal tax by act of Parliament. Anyone reading Bland's conclusions without reading the argument leading to them might get the impression that Bland would have agreed to Parliament's collection of a revenue from customs duties levied in the colonies; but Bland's demonstration of his conclusion showed that Parliament could not constitutionally charge duties in the colony upon either imports or exports. In fact, he even argued that the Navigation Acts were unconstitutional. Bland evidently included in the phrase "internal taxes" the very duties which other people called "external taxes."

Another pamphlet which objected specifically to internal taxes was Daniel Dulany's *Considerations on the Propriety of Imposing Taxes in the British Colonies.*[62] This probably had a wider circulation than any other pamphlet against the Stamp Act, and it has frequently been cited as the source of the distinction between internal and external taxes. Although the greater part of Dulany's pamphlet was devoted to general

[61] Williamsburg, 1766.

[62] Annapolis, 1765 (second edition). The succeeding quotations are taken from pp. 30–35.

arguments against the constitutionality of Parliamentary taxation, there were a few paragraphs in which he implied that internal taxes alone were unconstitutional. Thus he argued, on page 33, that before the Stamp Act, Parliament had never "imposed an internal Tax upon the Colonies *for the single Purpose of Revenue.*" He went on to deny the contention, which he attributed to the proponents of the Stamp Act, "That no Distinction can be supported between one Kind of Tax and another, an Authority to impose the one extending to the other." Contrary to this erroneous view, he said, "It appears to me, that there is a clear and necessary Distinction between an Act imposing a Tax *for the single Purpose of Revenue,* and those Acts which have been made for the Regulation of Trade, and have produced some Revenue in *Consequence of their Effect* and Operation as *Regulations of Trade.*" According to this distinction Parliament had the right to regulate trade by the imposition of duties, even though those duties should incidentally produce some revenue. Dulany closed the discussion of this point by affirming: "a Right to impose an internal Tax on the Colonies without their consent, *for the single Purpose of Revenue,* is denied; a Right to regulate their Trade without their Consent is admitted."

It will be observed that in the course of this discussion, which occupied two pages of the pamphlet, Dulany had not made entirely clear what he regarded as constitutional and what he considered unconstitutional. He said that internal taxes for the purpose of revenue were unconstitutional, and he said that duties on trade for the purpose of regulation were constitutional, even though an incidental revenue might attend them, but he failed to say explicitly how he regarded duties on trade for the single purpose of revenue. He failed, in other words, to say how he stood on external taxes; in fact he did not even use the words "external tax" at any point in the pamphlet. His readers would perhaps have been justified in thinking that Dulany admitted external taxes as constitutional, since he explicitly objected only to internal taxes. Yet, unless Dulany was simply confused about the matter, it would appear that in his use of the phrase "internal tax" he included all duties levied in the colonies for the single purpose of revenue. In no other way does Dulany's argument make sense, for he contrasted what he called an internal tax for the single purpose of revenue with duties for the purpose of regulation from which an incidental revenue might arise. The context indicates clearly that the point of the contrast was not the difference between internal taxes as opposed to duties on trade but the difference between an imposition on trade for the purpose of regulation and one for the purpose of revenue. Dulany emphasized the contrast by italicizing the phrases: *single purpose of revenue, incidental Revenue,* and *Regulations of Trade.* The whole force of the contrast is lost unless the phrase "internal tax" is taken to include duties on trade collected in the colonies for the purpose of revenue. That this was Dulany's understanding of the term is further indicated in the two paragraphs which follow those summarized above. Here Dulany demonstrated that the duties on trade which had hitherto been collected in the colony had been levied not for the purpose of revenue but for the purpose of regulating trade. The argument which he used to carry this point was drawn from the fact that the customs duties collected in North America brought only £1,900 a year into the treasury while they cost £7,600 a year to collect. Dulany had taken these figures from a pamphlet attributed to Grenville. Dulany concluded with some justice that

It would be ridiculous indeed to suppose, that the Parliament would raise a Revenue by Taxes in the Colonies to defray Part of the national Expence, the Collection of which Taxes would increase that Expence to a Sum more than three Times the Amount of the Revenue; but, the Impositions being considered in their true Light, as Regulations of Trade, the Expence arising from an Establishment necessary to carry them into Execution, is so far from being ridiculous, that it may be wisely incurred.

Thus Dulany demonstrated that Parliament could not levy what he called an internal tax for the purpose of revenue by showing that Parliament had never levied an external tax for the purpose of revenue. The conclusion seems inescapable that he used the phrase "internal tax" in a loose sense, to cover all taxes collected in the colonies, whether excise taxes or customs duties levied for the single purpose of revenue. That this was his meaning is also suggested by the remainder of the pamphlet, in which he argued against Parliamentary taxation in general terms, as when he started that "the Inhabitants of the Colonies claim an Exemption from *all* Taxes not imposed by their own Consent." (The italics are Dulany's.)

Dulany's pamphlet, though it was widely acclaimed as a defense of colonial rights, certainly employed a confusing terminology, and it would not be surprising if Englishmen at the time had gained the impression that there was some sort of distinction in it between the constitutionality of internal taxes as opposed to that of customs duties. Though Dulany never used the phrase "external tax" and though most of the pamphlet will make sense only if his use of the phrase "internal tax" is taken to include all taxes collected in the colonies, yet if American historians have derived the impression that he distinguished between internal and external taxes, it is not unreasonable to suppose that contemporary Englishmen received the same impression.

What does seem unlikely, however, is that British statesmen would have assumed, as American historians frequently seem to do, that Daniel Dulany was the proper spokesman for all the colonies. His pamphlet was only one of many, and the others ranged in attitude from complete submission to the authority of Parliament (as in Martin Howard's *Letter from a Gentleman at Halifax, to His Friend in Rhode Island*)[63] to complete defiance of Parliament (as in the *Considerations upon the Rights of the Colonists to the Privileges of British Subjects*).[64] Most of the pamphlets against the Stamp Act refrained from discussing the question of constitutional right and argued on the grounds of inexpediency or equity.[65] Those

63 Newport, 1765.

64 New York, 1766.

65 See for example: John Dickinson's *The Late Regulations Respecting the British Colonies on the Continent of America Considered* (London,

which concerned themselves with the constitutional aspects of the question devoted a major part of their attention to the doctrine of virtual representation.[66] This was an easy target, and in centering the constitutional controversy upon it the Americans gained a tactical victory; for when their opponents argued that the colonists might be taxed because they were virtually represented, this was tantamount to admitting that the power to tax depended upon representation. Daniel Dulany put his finger on the weakness of the ministerial position when he wrote to General Conway,

If the right to tax and the right to regulate had been imagined by Mr. Grenville to be inseparable why did he tax his ingenuity to find out a virtual Representation, why did not some able friend intimate to him his Hazard on the slippery ground, he chose, when the all powerful Sovereignty of Parliament might have afforded so safe a footing?[67]

In other words Grenville himself, by arguing for virtual representation (as his spokesman, Thomas Whately, did in *The*

1765); *A Letter to a Member of Parliament, Wherein the Power of the British Legislature, and the Case of the Colonists, Are briefly and impartially considered* (London, 1765); *The True Interest of Great Britain, with respect to her American Colonies, Stated and Impartially Considered* (London, 1766); *The Importance of the Colonies of North America, and the Interest of Great Britain with regard to them, considered* (London, 1766); *The Necessity of Repealing the American Stamp Act Demonstrated* (London, 1766); *The Late Occurences in North America, and Policy of Great Britain, Considered* (London, 1766); and Benjamin Franklin's *The General Opposition of the Colonies to the Payment of the Stamp Duty; and the Consequence of Enforcing Obedience by Military Measures; Impartially Considered* (London, 1766).

[66] See for example: Samuel Cooper, *The Crisis; or, A Full Defense of the Colonies* (London, 1766), 3–30; Maurice Moore, *The Justice and Policy of Taxing the American Colonies, in Great Britain, Considered* (Wilmington, N.C., 1765), 7–14; Richard Bland, *An Inquiry into the Rights of the British Colonies* (Williamsburg, 1766), 5–12; Daniel Dulany, *Considerations on the Propriety of imposing Taxes in the British Colonies* (Annapolis, 1765), 5–14.

[67] Sparks Manuscripts 44, bundle 7, f.10.

Regulations Lately Made concerning the Colonies, and the Taxes Imposed upon Them, considered),[68] had admitted that taxation was not a function of sovereignty but rather, as the colonies were contending, the prerogative of a representative body.

There was no reason why the pamphleteers on the American side should have made a distinction between internal and external taxes when arguing the case against virtual representation; and it is not surprising that with the possible exception of those discussed above, none of them seems to have employed the distinction for purposes of argument. The distinction did appear in some of the literature in support of the Stamp Act, where it served as a whipping boy. It was attributed to the Americans and then demolished under the heavy gunfire of constitutional history.[69] It hardly seems likely that the defenders of the Stamp Act would have attributed the distinction to the Americans simply in order to discredit the colonial position. It is much more likely that they and the members of Parliament really believed that the colonists did distinguish between internal and external taxes. The question remains as to how they gained this impression.

The source from which, in all probability, it was derived was the speeches made in Parliament by friends of the colonies during the debates on repeal of the Stamp Act and afterwards, not excepting the brilliant interview given at the bar of the House of Commons by Benjamin Franklin. The member of Parliament who heard that carefully rehearsed performance (or who read it afterwards in print) might very justly have concluded that the Americans had no objection to external taxes, for Franklin, the arch-American, at several points had stated that the Americans objected only to internal taxes.[70] When a

68 London, 1765.

69 See *The Rights of Parliament Vindicated, On Occasion of the late Stamp-Act. In which is exposed the conduct of the American Colonists* (London, 1766); *An Examination of the Rights of the Colonies upon Principles of Law* (London, 1766).

70 William Cobbett, ed., *Parliamentary History of England, from the Earliest Period to the Year 1803* (London, 1813), XVI, 137–60.

member had pointed out that the objection to internal taxes could with equal justice be applied to external taxes, Franklin had replied that the Americans did not reason in that way at present but that they might learn to do so from the English. The wit of Franklin's tongue obscured the fact that he was wrong, but the average member could scarcely have known that. Laughing at Franklin's clever answers, he would probably have forgotten the rather pertinent question put by a member of the opposition: "Do not the resolutions of the Pennsylvania Assembly say, all taxes?" This question was evidently asked by a member who knew something about Pennsylania's attitude. Franklin's answer to it was not as sprightly as his replies to some of the other questions. The best he could say was that if the Pennsylvania resolutions said all taxes, they meant only internal taxes. Actually it would have been impossible to tell from Franklin's testimony exactly what he thought the constitutional position of the Americans to be. At times he seemed to be saying that the Americans assented to external taxes; at other times, he implied that they consented only to the regulation of trade. The performance was a good piece of lobbying for repeal of the Stamp Act, but it gave no clear indication of the American position and certainly could have contributed to the idea that the Americans were willing to accept external taxes.

The speeches of Franklin's friend Richard Jackson, member of Parliament for Weymouth, and agent at various times for Pennsylvania, Connecticut, and Massachusetts, may also have contributed to a false impression of the colonial position. Jackson believed that Parliament had a clear right to tax the colonies by duties on trade. Since Parliament by its admitted right to regulate trade could prohibit any branch of colonial trade, he reasoned, Parliament could also tax any branch of colonial trade.[71] Jackson, moreover, had searched the precedents thoroughly and found that Parliament in the past had imposed external taxes on the trade of Chester and Durham and Wales

[71] Carl Van Doren, ed., *Letters and Papers of Benjamin Franklin and Richard Jackson 1753–1785* (Philadelphia, 1947), 123–24, 138–39.

before those areas were represented in Parliament. At the same time Parliament had refrained from taxing them internally until they were granted representation. When Jackson rehearsed these views before Parliament,[72] he must have been listened to as a man of some authority; for he had the reputation of being extraordinarily learned,[73] and he was, besides, the official agent for several colonies. The average member of Parliament could not have known that he had been elected agent for Massachusetts by the political maneuvers of the royal governor,[74] nor that the Connecticut Assembly had written him a letter deploring his insufficient insistence upon colonial rights,[75] nor that he owed his appointment in Pennsylvania to his friend Benjamin Franklin, who had also misrepresented the colonial position.[76]

What must also have impressed the uninformed member was the famous speech by William Pitt, when the Great Commoner had come out of his retirement to urge the repeal of the Stamp Act. On this occasion, Pitt had risen to a statement by George Grenville in which the latter had complained that he could not understand the distinction between internal and external taxes. "If the gentleman does not understand the difference between internal and external taxes," said Pitt, "I cannot help it."[77] Pitt's reply, if left there, might have been somewhat misleading. Anyone who listened to the whole of what he had to say would have known that Pitt, like the colonists, was distinguishing, not between internal and external taxes but between taxation and legislation. In an earlier speech he had stated that "Taxation is no part of the governing or legislative power,"[78] and now he went on to argue that "there is a

[72] Ibid., 194–96; Collections of the Connecticut Historical Society, XVIII, 316; Bradford, Massachusetts State Papers, 72–73.

[73] Van Doren, Letters and Papers of Benjamin Franklin and Richard Jackson, 1–2.

[74] Bernard Papers, III, 277–83.

[75] Collections of the Connecticut Historical Society, XVIII, 366–67.

[76] Van Doren, Letters and Papers of Benjamin Franklin and Richard Jackson, 87, 100.

[77] Parliamentary History, XVI, 105.

[78] Ibid., 99.

plain distinction between taxes levied for the purpose of raising a revenue, and duties imposed for the regulation of trade, for the accommodation of the subject; although, in the consequences, some revenue might incidentally arise from the latter."[79] Pitt was following the argument of Dulany, whom he had read and admired;[80] and if historians have misunderstood Dulany's argument, it is not unlikely that the members of Parliament may have misunderstood Pitt's. Though there was a manifest difference between Pitt's and Dulany's acceptance of trade regulations which might incidentally produce a revenue and Jackson's and Franklin's acceptance of external taxes as such, nevertheless all four men were arguing in behalf of the colonies. The average member may have lumped them all together and come out with the simple conclusion that Americans accepted external taxes.

This conclusion would have been strengthened a little later by a speech of Thomas Pownall. Pownall, speaking with some authority as the former governor of Massachusetts, said explicitly that the colonists *"never objected to external taxes—* to imposts, subsidies and duties. They know that the express conditions of their settlements and establishments were, that they should pay these—and therefore they never have had any disputes with government on this head—but have always found reason to be satisfied *in the moderation with which government hath exercised this power."*[81] Pownall had apparently never read any of the colonial statements. Perhaps he derived some of his ideas from his friend Benjamin Franklin.[82]

79 *Ibid.,* 105.

80 W. S. Taylor and J. H. Pringle, eds., *The Chatham Correspondence* (London 1838–40), III, 192; Moses C. Tyler, *The Literary History of the American Revolution 1763–1783* (New York, 1941), 111 and n.

81 *The Speech of Th-m-s P-n-ll, Esq. . . . in the H—se of C—m-ns, in favor of America* (Boston, 1769), 12.

82 Pownall cooperated with Franklin on a scheme for raising money in the colonies by interest-bearing paper currency. This scheme was proposed by Franklin as a substitute for the Stamp tax. For details see V. W. Crane, "Benjamin Franklin and the Stamp Act," *Publications of the Colonial Society of Massachusetts,* XXXII, 56–78. On Pownall's participation, see Pownall's letter to Hutchinson, Dec. 3, 1765, in Massachusetts Archives, XXV, 113.

Certainly his authority to represent the views of the colonists was long since out of date. But how was the average member to know that? All the friends of America in Parliament seemed to be of opinion that the Americans were resigned to external taxes.

Why the colonial advocates in Parliament should have joined in conveying so false an impression of the colonial position is not entirely clear. A number of reasons might be offered why Pownall or Jackson or Pitt argued as they did: Pownall may have been misinformed;[83] Jackson may have been speaking for himself rather than for the colonies; and Pitt was misunderstood. But Franklin's testimony is more difficult to explain, for Franklin must have been better acquainted with the colonial declarations than he appeared to be. Why should he have contributed to the general misunderstanding? Furthermore, why should all the proponents of colonial rights have misrepresented the colonies in the same way?

In the absence of direct information one can only suggest that political circumstances in 1766 required that every friend of the colonies in England refrain from urging the extreme claims put forward by the colonial assemblies and join in representing the colonies as more moderate than they actually were. The immediate object in 1766 was the repeal of the Stamp Act, and repeal was not to be attained by blunt denials of Parliament's authority. Though the colonists seemed to be unaware of this fact and continued on their intransigent course, their friends in England had to seek support where they could find it. They found it in the Rockingham administration, and consequently when they argued for repeal of the Stamp Act, they argued in Rockingham's terms. Now Rockinghams' terms, to judge from at least one account, were a recognition of the distinction between internal and external taxes. According to Charles Garth the administration refused

[83] That Pownall was an unreliable source of information is suggested by the fact that he himself had suggested a stamp tax in his book *The Administration of the Colonies*. Dennys De Berdt later wrote that he was "as irresolute as the Wind, in one days debate a friend to America the next quite with the Ministry." (*Publications of the Colonial Society of Massachusetts*, XIII, 377–78.)

to hear the petition of the Stamp Act Congress, because "it tended to question not only the Right of Parliament to impose internal Taxes, but external Duties."[84] Rockingham, it would appear, was prepared to settle the colonial issue by leaving internal taxes to the colonial assemblies. Though this was not as much as the colonies demanded, it was more than the rest of Parliament was willing to give, for most members were as ready to assert Parliament's right to levy all taxes as the colonists were to deny it.[85] Rockingham in fact was unable to repeal the Stamp Act on the basis of the distinction between internal and external taxes. Instead he was obliged to agree to the Declaratory Act, though worded in the ambiguous terms already noticed.[86] Rockingham, it is plain, needed all the support he could get, for he could not carry the rest of Parliament even as far as he and his own group were willing to go. In these circumstances it would have been undiplomatic, not to say reckless, for the friends of the colonies to embarrass him by insisting on the politically impossible claims of the colonial declarations. It seems unlikely that there was any formal agreement between the Rockingham group and the other colonial protagonists, whereby the latter agreed to soft-pedal the colonial claims to exclusive powers of taxation, but the pressure of politics undoubtedly dissuaded the friends of the colonies from giving publicity to the colonial declarations, and probably led them to cooperate with Rockingham in adopting a distinction which the colonists would never have allowed.

One conclusion in any case is clear: it was not the Americans who drew the line between internal and external taxes.

[84] *Maryland Historical Magazine*, VI, 285.

[85] This fact was reported to the colonists in several letters. See, for example, that of Jared Ingersoll in *Collections of the Connecticut Historical Society*, XVIII, 317–26, and that of Richard Jackson in *ibid.*, 349–51.

[86] Dennys De Berdt wrote to Samuel White at the time of repeal that there were three parties in Parliament so far as the Stamp Act was concerned, one for enforcing, one for repeal with a declaration of right, and one for repeal without a declaration. According to De Berdt the administration favored the last view but was obliged to take the middle position in order to gain a majority. (*Publications of the Colonial Society of Massachusetts*, XIII, 311–12.)

It was recognized in America at the time by such diverse political personalities as James Otis and Thomas Hutchinson that the distinction was an English one. Otis, as already noticed, in the pamphlet approved by the Massachusetts assembly in 1764, scouted the distinction as one that "some make in England."[87] Hutchinson, in the third volume of his history of Massachusetts, gave credit for it to Pitt. Though it is clear that Pitt did not originate it, Hutchinson evidently thought that he did and was equally certain that the Americans did not accept it; for he averred that in levying the Townshend duties, "government in England too easily presumed, that Mr. Pit's distinction between internal and external taxes would be favourably received in America."[88] There were members of Parliament in England, too, who realized that the distinction was not an American one, for in the debates on the Declaratory Act, Hans Stanley, the member for Southampton, embarrassed the Rockingham administration by pointing out that "The Americans have not made the futile Distinction between internal and external taxes,"[89] and Lord Lyttelton did the same thing in the House of Lords in the debate on the repeal of the Stamp Act, when he stated that "The Americans themselves make no distinction between external and internal taxes."[90] The colonial agents also realized that the colonists were talking bigger at home than their friends in England would admit, and the agents repeatedly requested their constituents to be less noisy about their rights. The colonists in return instructed the agents to be more noisy about them.[91]

The colonists were bumptious, blunt, and lacking in diplomacy, but they were not guilty of the constitutional frivolity

---

[87] *The Rights of the British Colonies asserted and proved* (Boston, 1764), 42.

[88] L. S. Mayo, ed., *History of the Province of Massachusetts Bay* (Cambridge, Mass., 1936), III, 130.

[89] *American Historical Review*, XVII, 566.

[90] *Parliamentary History*, XVI, 167.

[91] *Collections of the Connecticut Historical Society*, XVIII, 349–51, 366–67; *Collections of the Massachusetts Historical Society*, LXXIV, 39–54, 145–46; Massachusetts Archives, XXII, 361–63; *Publications of the Colonial Society of Massachusetts*, XIII, 332–33, 335, 337, 354.

with which they have been charged. When they objected to the Townshend duties in 1767, they had in no way changed the conception of Parliamentary power which they avowed at the time of the Stamp Act: they still admitted the authority of Parliament to regulate trade and to legislate in other ways for the whole empire; they still denied that Parliament had a right to tax them. These views they continued to affirm until the 1770's when they advanced to the more radical position of denying the authority of Parliament to legislate as well as to tax. Though this denial was generally accompanied by an allowance of Parliamentary legislation as a matter of convenience, there can be no question that the later position was constitutionally different from the earlier one. But that the colonists were guilty of skipping from one constitutional theory to another, like so many grasshoppers, is a Tory libel that has too readily been accepted by modern historians. American Revolutionary thought went through two stages, not three; the supposed first stage never existed. If anyone took a more advanced position because of the passage of the Townshend duties, it was not the colonists. They were already there.

CHAPTER II

REVISIONS IN NEED OF REVISING

❖❖❖❖❖❖❖❖❖❖❖❖❖❖❖❖❖❖❖❖❖❖

When one is obliged to discard a long held assumption about the past, it is natural to ask what else should be discarded with it. The fact that the colonists did not say what they were supposed to have said in 1765 raised the question whether they had said or done other things they were supposed to have. After completing the preceding essay, I went on to a full-length study of the Stamp Act crisis and to a brief survey of the whole Revolutionary period.*

In these efforts I became increasingly impressed—far more impressed than my previous reading in secondary works had led me to be—with the achievements of the men who carried out the Revolution. The Revolution, it seemed to me, was a far more significant event than I had been led to believe. The leading historians of my youth had approached it with scientific zeal, eager to undo a century and more of filiopietistic exaggeration, eager to reduce the Founding Fathers to life size and to show their human failings, especially their class

---

* E. S. and H. M. Morgan, *The Stamp Act Crisis: Prologue to Revolution* (Chapel Hill, 1953); E. S. Morgan, *The Birth of the Republic, 1763–89* (Chicago, 1957).

bias. These revisionists had done the job, but a little too well,
so that for one brought up on a diet of professional history the
original sources were full of surprises.

In the following essay I tried to delineate the ways in which
it seemed to me that historians had distorted the facts. At the
time when the article appeared, though this was not apparent
then, historical research was already moving in new directions.
Other young historians had also experienced the kind of sur-
prise that I had in finding the assumptions gained from their
mentors to be not quite so. The result was what has been called,
mistakenly I think, a "school" of historians who emphasized
consensus rather than class conflict in American history. The
so-called school was mainly the result of different scholars,
independently of one another, examining different episodes
and failing to find in them the social conflicts they had been
taught to expect. In any case, much of the revising of revisions
called for in this article has taken place, though I would not
claim it to be a result of this piece of exhortation. The revising
has even produced a reaction, in the efforts of radical, or "New
Left," historians (who are perhaps not a "school" either) to
restore, in a more sophisticated and qualified way, an emphasis
on internal conflict in the Revolution. But of that, more later.
I myself continue, as will be seen, to think of the Revolution
in terms of the problems I tried to pose here.†

DURING the past fifty years three ideas have inspired research
into the history of the eighteenth century in America and
England. The earliest of these to appear, and the most fruitful
of results, was the idea that American colonial history must be
seen in the setting of the British Empire as a whole. We are
all familiar today with the new insights and new discoveries
that have grown out of this view: the great works of George
Louis Beer and Charles McLean Andrews, the monumental
synthesis of Professor Lawrence Gipson, which now approaches

---

† The essay was delivered as a paper at a meeting of the Mississippi
Valley Historical Association in Pittsburgh on April 19, 1956. It was first
published in the *William and Mary Quarterly*, 3rd ser., XIV (Jan., 1957),
3–15.

its culmination. This has been a great idea, and it has done more than any other to shape our understanding of the colonial past.

A second idea, which has affected in one way or another most of us who study colonial history, is that the social and economic divisions of a people will profoundly influence the course of their history. This idea received early application to American history in Carl Becker's study of New York politics on the eve of the Revolution and in Charles Beard's *An Economic Interpretation of the Constitution*. New York politics before the Revolution, Becker said, revolved around two questions, equally important, the question of home rule and that of who should rule at home.[1] Subsequent historians have found in Becker's aphorism a good description of the Revolutionary period as a whole. The conflict between different social groups now looms as large in our histories of the Revolution as the struggle against England. Like all seminal ideas, this one has sometimes been used as a substitute for research instead of a stimulus to it. Historians have been so convinced of the importance of social and economic divisions that they have uttered the wildest kind of nonsense, for example, about the social and economic basis of a religious movement like the Great Awakening of the 1740's. The view has nevertheless been productive of important new insights and new information.

The third idea, although it has had scarcely any effect as yet on the study of American history, has furnished the principal impetus to recent research in British history. It is a more complex idea, growing out of the discoveries of Sir Lewis Namier. The effect of these discoveries has been to attach a new importance to local as opposed to national forces. "It has been the greatest of Sir Lewis Namier's achievements," says Richard Pares, "to exhibit the personal and local nature of political issues and political power at this time."[2] Namier and his disciples, of whom Pares is the most notable, have destroyed the traditional picture of British politics in the age of the

---

[1] Carl Becker, *The History of Political Parties in the Province of New York, 1760–1776* (Madison, Wis., 1909), 22.

[2] Richard Pares, *King George III and the Politicians* (Oxford, 1953), 2.

American Revolution. During this period, they tell us, there were no political parties in the modern sense, nor were there any political factions or associations with any principle or belief beyond that of serving selfish or local interests. The Rockingham Whigs, who made such a display of their opposition to the repressive measures against the colonies, were no different from the other squabbling factions except in their hypocritical pretense of standing for broader principles. And George III owed his control over Parliament not to bribery and corruption but simply to his constitutional position in the government and to his skill as a politician during a time when the House of Commons lacked effective leaders of its own.

I

Each of these three ideas, the imperial, the social or economic, and the Namierist, has had a somewhat similar effect on our understanding of the American Revolution. That effect has been to discredit, in different ways, the old Whig interpretation. The imperial historians have examined the running of the empire before the Revolution and pronounced it fair. The Navigation Acts, they have shown, were no cause for complaint. The Board of Trade did as good a job as could be expected. The Admiralty Courts were a useful means of maintaining fair play and fair trade on the high seas. Indeed, Professor Gipson tells us, the old colonial system "may not unfairly be compared to modern systems of state interference with the liberty of the subject in matters involving industry and trade, accepting the differences involved in the nature of the regulations respectively. In each case, individuals or groups within the state are forbidden to follow out lines of action that, while highly beneficial to those locally or personally concerned, are considered inimical to the larger national objectives."[3] In the light of such imperial benevolence and farsightedness, the

---

[3] Lawrence H. Gipson, *The British Empire before the American Revolution*, III (Caldwell, Idaho, 1936), 287.

unwillingness of the Americans to pay the trifling contribution demanded of them in the sixties and seventies becomes small and mean, and the resounding rhetoric of a Henry or an Otis or an Adams turns into the bombast of a demagogue.

The social and economic interpretation does nothing to redeem the fallen Revolutionary patriots but rather shows them up as hypocrites pursuing selfish interests while they mouth platitudes about democracy and freedom. Their objections to Parliamentary taxation are reduced to mere tax evasion, with the arguments shifting as the character of the taxes shifted. Their insistence on freedom and equality is shown to be insincere, because in setting up their own governments they failed to establish universal suffrage or proportional representation. They were, it would appear, eager to keep one foot on the lower classes while they kicked the British with the other.

Namier and his followers have little to say about the American revolutionists but devote themselves to scolding the English Whigs. Though the Namierists generally achieve a sophisticated objectivity with regard to persons and parties, they sometimes seem fond of beating the Whigs in order—one suspects—to displease the Whig historians. For example, the unflattering portrait of Charles James Fox that emerges from Richard Pares's brilliant study must surely be read in part as a rebuke to Sir George Otto Trevelyan, or rather to those who have accepted Trevelyan's estimate of Fox. This deflation of Fox and Burke and the other Rockingham Whigs, while accomplished with scarcely a glance in the direction of the colonies, nevertheless deprives the American revolutionists of a group of allies whose high-minded sympathy had been relied upon by earlier historians to help demonstrate the justice of the American cause.

By the same token the righteousness of the Americans is somewhat diminished through the loss of the principal villain in the contest. George III is no longer the foe of liberty, seeking to subvert the British constitution, but an earnest and responsible monarch, doing his job to the best of his abilities. And those abilities, we are told, while not of the highest order, were not small either. George, in fact, becomes a sympathetic figure, and one can scarcely escape the feeling that the Americans were rather beastly to have made things so hard for him.

While the imperial, the economic, and the Namierist approaches have thus contributed in different ways to diminish the prestige of the American Revolution and its promoters, it is a curious fact that none of the ideas has produced any full-scale examination of the Revolution itself or of how it came about. The imperial historians have hitherto been occupied primarily in dissecting the workings of the empire as it existed before the Revolutionary troubles. Although their works have necessarily squinted at the Revolution in every sentence, the only direct confrontations have been brief and inconclusive.

The social and economic interpretation has been applied more extensively to different aspects of the Revolution, but surprisingly enough we still know very little about what the social and economic divisions actually were in most of the colonies and states at the time of the Revolution. Professor Schlesinger's analysis of the role of the merchant class remains a fixed point of knowledge at the opening of the period, and Charles Beard's *Economic Interpretation of the Constitution* is a somewhat shakier foundation at the close of it, reinforced, however, by the work of Merrill Jensen.[4] Historians have bridged the gap between these two points with more assurance than information. There are, it is true, several illuminating studies of local divisions but not enough to warrant any firm conclusions about the role of economic and social forces in the Revolution as a whole. After thirty years we are only a little closer to the materials needed for such conclusions than J. Franklin Jameson was in 1926.

The Namierist approach, as already indicated, has been confined to events in England rather than America. Though the effect of such investigations has been to exonerate George III and discredit the English Whigs, the Revolution has not been

[4] Arthur M. Schlesinger, *The Colonial Merchants and the American Revolution* (New York, 1918); Merrill Jensen, *The Articles of Confederation* (Madison, Wis., 1940); *The New Nation* (New York, 1950).

a primary issue for Namier or Pares. One student of Professor Namier's, Eric Robson, made a preliminary excursion into the subject but confined his discussion primarily to military history.[5] And while Professor Charles Ritcheson has treated the place of the Revolution in British politics,[6] the implications of Namier's discoveries for developments on this side of the water remain unexplored.

Thus while the new ideas and new discoveries have altered our attitudes toward the American Revolution, they have done so for the most part indirectly, almost surreptitiously, without coming up against the Revolution itself. There is need for intensive and direct examination of all phases of the Revolution in the light of each of these ideas, and we may expect that in the next few years such examinations will be made.[7] I should

[5] Eric Robson, *The American Revolution in Its Political and Military Aspects* (London, 1955).

[6] Charles Ritcheson, *British Politics and the American Revolution* (Norman, Okla., 1954).

[7] In the twenty years since this was written, Lawrence Gipson completed his study of *The British Empire before the American Revolution*, with three volumes devoted to the coming of the Revolution. The volumes offer a detailed and judicious narrative of events, but they explain the American revolt against a benevolent imperialism by the analogy of a child maturing and casting off parental authority. The explanation is useful as a figure of speech but leaves the reader in doubt about the meaning of maturation as applied to a whole people rather than an individual. The Namier school has produced some intensive examinations of British politics in the Revolutionary period, in the works of Bernard Donoughue and P. D. G. Thomas, but the Namierist approach is not calculated to confront the causes of the Revolution except in terms of the series of short-range decisions that finally precipitated hostilities. There has been a reaction among some British political historians against the Namierist approach, but the historians involved in it have not yet dealt directly with the coming of the Revolution. The social and economic interpretation that stresses internal conflict has been sustained not only in further work by Merrill Jensen but in new studies by Jackson Turner Main, Staughton Lynd, Jesse Lemisch, Alfred Young, and J. K. Martin, to name only a few. The newer studies have uncovered a wealth of information about the political and economic aspirations, fulfilled and unfulfilled, of different social groups during the Revolutionary period; but they have not, I think, revived the earlier concept of the Revolution as the expression of an internal social conflict.

like to suggest, however, that we need not only to examine the Revolution in the light of the ideas but also to re-examine the ideas in the light of the Revolution; and in doing so we need also to examine them in relation to each other.

The Revolution is one of those brute facts which historians must account for, and it is a fact of central importance for ascertaining the meaning and limits of the three ideas we are discussing. I believe that each of the three needs revision and will take them up in order.

II

While everyone will acknowledge the importance of the imperial idea and of the discoveries made under its influence, the net effect of that idea has been to emphasize the justice and beneficence of the British imperial system as it existed before the Revolution. May we not therefore pose a question to the imperial historians: if the empire was as fairly administered as you show it to have been, how could the Revolution have happened at all? In their preliminary skirmishes with this problem, imperial historians have frequently implied that the American revolutionists were moved, in part at least, by narrow or selfish views and stirred up by evil-minded agitators. But if historians are to sustain such a view in any full-scale consideration of the Revolution, they face a very difficult task: they must explain men like George Washington, John Adams, Thomas Jefferson, and Benjamin Franklin as agitators or as the dupes of agitators, or as narrow-minded men without the vision to see beyond provincial borders. After all due allowance is made for patriotic myopia, this still seems to me to be an impossible undertaking. Anyone who studies the Revolution can scarcely emerge without some degree of admiration for the breadth of vision that moved these men. In twenty-five years they created a new nation and endowed it with a government that still survives and now has the longest continuous history of any government in existence outside of England. The idea that they were narrow-minded simply will not wash. Nor is it possible to see them as the dupes of their intellectual inferiors. Samuel Adams, Patrick Henry, and James Otis may perhaps be cast as demagogues without seeming out of place, but not the giants of the period. If the British government could not run the empire without bringing on evils that appeared insufferable to men like Washington, Jefferson, John Adams, and Franklin, then the burden of proof would seem to be on those who maintain that it was fit to run an empire.

When the imperial historians are ready to attempt the proof, they must face a second task: they must explain away the character which the Namierist historians have given to the British statesmen of the period. The Namierists, as already indicated, have emphasized the parochial character of English politics in this period. They have cut the Whigs down to size, but they have cut down everyone else on the British political scene likewise. If Parliament was dominated by local interests, what becomes of imperial beneficence and farsightedness?

The whole effect of the Namierist discoveries, so far as the colonies are concerned, must be to show that British statesmen in the 1760's and 1770's, whether in Parliament or in the Privy Council, were too dominated by local interests to be able to run an empire. There was no institution, no party, no organization through which imperial interests, as opposed to strictly British interests, could find adequate expression. In fact the Namierist view and the view of the imperial historians are directly at odds here: though neither group seems as yet to be aware of the conflict, they cannot both be wholly right, and the coming of the Revolution would seem to confirm the Namierist view and to cast doubt on the imperialist one. The achievements of the revolutionists and the failures of the British statesmen suggest in the strongest possible terms that it was the Americans who saw things in the large and the British who wore the blinders. If this is so, may it not be that the case for the beneficence and justice of the British Empire before the Revolution has been overstated?

In response to our argument *ad hominem* the imperialists may summon the aid of the economic interpretation to show that the Americans, however high-toned their arguments, were really moved by economic considerations of the basest kind. We may, however, call these considerations basic rather than base and offer our previous character witnesses against the economists too. There is no time to plead to every indictment here, but one may perhaps answer briefly the strongest yet offered, that of Charles Beard, and then suggest how the economic interpretation needs revision. Though Beard expressly disclaimed that his economic interpretation was the whole story, he gave not merely a one-sided view but a false one. All the evidence that Beard extracted from the records of the Constitutional Convention points toward the sordid conclusion that the delegates who held public securities also held undemocratic political views, motivated consciously or unconsciously by the desire to protect their investments. Beard consistently overlooked contradictory evidence. I will cite only two examples.

The first is his treatment of Roger Sherman, the delegate to the Constitutional Convention from Connecticut. Sherman, he notes, had risen from poverty to affluence and held nearly eight thousand dollars' worth of public securities. Sherman's corresponding political philosophy he represents by the following statement: "Roger Sherman believed in reducing the popular influence in the new government to the minimum. When it was proposed that the members of the first branch of the national legislature should be elected, Sherman said that he was 'opposed to the election by the people, insisting that it ought to be by the state legislatures. The people, he said, immediately should have as little to do as may be about the government. They want information and are constantly liable to be misled.' "[8]

The quotation certainly supports Beard's view, but Beard failed to indicate what Sherman said at other times in the Convention. On June 4, four days after the speech Beard quotes, Sherman was against giving the President a veto power, because he "was against enabling any one man to stop the

---

[8] Charles Beard, *An Economic Interpretation of the Constitution of the United States* (New York, 1913), pp. 213–14.

will of the whole. No one man could be found so far above all the rest in wisdom." On June 21 he argued again for election of the House of Representatives by the state legislatures, but after election by the people had been decided upon, spoke for annual elections as against triennial, because "He thought the representatives ought to return home and mix with the people." On August 14 he was in favor of substantial pay for congressmen, because otherwise "men ever so fit could not serve unless they were at the same time rich."[9] Whatever explanation may be offered for these views, they suggest a much broader confidence in the people than might be inferred from the single remark by which Beard characterized the man.

It cannot be said that the statements which Beard neglected are concerned with an aspect of Sherman's views not relevant to the problem Beard was examining: they are certainly as relevant as the statement he did quote. His treatment of Pierce Butler, the delegate from South Carolina, is similar. Beard notes that Butler held public securities and that he argued for apportionment of representation according to wealth.[10] He neglects to mention that Butler, in spite of his security holdings, opposed full payment of the public debt, "lest it should compel payment as well to the Blood-suckers who had speculated on the distresses of others, as to those who had fought and bled for their country."[11] The statement is relevant, but directly opposed, to Beard's thesis.

It requires only a reading of the Convention debates to see that Beard's study needs revision.[12] But the trouble with the economic interpretation, as currently applied to the whole Revolutionary period, goes deeper. The trouble lies in the

[9] *Records of the Federal Convention of 1787,* ed. Max Farrand (New Haven, 1911–37), I, 99, 362; II, 291.

[10] Beard, *Economic Interpretation,* pp. 81–82, 192.

[11] Farrand, *Records,* II, 392.

[12] Robert E. Brown's *Charles Beard and the Constitutian* (Princeton, 1956) appeared too late to be of use in preparation of this paper, but the reader will find in it abundant additional evidence of deficiencies in Beard's use of the Convention records. See also Forrest McDonald, *We the People: The Economic Origins of the Constitution* (Chicago, 1958).

assumption that a conflict between property rights and human rights has been the persistent theme of American history from the beginning. It was undoubtedly the great theme of Beard's day, and Beard was on the side of human rights, where decent men belong in such a conflict. From the vantage point of twentieth-century Progressivism, he lined up the members of the Constitutional Convention, found their pockets stuffed with public securities, and concluded that they were on the wrong side.

It was a daring piece of work, and it fired the imagination of Beard's fellow progressives.[13] Vernon L. Parrington has recorded how it "struck home like a submarine torpedo—the discovery that the drift toward plutocracy was not a drift away from the spirit of the Constitution, but an inevitable unfolding from its premises." As a result of Beard's work, Parrington was able to see that "From the beginning . . . democracy and property had been at bitter odds."[14]

Parrington went on to construct his own image of American history in these terms, and he too had a powerful influence. Together he and Beard virtually captured the American past for Progressivism, a performance all the more remarkable when we consider that they did not enlist the revered Founding Fathers of the Constitution on their side.

III

It is time, however, that we had another look at the conflict between human rights and property rights; and the Revolutionary period is a good place to begin, for however strong the conflict may later have become, it was not a dominant one then. Anyone who studies the Revolution must notice at once

[13] See Douglass Adair, "The Tenth Federalist Revisited," *William and Mary Quarterly*, 3rd ser., VIII (1951), 48–67; Richard Hofstadter, "Beard and the Constitution: The History of an Idea," *American Quarterly*, II (1950), 195–213.

[14] Vernon L. Parrington, *Main Currents in American Thought* (New York, 1927–30), III, 410.

the attachment of all articulate Americans to property. "Liberty and Property" was their cry, not "Liberty and Democracy." In the face of the modern dissociation of property from liberty, historians have often felt that this concern of the revolutionists for property was a rather shabby thing, and that the constitutional principles so much talked of, before 1776 as well as afterward, were invented to hide it under a more attractive cloak. But the Americans were actually quite shameless about their concern for property and made no effort to hide it, because it did not seem at all shabby to them. The colonial protests against taxation frankly and openly, indeed passionately, affirm the sanctity of property. And the passion is not the simple and unlovely passion of greed. For eighteenth-century Americans, property and liberty were one and inseparable, because property was the only foundation yet conceived for security of life and liberty: without security for his property, it was thought, no man could live or be free except at the mercy of another.

The revolutionists' coupling of property with life and liberty was not an attempt to lend respectability to property rights, nor was it an attempt to enlist the masses in a struggle for the special privileges of a small wealthy class. Property in eighteenth-century America was not associated with special privilege, as it came to be for later generations. Land was widely owned. A recent investigation has demonstrated that in Massachusetts, a key state in the Revolution, nearly every adult male could meet the property qualifications for the franchise.[15] We hear much from modern historians about the propertyless masses of the Revolutionary period, but it is altogether improbable that the mass of Americans were without property.

The Americans fought England because Parliament threatened the security of property. They established state constitutions with property qualifications for voting and officeholding in order to protect the security of property. And when the state governments seemed inadequate to the task, they set up the

15 Robert E. Brown, *Middle-Class Democracy and the Revolution in Massachusetts, 1691–1780* (Ithaca, N.Y., 1955).

federal government for the same purpose. The economic motive was present in all these actions, but it was present as the friend of universal liberty. Devotion to security of property was not the attitude of a privileged few but the fundamental principle of the many, inseparable from everything that went by the name of freedom and adhered to the more fervently precisely because it did affect most people so intimately.

What we have done in our social and economic interpretations of the Revolution is to project into eighteenth-century America a situation which existed in the nineteenth and early twentieth centuries, when property and the means of production became concentrated in the hands of a few, when liberty if it was to exist at all had to get along not only without the aid of property but in opposition to it. We seem now to be approaching a period when property, in another form, may again be widely distributed and may again become the friend rather than the enemy of liberty. Whether such is the case or not, as historians we should stop projecting into the eighteenth century the particular economic and social antagonisms that we have found in later generations. We may still believe that the American Revolution was in part a contest about who should rule at home, but we should beware of assuming that people took sides in that contest according to whether or not they owned property. And we should totally abandon the assumption that those who showed the greatest concern for property rights were not devoted to human rights.

The challenge of the Revolution to the Namier school of historians is less direct and less crucial, but it does pose one or two questions which these historians seem not to have confronted. The first is whether the new judgment of George III has not raised that monarch's reputation a little too high. Granted that George was neither the fool nor the knave he has hitherto been thought, granted that he was moved by a desire to maintain Parliamentary supremacy rather than regal supremacy, it is nevertheless true that under his leadership England lost an important, if not the most important, part of her empire. The loss was not inevitable. All the objectives of the Americans before 1776 could have been attained within the

empire, and would have cost the mother country little or
nothing. George undoubtedly received a good deal of assistance
from other politicians in losing the colonies, but the contention of the Namierists has been that the King still held a position of central responsibility in the British government in the
1760's and 1770's, a responsibility which they have shown that
he shouldered and carried. If he was responsible then he must
be held responsible. He must bear most of the praise or blame
for the series of measures that alienated and lost the colonies,
and it is hard to see how there can be much praise.

The other question that the Revolution poses for the
Namierists may be more fundamental. Virtually no one in
British politics, they argue, had any political principles that
reached beyond local or factional interests. The argument,
though convincingly presented, presumes a consistent hypocrisy
or delusion on the part of the Whig opposition. It may be
that the Whigs were hypocritical in their attack on George III
and their support of the Americans. But if so why were they
hypocritical in just the way they were? Why did they appeal
to principles of government that later won acceptance? Can we
be sure that it was only in order to attack their opponents?
Can we be sure they were on the right side for the wrong
reasons? I do not pretend to know the answers to these questions, but I am not quite comfortable about judgments of
history in which people are condemned for being prematurely
antimonarchical.

IV

What I would suggest in conclusion is that the Whig interpretation of the American Revolution may not be as dead as
some historians would have us believe, that George Bancroft
may not have been so far from the mark as we have often
assumed. Is it not time to ask again a few of the old questions
that he was trying to answer? Let us grant that local interests
were the keynote of British politics; we must still ask: how
did the Americans, living on the edge of empire, develop the

breadth of vision and the attachment to principle which they displayed in that remarkable period from 1763 to 1789? While English politics remained parochial and the empire was dissolving for lack of vision, how did the Americans generate the forces that carried them into a new nationality and a new human liberty?

The answer, I think, may lie in a comparatively neglected field of American scholarship. During the past fifty years our investigations of the colonial period have been directed primarily by the imperial idea and the social and economic one. We have seen the colonists as part of the empire or else we have seen them as the pawns of sweeping economic and social forces. What we have neglected is the very thing that the English have been pursuing in the study of their institutions. We have neglected, comparatively speaking at least, the study of local institutions, and it is in such a study that we may perhaps discover the answer to the fundamental question that moved Bancroft, the question of how a great nation with great principles of freedom was forged from thirteen quarrelsome colonies. What kind of institutions produced a Jefferson, a Madison, a Washington, a John Adams? Not imperial institutions certainly. The imperial machinery had no place for Americans except in performing local services. No American ever sat on the Board of Trade or the Privy Council. Few Americans ever came in contact with imperial offices. It was in local American institutions that these men gained their political experience.

Two generations ago Herbert Baxter Adams thought he had the clue to the question of where American liberty began, and he put a host of graduate students to work studying the local institutions of the colonies. As we all know, they did not find precisely what Adams was looking for, but they produced a prodigious number of studies, which are still the principal source of historical information about many colonial institutions. Some have been superseded by more recent scholarship, but we need more new studies of this kind, which will take advantage of what we have learned since Adams's time about the imperial setting and about social and economic forces.

We need to know how the individual's picture of society was formed. We need to study the social groupings in every colony: towns, plantations, counties, churches, schools, clubs, and other groups which occupied the social horizons of the individual colonist. We need to study political parties and factions in every colony. We need to study the way government worked at the local level. We need to study the county courts and the justices of the peace. We need to study the distribution of land and other forms of wealth from decade to decade and from place to place. We need to know so elementary a thing as the history of representation and the history of taxation in every colony. We have always known that the Revolution had something to do with the phrase, "no taxation without representation," and yet, after two generations of modern scholarship, how many scholars have studied the history of taxation in the colonies? Who really knows anything about the history of representation?

Without abandoning what we have gained from the imperial idea and from economic interpretations, we must dissect the local institutions which produced the American Revolution, the institutions from which were distilled the ideas that enabled men of that age to stand as the architects of modern liberty. The task has not been wholly neglected. A number of scholars have been quietly working at it. I will not attempt to name them here, but their discoveries are sufficient to show that this is the direction which scholarship in colonial history should now take and that the rewards will not be small.

CHAPTER III

THE REVOLUTION CONSIDERED AS AN INTELLECTUAL MOVEMENT

❖❖❖❖❖❖❖❖❖❖❖❖❖❖❖❖❖❖❖❖❖❖❖

In the study of history, I have come to believe, it is always dangerous to assume that men do not mean what they say, that words are a façade which must be penetrated in order to arrive at some fundamental but hidden reality. The historian is seldom in a position to know that a man meant more or less than he put into his words. And the search for hidden truths can lead one to overlook or to reject the obvious, unhidden meanings that fairly leap from the records. In examining what the American colonists had to say about Parliamentary taxation, I was struck by the intellectual force of the ideas which had so often been dismissed as window dressing. The Revolution, I began to think, might profitably be thought of as an intellectual movement.

One way of approaching the subject in this light was biographical. In studying the Stamp Act crisis, I had come across the papers of a New England clergyman who exhibited a lively curiosity in everything going on around him. Ezra Stiles collected information on an enormous variety of matters and recorded his reactions in voluminous diaries, letters, and notebooks. Among the things that interested him most profoundly *was the train of events that produced the American Revolution and the formation of the United States. With the help of his papers, running to thousands of manuscript pages, it was possible to trace the Revolution in one man's mind, from loyal British colonist to independent American—to see, in other words, the making of an American.**

The life of Ezra Stiles occupied me, off and on, for ten years, and through his eyes I was able to refine my understanding of the Revolution as an intellectual movement. The piece that follows is not about Ezra Stiles, but much of it is the result of the years I spent in his company.†

IN 1740 America's leading intellectuals were clergymen and thought about theology; in 1790 they were statesmen and thought about politics. A variety of forces, some of them reaching deep into the colonial past, helped to bring about the transformation, but it was so closely associated with the revolt from England that one may properly consider the American Revolution, as an intellectual movement, to mean the substitution of political for clerical leadership and of politics for religion as the most challenging area of human thought and endeavor.

I

The American colonies had been founded during the seventeenth century, when Englishmen were still animated by the great vision of John Calvin, the vision of human depravity and divine perfection. Every human being from Adam onward must be counted, Calvin insisted, in the ranks of "those whose feet are swift to shed blood, whose hands are polluted with

---

* E. S. Morgan, *The Gentle Puritan: A Life of Ezra Stiles, 1727–1795* (New Haven, 1962).

† The essay was first published in A. M. Schlesinger, Jr., and Morton White, eds., *Paths of American Thought* (Boston, 1963), 11–33, and is reprinted here with the permission of the publisher, Houghton Mifflin Co.

rapine and murder, whose throats are like open sepulchres, whose tongues are deceitful, whose lips are envenomed, whose works are useless, iniquitous, corrupt, and deadly, whose souls are estranged from God, the inmost recesses of whose hearts are full of pravity, whose eyes are insidiously employed, whose minds are elated with insolence—in a word, all whose powers are prepared for the commission of atrocious and innumerable crimes." If a man did not actually commit such crimes, it was not for want of a desire to. God might furnish restraints of one sort or another to prevent "the perverseness of our nature from breaking out into external acts, but does not purify it within."[1]

The official church of England, born of a licentious monarch's divorce, had never fully shared in Calvin's vision. Though it absorbed much of his theology during the reign of Queen Elizabeth I, it retained a more flattering view than his of human capacities and priestly powers. The more thoroughgoing English Calvinists, the Puritans, were hopeful of effecting further reforms, but during the late 1620's and 1630's the Church and the king who headed it drew ever closer to old Roman Catholic doctrines. In the 1640's the Puritans resorted to arms, killed the king, purged the Church, and turned England into a republic. But in 1660 the monarchy was restored. Puritans, now called dissenters, were dismissed from office in both church and state; and the Church of England resumed its old ways, unimpeded by Calvinism.

It is no coincidence that England's American colonies were settled before 1640 or after 1660. Emigration offered a substitute for revolution to thousands of men and women who were discontented with the Church of England and with the government that fostered it. Puritans settled all the New England colonies, overran the Catholic refuge of the Calvert family in Maryland, and later furnished substantial numbers of settlers to New York, New Jersey, and the Carolinas. They came even to Virginia, where the majority of settlers, though remaining within the Church of England, did not share in its high-church

[1] John Calvin, *Institutes of the Christian Religion*, trans. John Allen (sixth American edition, Philadelphia, 1932), I, 263.

movement. After the Restoration, the colonies attracted large numbers of English Quakers and Scotch-Irish Presbyterians, not to mention French Huguenots and German Protestants of various denominations. Anglicans came too, and the Anglican Church was supported by law in several colonies, but the flavor of American colonial life was overwhelmingly that of the Reformation.[2]

The intellectual center of the colonies was New England, and the intellectual leaders of New England were the clergy, who preached and wrote indefatigably of human depravity and divine perfection. These two axioms, for the Puritans as for Calvin himself, required the eternal damnation of most of mankind. And since God knew all and decreed all from eternity, it followed that He had determined in advance who should be damned and who should be saved. One of the principal tasks of the ministry was to explain to men how bad they were, so bad that they all deserved damnation. That God had chosen to save any was simply through mercy, another attribute of His perfection. No man deserved salvation, no one was less guilty than another, so that God's choice rested only in Himself.

To explain these doctrines was the easiest part of the preacher's task, for most of his audience were already persuaded of them. A more difficult assignment was to assist men in discerning where they stood in the divine scheme. No man could be certain whether he was saved until the day of judgment, but there were stages in the process of redemption that took place in this life; and ministers devoted much of their preaching and writing to descriptions of them. One of the first stages was conviction, a full recognition of man's helpless and hopeless condition. A man destined for damnation could reach this stage, but not the next one, conversion. Conversion was an act of God, infusing a man's soul with the Holy Spirit, "justifying" him through the attribution of Christ's merits. Con-

[2] Cf. Frederick B. Tolles, *Quakers and the Atlantic Culture* (New York, 1960), 11; Babette M. Levy, "Early Puritanism in the Southern and Island Colonies," American Antiquarian Society, *Proceedings*, LXX (1960), 69–348.

version, for the Puritan, was so clear and precise an experience that a man who had undergone it could often specify the time and place. After conversion came sanctification, a gradual improvement in conduct, approximating, though only outwardly, the obedience which God had demanded of Adam. Sanctification could never be complete in this world, but it might be sufficiently marked to be discernible. Guided by the clergy, Puritans and other Calvinist Protestants became familiar with the morphology of redemption and expert in searching their own souls for signs of metamorphosis.

Just as the Puritans' theology revolved around human depravity and divine perfection, so did their political theory. And Puritan ministers instructed their congregations in politics as well as religion. They taught that society originates in a contract between God on the one hand and the people on the other, whereby if the people agreed to abide by His commands (though again, only outwardly, for true, inner obedience was beyond them) He would assure them outward prosperity. Having made such an agreement, the people, in another compact, voluntarily subjected themselves to a king or to other civil rulers. This was the origin of government; and the purpose of government was to restrain the sinfulness of man, to prevent and punish offenses against God. As long as a king enforced God's commands, embodying them in human laws, the people owed him obedience and assistance. If, however, moved by his own depravity, he violated God's commands or failed to enforce them, he broke the compact on which his political authority rested, and it was the people's duty to remove him lest God visit the whole community with death and destruction.[3]

These ideas had developed in England at a time when reigning monarchs exhibited (by Puritan standards) far too much depravity. Three generations of Puritans nervously scolded their kings and queens and momentarily expected

[3] Perry Miller, *The New England Mind: The Seventeenth Century* (New York, 1939), 398–431; E. S. Morgan, *The Puritan Dilemma* (Boston, 1958), 18–100.

God's wrath to descend on England. Finally, in 1649, they did away with both king and kingship. But even after monarchy ended, human depravity remained, and Englishmen faced the problem of controlling it in the new context of a republic. Ideas about the maintenance of purity, probity, and stability in a republic were offered by a number of men, the most influential of whom was James Harrington. In his *Oceana* (1656) Harrington associated republican government with widespread distribution—approaching equality—of property. He also advocated religious toleration, rotation in public office, and separation of governmental powers. With the restoration of the monarchy, Harrington's work continued for several generations to excite the admiration of a small group of British political thinkers, who probed the nature of government and speculated about methods of keeping it responsible to the people.[4] The best known of them, John Locke, re-emphasized the idea of a compact between rulers and people in order to justify the exclusion of James II from the throne.[5]

The English republican writers were read in the colonies, and Locke's political doctrines were assimiliated by American clergymen and dispensed in their sermons along with the older ideas. Every generation learned of its duty to pull down bad rulers and to uphold good ones. The colonists did not, however, develop a separate school of republican political theory. The clergy, who continued to be the principal exponents of political ideas and the most influential members of the community, devoted their creative intellectual efforts to theology, and their congregations continued to search souls. Every Sunday they attended at the meetinghouse morning and afternoon to hear the theological expositions that were always the principal ingredient in a Puritan church service. Then they went home to write in their diaries and measure their lives against what they had learned in the sermons. Daily they read their

[4] In *The Eighteenth-Century Commonwealthman* (Cambridge, Mass., 1959), Caroline Robbins has identified and discussed this political tradition.

[5] Peter Laslett, "The English Revolution and Locke's Two Treatises," *Cambridge Historical Journal*, XII (1956), 40–55.

Bibles and prayed, in private and with their families. Theology was as much a part of their lives as meat and drink.

By the middle of the eighteenth century, however, a change had begun. A series of developments, culminating in the Revolution, combined to effect a weakening of popular interest in theology and a decline in clerical leadership.

II

The first development, and the most difficult to assess, was the growth in England and Europe, transmitted gradually to America, of a new confidence in human reason. The achievements of Sir Isaac Newton and of other seventeenth-century astronomers and mathematicians belied the low estimate hitherto entertained of man's capacity to understand, without the assistance of divine revelation, God's government of the universe. The Enlightenment, as the new attitude came to be called, promised to reveal the mysteries of creation simply through the application of human intelligence.

New England ministers at first perceived no threat to religion from the Enlightenment. Although they thought poorly of human reason, they were themselves assiduous in making the most of it. They had applied it primarily to the Bible, but they now welcomed every new piece of observational knowledge in the assurance that it would help to fill out the data derived from the Bible. With the success of Newton to spur them, they began to pay more attention to the physical world and made observations of plants and animals, of comets and stars; and they sent these observations to England to assist the progress of knowledge about God's wonderful universe.

It became apparent only gradually—first in England, then in America—that reason, instead of assisting revelation, might replace it. Though Newton himself retained a firm belief in the Scriptures and spent his later years unraveling biblical prophecies, many of his admirers became deists, who believed that God reveals Himself only through the operation of His universe and not through prophets, priests, or holy scriptures. In America deism claimed few adherents before the last quarter of the eighteenth century; and it seems probable that the Enlightenment appreciably lowered the prestige of the clergy only after they had already lost much of their influence through the paradoxical operation of a religious revival.

The Great Awakening of the 1740's began when a young English minister, George Whitefield, showed American preachers how to convey the full meaning of human depravity. Traveling throughout the colonies, he preached wherever he could find an audience, whether inside a church or under a tree, and everywhere his message was the same: men deserve hell. Whitefield's talent lay in depicting the torments of hell dramatically and vividly. He could weep at will, over the fate of the men and women before him; he could impersonate God delivering the awful sentence against them. When he wept they did too, and when he pronounced the sentence against them, they fell to the ground in agony.[6]

Whitefield had already earned some notoriety by these methods before crossing the ocean. In the colonies his success was overwhelming. People flocked to him as to a new messiah. Though Anglicans remained largely unmoved, most Americans had been brought up on the doctrine of the depravity of man, and they could not find any expression of it too strong. Whitefield merely brought them a new and more emotional appreciation of truths they had known all along. Other preachers quickly imitated his methods and outdid him in the extravagance of their gestures. Gilbert Tennent of Pennsylvania made a specialty of roaring with holy laughter at sinners whom he had awakened to their helpless condition. James Davenport of Long Island liked to preach at night, when

[6] On Whitefield, see Luke Tyerman, *The Life of the Rev. George Whitefield* (New York, 1877), and John Gillies, *Memoirs of Rev. George Whitefield* (New Haven, 1834). Originally published in 1772, Gillies's work was considerably expanded in later editions. On Whitefield in New England, see Edwin L. Gaustad, *The Great Awakening in New England* (New York, 1957).

smoking candles and torches gave verisimilitude to his fiery denunciations.[7] These self-appointed apostles and dozens more like them imitated Whitefield not only in their manner of preaching but in wandering from place to place to deliver their fearful message.

Terror was the object; and terror was right. If a man faces eternal, unbearable pain, deserves it, and can do nothing to avoid it, he ought to be terrified. The preachers had another word for it, familiar to all Calvinists: they called it conviction, the awareness, denied to the complacent, of one's hopeless condition. The great thing about the new preaching was that it destroyed complacency and brought conviction to thousands. And the great thing about conviction was that conversion could be expected in many cases to follow it. Calvinist ministers for two centuries had described the divine process, and in the Great Awakening the course of conviction and conversion ran true to form. Not everyone who trembled in terror rose to the joy of conversion, but hundreds did.

As the churches filled with them, it seemed apparent that God approved the new method of preaching and the men who practiced it. Whether He also approved the older methods was questionable. Men and women who had worshiped for years without result under the guidance of an erudite but undramatic minister found grace after a few hours at the feet of some wandering apostle. The itinerant was often a layman who had never been to college and knew no Greek, Latin, or Hebrew, but had a way with an audience. If God selected him to do so much without learning, was learning perhaps more a hindrance than a help to true religion? The thought occurred to many converts and was encouraged by the increasingly confident, not to say arrogant, posture of the itinerants. Whitefield had warned broadly against ministers who preached an unknown and unfelt Christ. His followers did not hesitate to

7 Charles Chauncy, *Seasonable Thoughts on the State of Religion in New England* (Boston, 1743), 127, 151–68; *Boston Weekly News-Letter*, June 24–July 1, 1742; "Diary of Joshua Hempstead," New London Historical Society, *Proceedings*, I (1901), 379ff.

name individual ministers as dead of heart, blind leaders of the blind.

After such a pronouncement, a congregation, or a substantial portion of it, might desert their old minister. If they were a majority, they could dismiss him; if a minority, they might secede to form a church of their own, with some newly discovered prophet to lead them. Congregations had left their ministers before, especially in New England, but never before had the desertions been so many or so bitter.

At first the deserted clergymen merely looked upon the Awakening with skepticism. But as its exponents (known to the time as New Lights) became more and more extravagant, skepticism spread and grew to hostility. Ministers who had spent their lives in the study of theology, and who had perhaps been touched by the Enlightenment, were appalled at the ignorance of New Light preachers and dismissed their convictions and conversions as hysteria. Many of these opposers (Old Lights), though reluctant to recognize the fact, were already several steps down the road that led to Arminianism, Universalism, Unitarianism, and deism. The most outspoken of them, Charles Chauncy, eventually became a Universalist. But most of them pulled up short of these extremes, and those who went the whole way found few followers. The majority, clinging to the old doctrines of Calvinism, mitigated in some measure by the Enlightenment, were a humane and pious group, perhaps the most likable of New England clergymen. Some of them retained or rewon the loyalty of large congregations. But they never regained the broad influence they had enjoyed over the colonial community before the Great Awakening.

The failure of the Old Light clergy to retain intellectual leadership was due partly to the fact that they failed to win the minds of the next generation of ministers. The New Lights, in spite of their ignorance, enjoyed the blessing of Jonathan Edwards, America's foremost intellectual. It was inevitable that bright young divinity students should follow his lead. Edwards, the most brilliant theologian the country ever produced, had already generated a minor awakening of his own at Northampton, Massachusetts, six years before the Great Awakening. By comparison with Whitefield his technique was muted: he talked almost in a monotone, and never resorted to dramatic gestures, but when he spoke of eternal torments in as matter-of-fact a manner as he spoke of the weather, the effect on a New England audience could be devastating. Observing the beneficial effects of terror, Edwards applauded when Whitefield and Tennent brought the fires of hell to New England.

In ensuing years Edwards wrote a series of treatises to demonstrate the importance of the emotions or "affections" in religion and to affirm, more rigorously than ever before in New England, the dogmas of divine perfection and human depravity. By the time he died in 1758, he had gathered a tight band of followers, who continued his doctrines and developed them into a theological system known as the New Divinity.[8] The high priest of the movement was Samuel Hopkins, who preached at Great Barrington, Massachusetts, and later at Newport, Rhode Island. Other leading figures were Edwards's son, Jonathan Jr., of New Haven, and Joseph Bellamy, who from the small village of Bethlehem, Connecticut, earned the title of pope of Litchfield County.

New Divinity men were often rough and domineering with their congregations, exploding in angry denunciations; and their doctrines matched their manners. It was wrong, they said, for the unregenerate to pray, since an unregenerate man, lacking real love for God, could not pray without hypocrisy and would anger God further by his futile efforts. The only way in which the unregenerate could contribute to the glory of God was to rejoice in their own damnation—an attitude which their very unregeneracy made improbable. The New Divinity also called for a restoration of the standards of church

8 On Edwards, see Ola Winslow, *Jonathan Edwards* (New York, 1940); Perry Miller, *Jonathan Edwards* (New York, 1949). On the New Divinity, see F. H. Foster, *A Genetic History of the New England Theology* (Chicago, 1907); Joseph Haroutunian, *Piety versus Moralism* (New York, 1932).

membership that had prevailed in New England before the Half-Way Covenant of 1662: a man could join the church only if he demonstrated to the satisfaction of the other members that God had predestined him to eternal salvation. Only such persons were entitled to take communion or to have their children baptized. The remainder of the community could only listen to the minister's preaching, in hopes that God would use this means to achieve a salvation already determined though as yet undisclosed.

The New Divinity had a consistency and rigor that young intellectuals found challenging. It was the fashionable, avant-garde movement of the seventeen-fifties, sixties, seventies, and to some extent the eighties. During these years many young men had already begun to find politics or the law more satisfying intellectually than religion, but insofar as religion continued to draw young minds, they gravitated to men like Bellamy and Hopkins for guidance. As a result, by 1792 the New Divinity claimed half the pulpits in Connecticut (and an increasing number in the rest of New England), together with virtually all the candidates for the ministry—this on the testimony of Ezra Stiles, president of Yale from 1778 to 1795, who despised the New Divinity and lamented its attraction for the young men he had educated.[9]

But the success of the New Divinity among the rising generation of clergy was not matched among the people at large. Its harsh doctrines could be sustained only by intellectual or religious fervor, and the religious fervor of Americans was already waning before the complexities of the system had been completely worked out. Even as Jonathan Edwards turned out his massive justifications of the Great Awakening, that movement subsided in the manner of later religious revivals. By the time Edwards had devised an intellectual foundation for emotionalism in religion, he had begun to lose his popular audience. When he announced that he would apply new

[9] *The Literary Diary of Ezra Stiles,* ed. F. B. Dexter (New York, 1901), III, 464. Cf. Conrad Wright, *The Beginnings of Unitarianism in America* (Boston, 1955), 252–59.

standards of church membership, excluding all but the demon-
strably regenerate from the sacraments, his church at Northampton dismissed him. America's greatest intellectual of his
time spent most of his later years preaching, for want of a
wider audience, to the Indians, who perhaps least of any
group in America could understand him.

The careers of Edwards's disciples were somewhat more
fortunate but not dissimilar. Samuel Hopkins, ministering to
a large congregation at Great Barrington, saw it dwindle away
until he was obliged to leave. At Newport, Rhode Island, he
found another large congregation and again watched it decline.
The history of New Haven's Second Church, formed during
the Great Awakening by a seceding New Light minority from
New Haven's First Church, reveals the same development. The
new church prospered under the ministry of the Reverend
Samuel Bird. But after Jonathan Edwards, Jr., took charge
in 1769 and the relative simplicity of New Light gave way to
the complexities of New Divinity, the congregation diminished
until by 1795 there were not enough left or willing to support
him.[10]

Hopkins and Jonathan Edwards, Jr., enjoyed the admiration
of their ministerial colleagues, as did many other fearlessly
consistent theologians of the New Divinity, but few of them
could retain a popular following. Even while they justified
emotionalism in religion, their sermons became complex, ab-
struse, metaphysical, devoted to details of theology that the
layman found incomprehensible. During a revival of religion,
their arid doctrines might still send shudders of horror through
a receptive audience, but most of the time their congregations
found them simply dull.

Their fault lay in addressing themselves more to each other
than to their people. Engrossed in the details of their system,
they delighted in exploring new elements of consistency in it
and neglected the central problems of Christianity, until they
scarcely knew how to deal with the elementary questions of
salvation that their people put to them. Nowhere is the para-

10 Stiles, *Diary*, III, 344, 438, 562.

dox of the New Divinity's intellectual success and popular failure more graphically demonstrated than in a letter from a young minister to his mentor. Medad Rogers, after graduating from Yale in 1777, had studied theology with Benjamin Trumbull, the New Divinity minister of North Haven. When Rogers began to preach, he discovered for the first time that he did not know the answers to the questions that Christians have always had to wrestle with.

"Sir," he wrote to Trumbull,

if you do not think I deserve more reproof than direction, some of your kind instructions, would be most timely to me—as also some directions how we should begin, spend, and end the day—What to say to those under concern for a future existence, when they enquire how they shall come to the foot of a sovereign God. They try to, but cannot. They would bow to Christ's sceptre but are not able. How are we to blame, say they? We would be saved but can't be saved. How are such to be dealt with? As also, if God hath decreed all things, why is he not the Author of sin? How can any man do otherwise than he does? If God hath elected a particular number, what is there for the others to do? Why had we not Just as good lie still and do nothing? Where is the criminality of their conduct in not embracing the Gospel offers, when they were not elected? What Justice, say they, in punishing those who miss of Salvation, for not accepting the offer, when they were not elected to it? Is not God partial? If we are to be saved we shall, if not we shall be cast away. Then, what good do our works do? Will persons who lived morally honest lives, have any respect shown them upon that account, in the day of Judgment, if they appear on the left hand of the Judge? Sir, if you could find yourself willing and at leasure Just to touch upon some, or all of these, you would do me a very great favour, and perhaps be a greater monument of glory to you, Kind sir, at last, than if you had written an hundred thousand volumes of Phylosophy, Rhetorick, Logick, and History.[11]

Trumbull's answer to Rogers is not preserved. But the very fact that a young minister should ask such questions speaks

[11] Rogers to Trumbull, March 17, 1783, Benjamin Trumbull Correspondence, Yale University Library.

volumes about the state of religion in New England. The clergy for the first time in their history had lost contact with the people. In the seventeenth century when Roger Williams debated fine points of theology with John Cotton, or Increase Mather with Solomon Stoddard, people had not been bored. But the New Divinity ministers were unable to carry their congregations with them.

In earlier decades when a people became disgruntled with their minister, they had replaced him. But the American population had increased so rapidly that there were not enough ministers to go around; and since the New Divinity claimed such a large percentage of ministerial candidates, congregations were regularly faced with the necessity of taking a New Divinity man or leaving their pulpit vacant. The resultant discontent contributed in the last quarter of the eighteenth century to the rapid growth of Anglicanism, Methodism, deism, and what people at the time called "nothingarianism," a total indifference to religion. The clergy, once the most respected members of the community, became the objects of ridicule and contempt, especially in Connecticut, the stronghold of the New Divinity. In 1788, when the ministers of the state published a rebuke to the people for their neglect of public worship, the newspapers carried some rude answers. "We have heard your animadversions," said one, "upon our absence from Sabbath meetings, and humbly conceive if you wish our attendance there, you would make it worth our while to give it. To miss a sermon of the present growth, what is it but to miss of an opiate? And can the loss of a nap expose our souls to eternal perdition?"[12]

Such indifference to religion, edged with hostility to the clergy, was the end product of the developments we have been tracing from the 1740's. But though the clergy could blame themselves for much of their loss of prestige and for much of the decline of popular interest in religion, it was Parliament's attempt to tax the colonists in the 1760's that caused Ameri-

[12] *New Haven Gazette and Connecticut Magazine,* July 31, Oct. 9, 1788.

cans to transfer to politics the intellectual interest and energy that were once reserved for religion. This reorientation was directed partly by the clergy themselves. They had never stopped giving instruction in political thought; and (except for the Anglicans) throughout the 1760's and 1770's they publicly and passionately scored the actions of George III and his Parliament against the standards by which their English Puritan predecessors had judged and condemned Charles I.

Presbyterian and Congregational ministers also raised the alarm when a movement was set afoot for the establishment in the colonies of state-supported bishops. The American clergymen developed no new general ideas about government—there was no New Light in political thought, no New Politics to match the New Divinity—but the old ideas and those imported from English political theorists served well enough to impress upon their congregations the tyrannical nature of taxation without representation, and of bishops who might establish ecclesiastical courts with jurisdiction extending beyond their own denomination.

Although the clergy were a powerful influence in molding American political opinion during the Revolutionary period, they did not recover through politics the intellectual leadership they had already begun to lose. Their own principles barred them from an active role in politics. While they had always given political advice freely and exercised their influence in elections, most of them would have considered it wrong to sit in a representative assembly, on a governor's council, or on the bench. To them as to their Puritan ancestors the clerical exercise of temporal powers spelled Rome. A minister's business was, after all, the saving of souls. By the same token, however outraged he might be by the actions of the English government, however excited by the achievement of American independence, a minister could not devote his principal intellectual effort to the expounding of political ideas and political principles. As the quarrel with England developed and turned into a struggle for independence and nationhood, though the ministers continued to speak up on the American side, other voices commanding greater attention were raised by men who were free to make a career of politics and prepared to act as well as talk.

III

There had always, of course, been political leaders in the colonies, but hitherto politics had been a local affair, requiring at most the kind of talents needed for collecting votes or pulling wires. A colonial legislative assembly might occasionally engage in debates about paper money, defense, or modes of taxation; but the issues did not reach beyond the borders of the colony involved and were seldom of a kind to challenge a superior mind. No American debated imperial policy in the British Parliament, the Privy Council, or the Board of Trade. The highest political post to which a man could aspire in the colonies was that of governor, and everywhere except in Connecticut and Rhode Island, this was obtained not through political success but through having friends in England. Few native Americans ever achieved it or even tried to.

But the advent of Parliamentary taxation inaugurated a quarter century of political discussion in America that has never since been matched in intensity. With the passage of the Stamp Act in 1765, every colonial legislature took up the task of defining the structure of the British Empire; and as colonial definitions met with resistance from England, as the colonies banded together for defense and declared their independence, politics posed continental, even global, problems that called forth the best efforts of the best American minds. In no other period of our history would it be possible to find in politics five men of such intellectual stature as Benjamin Franklin, John Adams, Alexander Hamilton, James Madison, and Thomas Jefferson; and there were others only slightly less distinguished.

Whether they hailed from Pennsylvania or Virginia, New England or New York, the men who steered Americans through the Revolution, the establishment of a new nation, and the framing of the Constitution did not for the most part repudiate the political ideas inherited from the period of clerical dominance. Like the clergy, they started from a conviction of human depravity; like the clergy, they saw government originating in compact, and measured governmental performance against an absolute standard ordained by God. Like the clergy too, they found inspiration in the example of seventeenth-century Englishmen. Sometimes they signed their own attacks on George III or his ministers with the names of John Hampden, John Pym, or other Parliamentary heroes in the struggle against Charles I. They read the works of Harrington and of Harrington's later admirers; and after the Declaration of Independence, when they found themselves in a position similar to that of England in the 1650's, they drew heavily on the arsenal of political ideas furnished by these latter-day republicans.

Indeed, most of the ideas about government which American intellectuals employed first in their resistance to Parliament, and then in constructing their own governments, had been articulated earlier in England and were still in limited circulation there. The social compact, fundamental law, the separation of powers, human equality, religious freedom, and the superiority of republican government were continuing ideals for a small but ardent group of Englishmen who, like the Americans, believed that the British constitution was basically republican and drew inspiration from it while attacking the ministers and-monarch who seemed to be betraying it.[13] It is perhaps no accident that the work in which Americans first repudiated monarchy, *Common Sense,* was written by an Englishman, Thomas Paine, who had come to America only two years before.

But if Englishmen supplied the intellectual foundations both for the overthrow of English rule and for the construction of republican government, Americans put the ideas into practice and drew on American experience and tradition to devise refinements and applications of the greatest importance. That

[13] See again Robbins, *Eighteenth-Century Commonwealthman.*

republican ideas, which existed in a state of obscurity in England, should be congenial in the colonies was due in the first place to the strong continuing Calvinist tradition which had been nourished over the years by the American clergy. But fully as important was the fact that during a hundred and fifty years of living in the freedom of a relatively isolated and empty continent, the colonists had developed a way of life in which republican ideas played a visible part. When Parliamentary taxation set Americans to analyzing their relationship to the mother country, they could not escape seeing that the social, economic, and political configuration of America had diverged from that of England in ways that made Americans better off than Englishmen. And the things that made them better off could be labeled republican.

England's practical experience with republicanism had lasted only eleven years. With the return of Charles II in 1660, Englishmen repudiated their republic and the Puritans who had sponsored it. Though a small minority continued to write and talk about republicanism and responsible government, they wielded no authority. The House of Commons grew more powerful but less common, and the main current of English national life flowed in the channels of monarchy, aristocracy, and special privilege. Americans, by contrast, though formally subjects of the king, had lived long under conditions that approximated the ideals of the English republican theorists. Harrington thought he had found in the England of his day the widespread ownership of property that seemed to him a necessary condition for republican government; but throughout the colonies ownership of property had always been more widespread than in England. Furthermore no member of the nobility had settled in America, so that people were accustomed to a greater degree of social as well as economic equality than existed anywhere in England.

During the 1640's and 1650's England had seen a rapid multiplication of religious sects, which produced a wide belief in religious freedom, but after the Anglican Church had reimposed its controls in the 1660's, the most that other denominations could hope for was toleration. In America, religious diversity had steadily increased, and with it came a religious freedom which, if still imperfect, surpassed anything England had ever known.

Though the English people had twice removed an unsatisfactory king, in 1649 and 1688, the English government remained far less responsible and far less responsive to the people than any colonial government. The voting population had expanded during the seventeenth century, but in 1760 it embraced less than a quarter of the adult males, while in the colonies it probably included the great majority of them. In England, the government paid hundreds of officeholders whose offices, carrying no duties, existed solely for the enrichment of those who held them. In the colonies such sinecures were few. Americans thought that government existed to do a job, and they created no offices except for useful purposes.

Thus when the quarrel with Parliament began, the colonists already had what English reformers wanted. And the colonists were inclined to credit their good fortune not to the accident of geography but to their own superior virtue and political sophistication. The interpretation was not without foundation: since Calvinist traditions were still strong among them and since they had often learned of British republican ideas through the sermons of Calvinist clergymen, Americans retained what the Enlightenment had dimmed in England and Europe, a keen sense of human depravity and of the dangers it posed for government. Although their own governments had hitherto given little evidence of depravity, by comparison with those of Europe, they were expert at detecting it in any degree. They had always been horrified by the open corruption of British politics and feared it would lead to tyranny. When Parliament attempted to tax them and sent swarms of customs collectors, sailors, and soldiers to support the attempt, their fears were confirmed. In resisting the British and in forming their own governments, they saw the central problem as one of devising means to check the inevitable operation of depravity in men who wielded power. English statesmen had succumbed to it. How could Americans avoid their mistakes?

IV

In the era of the American Revolution, from 1764 to 1789, this was the great intellectual challenge. Although human depravity continued to pose as difficult theological problems as ever, the best minds of the period addressed themselves to the rescue, not of souls, but of governments, from the perils of corruption. Of course the problem was not new, nor any more susceptible of final solution than it had been in an earlier time, but Americans in the Revolutionary period contributed three notable principles to men's efforts to deal with it.

The first principle, which evolved from the struggle with Parliament, was that the people of one region ought not to exercise dominion over those of another, even though the two may be joined together. It was an idea that overlapped and greatly facilitated the slower but parallel development of the more general belief in human equality. In objecting to British taxation in 1764 the colonists had begun by asserting their right to equal treatment with the king's subjects in Great Britain: Englishmen could not be taxed except by their representatives; neither therefore could Americans. Within a year or two the idea was extended to a denial that Parliament, representing the electors of Great Britain, could exercise any authority over the colonies. The empire, according to one American writer, was "a confederacy of states, independent of each other, yet united under one head," namely the king. "I cannot find," said another, "that the inhabitants of the colonies are dependent on the people of Britain, or the people of Britain on them, any more than Kent is on Sussex, or Sussex on Kent."[14]

It took varying lengths of time for other Americans to reach the position thus anonymously expressed in the press in 1765 and 1766. Franklin stated it later in 1766;[15] Jefferson, James Wilson, and John Adams had all expressed it by the beginning

[14] E. S. Morgan, *Prologue to Revolution: Sources and Documents on the Stamp Act Crisis* (Chapel Hill, 1959), 73, 91.

[15] Verner Crane, *Benjamin Franklin's Letters to the Press, 1758–1775* (Chapel Hill, 1950), p. xlii.

of 1775.[16] It was frequently buttressed by the citation of precedents from English constitutional history, but it rested on a principle capable of universal application, the principle stated in the preamble of the Declaration of Independence, that every people is entitled, by the laws of nature and of nature's God, to a separate and equal station.

Before Independence this principle offered a means of reorganizing the British Empire so as to defeat the tyranny which Americans thought English statesmen were developing in the extension of taxation. If a British legislature, in which the colonists were not represented, could govern them, then neither British nor colonial freedom could be safe. Americans without a voice in the government could not defend their rights against corrupt rulers. Englishmen, relieved of expenses by American taxation, might rejoice for the moment, but their rulers, no longer dependent on them financially, would be able to govern as they pleased and would eventually escape popular control altogether. The only solution was to give each legislature power only over the people who chose it.

In the 1770's England was unwilling to listen to the colonial arguments, but ultimately adopted the American principle in forming the Commonwealth of Nations. The independent United States applied the principle not only in the confederation of states but in the annexation of other areas. When Virginia in 1781 offered the United States Congress her superior claim to the old Northwest, it was with the stipulation that the region be divided into separate republican states, each of which was to be admitted to the union on equal terms with the old ones. The stipulation, though not accepted by Congress at the time, was carried out in Jefferson's land ordinance of 1784 and in the Northwest Ordinance of 1787 which superseded it. The United States never wavered from the principle until after the Spanish-American War, when it

16 Thomas Jefferson, *A Summary View of the Rights of British America* (Williamsburg, 1774); James Wilson, *Considerations on the Nature and the Extent of the Legislative Authority of the British Parliament* (Philadelphia, 1774); John Adams, *Works,* ed. C. F. Adams (Boston, 1850–56), IV, 3–177.)

temporarily accepted government of areas which it had no intention of admitting to the union on equal terms.

The second contribution of the American revolutionists was an application of the assumption, implicit in the whole idea of a compact between rulers and people, that a people can exist as a people before they have a government and that they can act as a people independently of government. The Puritans had distinguished between the compact of a group of individuals with God, by which they became a people, and the subsequent compact between this people and their rulers, by which government was created. John Locke had similarly distinguished between the dissolution of society and of government, and so, at least tacitly, had the revolutionists. They would have been more daring, not to say foolhardy, if they had undertaken to destroy the bonds of society as well as of government. But in their haste to form new governments after the royal government in each colony dissolved, the revolutionists followed a procedure that did not clearly distinguish the people from the government. Provincial congresses, exercising a *de facto* power, drafted and adopted permanent constitutions, which in most cases then went into effect without submission to a popular vote.

When the Massachusetts provincial congress proposed to follow this procedure in 1776, the citizens of the town of Concord pointed out the dangerous opening which it offered to human depravity. A *de facto* government that legitimized itself could also alter itself. Whatever safeguards it adopted against corruption could easily be discarded by later legislators: "a Constitution alterable by the Supreme Legislative is no Security at all to the Subject against any Encroachment of the Governing part on any or on all of their Rights and priviliges." The town therefore suggested that a special popularly elected convention be called for the sole purpose of drafting a constitution, which should then be submitted to the people for approval.[17]

17 Robert J. Taylor, ed., *Massachusetts, Colony to Commonwealth: Documents on the Formation of Its Constitution, 1775–1780* (Chapel Hill, 1961), 45.

It is impossible to determine who was responsible for Concord's action, but the protest displays a refinement in the application of republican ideas that does not appear to have been expressed before. Concord's suggestion was eventually followed in the drafting and adoption of the Massachusetts constitution of 1780 and of every subsequent constitution established in the United States. By it the subservience of government to the people was secured through a constitution clearly superior to the government it created, a constitution against which the people could measure governmental performance and against which each branch of government could measure the actions of the other branches. The separation of governmental powers into a bicameral legislature, an executive, and a judiciary, which was an older and more familiar way of checking depravity, was rendered far more effective by the existence of a written constitution resting directly on popular approval. The written constitution also proved its effectiveness in later years by perpetuating in America the operation of judicial review, of executive veto, and of a powerful upper house of the legislature, all of which had been or would be lost in England, where the constitution was unwritten and consisted of customary procedures that could be altered at will by Parliament.

V

Thus by the time the Revolution ended, Americans had devised a way to establish the superiority of the people to their government and so to control man's tyranny over man. For the same purpose Americans had formulated the principle that no people should exercise dominion over another people. But the way in which they first employed the latter principle in running the new nation did not prove satisfactory. As thirteen separate colonies the people of America had joined to combat Parliamentary taxation, and the result had been thirteen independent republics. It had been an exhilarating experience, and it had led them almost from the beginning to think of themselves in some degree as one people. But the thought was not completed: they did not coalesce into one republic with one government. Instead, as thirteen separate and equal peoples, they set up a "perpetual union" in which they were joined only through a Congress in which each state had one vote. They gave the Congress responsibility for their common concerns. But they did not give it the ordinary powers of a government to tax or legislate.

Because of the straightforward equality of the member states and because the Congress did not possess the means by which governments generally ran to tyranny, the confederation seemed a safe shape in which to cast the new nation. Actually danger lurked in the fact that the Congress had insufficient power to carry out the responsibilities which the states assigned to it. After the British troops were defeated and the need for united action became less obvious, state support of the Congress steadily declined. Without coercive powers, the Congress could not act effectively either at home or abroad, and the nation was increasingly exposed to the danger of foreign depredations. At the same time, the state governments were proving vulnerable to manipulation by corrupt or ambitious politicians and were growing powerful at the expense not only of the Congress but of the people. Some undertook irresponsible inflationary measures that threatened property rights. Unless the state governments were brought under more effective control, local demagogues might destroy the union and replace the tyranny of Parliament with a new domestic brand.

Although a few men foresaw the drawbacks of a weak Congress from the beginning, most people needed time to show them. The Massachusetts legislature, perceiving that the experience of the state could be applied to the whole United States, in 1785 suggested a national constitutional convention to create a central authority capable of acting effectively in the interests of the whole American people. But in 1785, Americans were not yet convinced that what they had was inadequate. The Massachusetts delegates to the Congress replied to their state's suggestion with the same arguments that had in the first place prompted Americans to base their union on a weak coordinative Congress rather than a real national government: it would be impossible, they said, to prevent such a government from escaping popular control. With headquarters remote from most of its constituents, with only a select few from each state engaged in it, a national government would offer too many opportunities for corruption.[18] The fear was supported by the views of respected European political thinkers. Montesquieu, who had been widely read in America, maintained that republican government was suited only to small areas. A confederation of republics might extend far, but a single republican government of large extent would either fall a prey to the ambitions of a few corrupt individuals, or else it would break up into a number of smaller states.[19]

These sentiments were so widely held that they prevented any effort to establish a national government until 1787. And when a convention was finally called in that year it was charged, not to create a new government, but simply to revise the Articles of Confederation. The members of the convention, without authorization, assumed the larger task and turned themselves into a national Constitutional Convention. They did so because they became convinced that, contrary to popular belief, a large republic would not necessarily succumb to corruption. The man who persuaded the Convention, insofar as any one man did it, was James Madison, one of the delegates from Virginia.

In the month before the Convention assembled, Madison had drawn up some observations on the "Vices of the Political System of the United States." Following a hint thrown out by David Hume, he reached the conclusion that "the inconveniencies of popular States contrary to the prevailing Theory, are in proportion not to the extent, but to the narrowness of their limits." In the state governments that had operated since 1776, the great defect was a tendency of the majority to tyrannize over the minority. Madison took it as axiomatic that "in

18 Edmund C. Burnett, ed., *Letters of Members of the Continental Congress* (Washington, 1921–36), VIII, 206–10.

19 Montesquieu, *Spirit of the Laws* (New York, 1949), 120 (Book VIII, c. 16).

republican Government the majority however composed, ultimately give the law." Unless a way could be found to control them, the majority would inevitably oppress the minority, because the individuals who made up the majority were as susceptible as any king or lord to the operation of human depravity. The most effective curb, Madison suggested, was to make the territory of the republic so large that a majority would have difficulty forming. Men being hopelessly selfish would inevitably seek to capture the government for selfish purposes, and in a small republic they might easily form combinations to secure the necessary majority. But in a large republic, "the Society becomes broken into a greater variety of interests, of pursuits of passions, which check each other, whilst those who may feel a common sentiment have less opportunity of communication and concert."[20]

This insight, later given classic expression in the tenth *Federalist* paper, was the most fruitful intellectual achievement of the Revolutionary period, the third of the three principles mentioned earlier. It gave Madison and his colleagues at Philadelphia the courage to attempt a republican government for the whole nation. The constitution which they drew up would provide the American peoples with a government that would effectively make them one people. The government would incorporate all the protections to liberty that they still cherished from their British heritage; it would preserve both imported and home-grown republican traditions; and it would employ the political principles developed during the Revolution. It would be a government inferior to the people and one in which no people should have dominion over another, a government in which almost every detail was prompted by the framers' determination to control the operation of human depravity. Many Americans, doubting that the safeguards would work, opposed the adoption of the Constitution. But the character of American politics from 1789 to the present day has borne out Madison's observation: majorities

[20] James Madison, *Writings*, ed. Gaillard Hunt (New York, 1900–1910), II, 361–69.

in the United States have been composed of such a variety of interests that they have seldom proved oppressive, and the national government has been a stronger bulwark of freedom than the state governments.

The establishment of a national republic renewed the challenge which the contest with Great Britain had presented to the best minds of America. In the Constitutional Convention and in the conduct of the new national government, Americans found scope for talents that the Revolution had uncovered. Jefferson, Hamilton, Madison, and John Adams received from national politics the stimulus that made them great. The writings in which they embodied their best thoughts were state papers.

In the course of the nineteenth century the stimulus was somehow lost, in hard cider, log cabins, and civil war. Intellect moved away from politics; and intellectual leadership, having passed from clergy to statesmen, moved on to philosophers, scientists, and novelists. But during the brief period when America's intellectual leaders were her political leaders, they created for their country the most stable popular government ever invented and presented to the world three political principles which men have since used repeatedly and successfully to advance human freedom and responsible government.

CHAPTER IV

THE PURITAN ETHIC AND THE AMERICAN REVOLUTION

❖❖❖❖❖❖❖❖❖❖❖❖❖❖❖❖❖❖❖❖❖❖❖

In acquainting myself with Ezra Stiles, as well as in earlier efforts to understand the Revolution, I read several newspapers of the period. There, as in pamphlets and letters, an unexpected theme presented itself insistently. It appeared most strikingly in arguments for the successive non-importation agreements. The ostensible purpose of the agreements was to bring pressure on Parliament to repeal its objectionable measures: the Sugar Act, the Stamp Act, the Townshend Acts, the Coercive Acts. To be effective, non-importation had to be universal, and the colonists exhorted themselves to keep the agreements. Yet the exhortations seldom stressed solidarity. Instead, the authors praised austerity for its own sake or for the sake of the virtue and good character that austerity would foster. Doing without British imports, it seemed, would be good for the soul, whatever Parliament did.

If one took the words at face value, then the Revolution was shaped by forces that reached well beyond the immediate quarrel over Parliamentary taxation. I was prepared to take the words at face value, for, whatever may have been the motives, the authors were appealing to attitudes and values

*that they believed their countrymen shared. My next step in
thinking about the Revolution was therefore to begin a study
of attitudes toward work and wealth in America, particularly
the attitude embodied in the arguments for non-importation,
the attitude that for want of a better phrase I call the Puritan
Ethic. I wished to carry the study back to the first settlements
and even beyond, to the expectations that previous experience
had induced in the settlers. But first I wished to identify and
explore the more obvious ways in which the Puritan Ethic
affected the course of the Revolution. In order to do so, I read
for several years in the publications of the time and in the
great collections of public and private papers of the Founding
Fathers. Before turning back to the period of discovery and
settlement, I tried to assess, in the essay that follows,* what I
had learned about the Revolution as an ethical movement.*

THE American Revolution, we have been told, was radical and
conservative, a movement for home rule and a contest for rule
at home, the product of a rising nationality and the cause of
that nationality, the work of designing demagogues and a
triumph of statesmanship. There were evidently many revolutions, many contests, divisions, and developments that deserve
to be considered as part of the American Revolution. This
paper deals in a preliminary, exploratory way with an aspect of
the subject that has hitherto received little attention. Without
pretending to explain the whole exciting variety of the Revolution, I should like to suggest that the movement in all its
phases, from the resistance against Parliamentary taxation in
the 1760's to the establishment of a national government and
national policies in the 1790's was affected, not to say guided,
by a set of values inherited from the age of Puritanism.

These values or ideas, which I will call collectively the Puri-

---

* The essay, in a shortened version, was delivered as a lecture under
the auspices of the Charles Warren Center at Harvard University in 1966
and was first published in the *William and Mary Quarterly*, XXIV (Jan.,
1967), 3–43.

tan Ethic,[1] were not unconscious or subconscious, but were deliberately and openly expressed by men of the time. The men who expressed them were not Puritans, and few of the ideas included in the Puritan Ethic were actually new. Many of them had existed in other intellectual contexts before Puritanism was heard of, and many of them continue to exist today, as they did in the Revolutionary period, without the support of Puritanism. But Puritanism wove them together in a single rational pattern, and Puritans planted the pattern in America. It may be instructive, therefore, to identify the ideas as the Puritans defined and explained them before going on to the way in which they were applied in Revolutionary America after they had emerged from the Puritan mesh.

I

The values, ideas, and attitudes of the Puritan Ethic, as the term will be used here, clustered around the familiar idea of "calling." God, the Puritans believed, called every man to serve Him by serving society and himself in some useful, productive occupation. Before entering on a trade or profession, a man must determine whether he had a calling to undertake it. If he had talents for it, if it was useful to society, if it was appropriate to his station in life, he could feel confident that God called him to it. God called no one to a life of prayer or to a life of ease or to any life that added nothing to the common good. It was a "foul disorder in any Commonwealth that there should be suffered rogues, beggars, vagabonds." The life of a monk or nun was no calling because prayer must be the

---

[1] I have chosen this term rather than the familiar "Protestant Ethic" of Max Weber, partly because I mean something slightly different and partly because Weber confined his phrase to attitudes prevailing while the religious impulse was paramount. The attitudes that survived the decline of religion he designated as the "spirit of capitalism." In this essay I have not attempted to distinguish earlier from later, though I am concerned with a period when the attitudes were no longer dictated primarily by religion.

daily exercise of every man, not a way for particular men to make a living. And perhaps most important, the life of the carefree aristocrat was no calling: "miserable and damnable is the estate of those that being enriched with great livings and revenues, do spend their days in eating and drinking, in sports and pastimes, not employing themselves in service for Church or Commonwealth."[2]

Once called to an occupation, a man's duty to the Maker who called him demanded that he labor assiduously at it. He must shun both idleness or neglect of his calling, and sloth, or slackness in it. Recreation was legitimate, because body and mind sometimes needed a release in order to return to work with renewed vigor. But recreation must not become an end in itself. One of the Puritans' objections to the stage was that professional players made recreation an occupation and thereby robbed the commonwealth of productive labor. The emphasis throughout was on productivity for the benefit of society.

In addition to working diligently at productive tasks, a man was supposed to be thrifty and frugal. It was good to produce but bad to consume any more than necessity required. A man was but the steward of the possessions he accumulated. If he indulged himself in luxurious living, he would have that much less with which to support church and society. If he needlessly consumed his substance, either from carelessness or from sensuality, he failed to honor the God who furnished him with it.

In this atmosphere the tolerance accorded to merchants was grudging. The merchant was suspect because he tended to encourage unnecessary consumption and because he did not actually produce anything; he simply moved things about. It was formally recognized that making exchanges could be a useful service, but it was a less essential one than that performed by the farmer, the shoemaker, or the weaver. Moreover, the merchant sometimes demeaned his calling by practicing it to the detriment rather than the benefit of society: he took advantage of his position to collect more than the value of his services, to charge what the market would bear. In short, he

2 William Perkins, *Workes* (London, 1626–31), I, 755–56.

sometimes engaged in what a later generation would call speculation.

As the Puritan Ethic induced a suspicion of merchants, it also induced, for different reasons, suspicion of prosperity. Superficial readers of Max Weber have often leapt to the conclusion that Puritans viewed economic success as a sign of salvation. In fact, Puritans were always uncomfortable in the presence of prosperity. Although they constantly sought it, although hard work combined with frugality could scarcely fail in the New World to bring it, the Puritans always felt more at ease when adversity made them tighten their belts. They knew that they must be thankful for prosperity, that like everything good in the world it came from God. But they also knew that God could use it as a temptation, that it could lead to idleness, sloth, and extravagance. These were vices, not simply because they in turn led to poverty, but because God forbade them. Adversity, on the other hand, though a sign of God's temporary displeasure, and therefore a cause for worry, was also God's means of recalling a people to Him. When God showed anger man knew he must repent and do something about it. In times of drought, disease, and disaster a man could renew his faith by exercising frugality and industry, which were good not simply because they would lead to a restoration of prosperity, but because God demanded them.

The ambivalence of this attitude toward prosperity and adversity was characteristic of the Puritans: it was their lot to be forever improving the world, in full knowledge that every improvement would in the end prove illusory. While rejoicing at the superior purity of the churches they founded in New England, they had to tell themselves that they had often enjoyed more godliness while striving against heavy odds in England. The experience caused Nathaniel Ward, the "simple cobbler of Aggawam," to lament the declension that he was sure would overtake the Puritans in England after they gained the upper hand in the 1640's: "my heart hath mourned, and mine eyes wept in secret, to consider what will become of multitudes of my dear Country-men [in England], when they shall enjoy what they now covet."[3] Human flesh was too proud to stand success; it needed the discipline of adversity to keep it in line. And Puritans accordingly relished every difficulty and worried over every success.

This thirst for adversity found expression in a special kind of sermon, the Jeremiad, which was a lament for the loss of virtue and a warning of divine displeasure and desolation to come. The Jeremiad was a rhetorical substitute for adversity, designed to stiffen the virtue of the prosperous and successful by assuring them that they had failed. Nowhere was the Puritan Ethic more assiduously inculcated than in these laments, and it accordingly became a characteristic of the virtues which that ethic demanded that they were always seen to be expiring, if not already dead. Industry and frugality in their full vigor belonged always to an earlier generation, which the existing one must learn to emulate if it would avoid the wrath of God.

These ideas and attitudes were not peculiar to Puritans. The voluminous critiques of the Weber thesis have shown that similar attitudes prevailed widely among many groups and at many times. But the Puritans did have them, and so did Americans in the time of the Revolution and indeed for long after it. It matters little by what name we call these attitudes or where they came from. "The Puritan Ethic" is used here simply as an appropriate shorthand phrase to designate them, and should not be taken to imply that the American revolutionists were Puritans.[4]

The Puritan Ethic as it existed among the Revolutionary generation had in fact lost for most men the endorsement of an omnipresent angry God. The element of divinity had not entirely departed, but it was a good deal diluted. The values and precepts derived from it, however, remained intact and were reinforced by contemporary expositions of history that

[3] Nathaniel Ward, *The Simple Cobbler of Aggawam in America* (London, 1647), 41.

[4] For a lively dissent from the extension of the term south of the Mason-Dixon line, see C. Vann Woodward, "The Southern Ethic in a Puritan World," *William and Mary Quarterly*, XXV (1968), 343–70.

attributed the rise and fall of empires to the acquisition and loss of the same virtues that God had demanded of the founders of New England. Rome, it was learned, had risen while its citizens worked at their callings and led lives of simplicity and frugality. Success as usual had resulted in extravagance and luxury. "The ancient, regular, and laborious life was relaxed and sunk in Idleness," and the torrent of vices thus let loose had overwhelmed the empire. In modern times the frugal Dutch had overthrown the extravagant Spanish.[5] The lesson of history carried the same imperatives that were intoned from the pulpit.

Whether they derived their ideas from history thus interpreted or from the Puritan tradition or elsewhere, Americans of the Revolutionary period in every colony and state paid tribute to the Puritan Ethic and repeated its injunctions. Although it was probably strongest among Presbyterians and Congregationalists like Benjamin Rush and Samuel Adams, it is evident enough among Anglicans like Henry Laurens and Richard Henry Lee and even among deists like Franklin and Jefferson. Jefferson's letters to his daughters sometimes sound as though they had been written by Cotton Mather: "It is your future happiness which interests me, and nothing can contribute more to it (moral rectitude always excepted) than the contracting a habit of industry and activity. Of all the cankers of human happiness, none corrodes it with so silent, yet so baneful a tooth, as indolence." "Determine never to be idle. No person will have occasion to complain of the want of time, who never loses any. It is wonderful how much may be done, if we are always doing."[6] And Jefferson of course followed his own injunction: a more methodically industrious man never lived.

The Puritan Ethic whether enjoined by God, by history, or by philosophy, called for diligence in a productive calling,

---

[5] Purdie and Dixon's *Virginia Gazette* (Williamsburg), Sept. 5, 1771. Cf. *Pennsylvania Chronicle* (Philadelphia), Feb. 9–16, May 4–11, 1767; *Newport Mercury*, March 7, 1774; and *Boston Evening Post*, Nov. 30, 1767.

[6] To Martha Jefferson, March 28, May 5, 1787, in Julian Boyd *et al.*, eds., *The Papers of Thomas Jefferson* (Princeton, 1950–   ), XI, 250, 349.

beneficial both to society and to the individual. It encouraged frugality and frowned on extravagance. It viewed the merchant with suspicion and speculation with horror. It distrusted prosperity and gathered strength from adversity. It prevailed widely among Americans of different times and places, but those who urged it most vigorously always believed it to be on the point of expiring and in need of renewal.

The role of these ideas in the American Revolution—during the period, say, roughly from 1764 to 1789—was not explicitly causative. That is, the important events of the time can seldom be seen as the result of these ideas and never as the result solely of these ideas. Yet the major developments, the resistance to Great Britain, independence, the divisions among the successful revolutionists, and the formulation of policies for the new nation, were all discussed and understood by men of the time in terms derived from the Puritan Ethic. And the way men understood and defined the issues before them frequently influenced their decisions.

II

In the first phase of the American Revolution, the period of agitation between the passage of the Sugar Act in 1764 and the outbreak of hostilities at Lexington in 1775, Americans were primarily concerned with finding ways to prevent British authority from infringing what they considered to be their rights. The principal point of contention was Parliament's attempt to tax them; and their efforts to prevent taxation, short of outright resistance, took two forms: economic pressure through boycotts and political pressure through the assertion of political and constitutional principles. Neither form of protest required the application of the Puritan Ethic, but both in the end were affected by it.

The boycott movements were a means of getting British merchants to bring their weight to bear on Parliament for the specific purpose of repealing tax laws. In each case the boycotts began with extralegal voluntary agreements among citizens not to consume British goods. In 1764–65, for instance, artisans agreed to wear only leather working clothes. Students forbore imported beer. Fire companies pledged themselves to eat no mutton in order to increase the supply of local wool. Backed by the nonconsumers, merchants of New York, Philadelphia, and Boston agreed to import no British goods until the repeal of the Stamp Act. The pressure had the desired effect: the Stamp Act was repealed and the Sugar Act revised. When the Townshend Acts and later the Coercive Acts were passed, new non-consumption and non-importation agreements were launched.[7]

From the outset these colonial boycott movements were more than a means of bringing pressure on Parliament. That is to say, they were not simply negative in intent. They were also a positive end in themselves, a way of reaffirming and rehabilitating the virtues of the Puritan Ethic. Parliamentary taxation offered Americans the prospect of poverty and adversity, and, as of old, adversity provided a spur to virtue. In 1764, when Richard Henry Lee of Virginia got news of the Sugar Act, he wrote to a friend in London: "Possibly this step of the mother country, though intended to oppress and keep us low, in order to secure our dependence, may be subversive of this end. Poverty and oppression, among those whose minds are filled with ideas of British liberty, may introduce a virtuous industry, with a train of generous and manly sentiments. . . ."[8] And so it proved in the years that followed: as their Puritan forefathers had met providential disasters with a renewal of the virtue that would restore God's favor, the Revolutionary generation met taxation with a self-denial and industry that they hoped would restore their accustomed freedom and enable them to identify with their virtuous ancestors.

The advocates of non-consumption and non-importation, in urging austerity on their countrymen, made very little of the

---

[7] Arthur M. Schlesinger, *The Colonial Merchants and the American Revolution, 1763–1776* (New York, 1918), remains the best account of these movements.

[8] To [Unknown], May 31, 1764, in James C. Ballagh, ed., *The Letters of Richard Henry Lee* (New York, 1911), I, 7.

effect that self-denial would have on the British government. Instead they rejoiced in non-importation and non-consumption as means of renewing ancestral virtues, and reminded Americans that they had been "of late years insensibly drawn into too great a degree of *luxury* and *dissipation*."[9] Parliamentary taxation was a blessing in disguise, because it produced the non-importation and non-consumption agreements. "Luxury," the people of the colonies were told, "has taken deep root among us, and to cure a people of luxury were an Herculean task indeed; what perhaps no power on earth but a British Parliament, in the very method they are taking with us, could possibly execute."[10] Parliamentary taxation, like an Indian attack in earlier years, was thus both a danger to be resisted and an act of providence to recall Americans from declension: "The Americans have plentifully enjoyed the delights and comforts, as well as the necessaries of life, and it is well known that an increase of wealth and affluence paves the way to an increase of luxury, immorality and profaneness, and here kind providence interposes; and as it were, obliges them to forsake the use of one of their delights, to preserve their liberty."[11] The principal object of this last homily was tea, which, upon being subjected to a Parliamentary duty, became luxurious and enervating. Physicians even discovered that it was bad for the health.[12] Importations, it now appeared, were mainly luxuries, "Baubles of Britain," "foreign trifles."[13]

In these appeals for self-denial, the Puritan Ethic acquired a value that had been only loosely associated with it hitherto: it became an essential condition of political liberty. Americans like Englishmen had long associated liberty with property. They now concluded that both rested on virtue. An author

[9] *Boston Evening Post*, Nov. 16, 1767.

[10] *Virginia Gazette* (Purdie and Dixon), June 1, 1769 (reprinted from *New York Chronicle*).

[11] *Newport Mercury*, Dec. 13, 1773.

[12] *Ibid.*, Nov. 9, 1767, Nov. 29, 1773, Feb. 14, 28, 1774.

[13] *Boston Evening Post*, Nov. 9, 16, 1767; to Arthur Lee, Oct. 31, 1771, in H. A. Cushing, ed., *The Writings of Samuel Adams* (New York, 1904–8), II, 267.

who signed himself "Frugality" advised the readers of the *Newport Mercury,* "We may talk and boast of liberty; but after all, the industrious and frugal only will be free,"[14] free not merely because their self-denial would secure repeal of Parliamentary taxes, but because freedom was inseparable from virtue, and frugality and industry were the most conspicuous public virtues. Bostonians were told that "by consuming *less* of what we are not really in want of, and by industriously cultivating and improving the natural advantages of our own country, we might save our *substance, even our lands,* from becoming the property of others, and we might effectually preserve our *virtue* and our *liberty,* to the latest posterity." Liberty, virtue, and property offered a powerful rallying call to Americans. Each supported the others; but virtue was the *sine qua non* of the trio, for while liberty would expire without the support of property, property itself could not exist without industry and frugality. Expounding this point, the *Pennsylvania Journal* assured its readers that "Our enemies very well know that dominion and property are closely connected; and that to impoverish us, is the surest way to enslave us. Therefore, if we mean still to be free, let us unanimously lay aside foreign superfluities, and encourage our own manufacture. SAVE YOUR MONEY AND YOU WILL SAVE YOUR COUNTRY!"[15]

There was one class of Americans who could take no comfort in this motto. The merchants, on whom non-importation depended, stood to lose by the campaign for austerity, and it is not surprising that they showed less enthusiasm for it than the rest of the population. Their lukewarmness only served to heighten the suspicion with which their calling was still viewed. "Merchants have no country," Jefferson once remarked. "The mere spot they stand on does not constitute so strong an attachment as that from which they draw their gains."[16] And John

<hr>

14 Feb. 28, 1774.

15 *Boston Evening Post,* Nov. 16, 1767; *Pennsylvania Journal* (Philadelphia), Dec. 10, 1767.

16 To Horatio Spafford, March 17, 1817, quoted in Boyd, ed., *Jefferson Papers,* XIV, 221.

Adams at the Continental Congress was warned by his wife's uncle that merchants "have no Object but their own particular Interest and they must be Contrould or they will ruin any State under Heaven."[17]

Such attitudes had been nourished by the merchants' behavior in the 1760's and 1770's. After repeal of the Stamp Act, Silas Downer, secretary of the Sons of Liberty in Providence, Rhode Island, wrote to the New York Sons of Liberty that "From many observations when the Stamp Act was new, I found that the Merchants in general would have quietly submitted, and many were zealous for it, always reciting the Difficulties their Trade would be cast into on Non Compliance, and never regarding the Interest of the whole Community. . . ."[18] When the Townshend Acts were passed, it was not the merchants but the Boston town meeting that took the lead in promoting non-importation, and after repeal of the Acts the merchants broke down and began importing while the duty on tea still remained. Samuel Adams had expected their defection much sooner, for he recognized that the non-importation agreements had "pressed hard upon their private Interest" whereas the majority of consumers could participate under the "happy Consideration that while they are most effectually serving their Country they are adding to their private fortunes."[19]

The merchants actually had more than a short-range interest at stake in their reluctance to undertake non-importation. The movement, as we have seen, was not simply a means of securing repeal of the taxes to which merchants along with other colonists were opposed. The movement was in fact anticommercial, a repudiation of the merchant's calling. Merchants, it was said, encouraged men to go into debt. Merchants pandered to luxury. Since they made more on the sale of superfluous

17 Cotton Tufts to John Adams, April 26, 1776, in L. H. Butterfield *et al.*, eds., *Adams Family Correspondence* (Cambridge, Mass., 1963–), I, 395.

18 Letter dated July 21, 1766, Peck Manuscripts, III, 3, Rhode Island Historical Society, Providence.

19 To Stephen Sayre, Nov. 16, 1770, in Cushing, ed., *Writings of Samuel Adams*, II, 58.

baubles than on necessities, they therefore pressed the sale of them to a weak and gullible public. What the advocates of non-importation demanded was not merely an interruption of commerce but a permanent reduction, not to say elimination, of it. In its place they called for manufacturing, a palpably productive, useful calling.

Encouragement of manufacturing accompanied all the non-importation, non-consumption movements. New Yorkers organized a society specifically for that purpose and offered bounties for the production of native textiles and other necessaries. The non-consumption of mutton provided new supplies of wool, and housewives turned it into thread in spinning matches (wheelwrights did a land-office business in spinning wheels). Stores began selling American cloth, and college students appeared at commencement in homespun. Tories ridiculed these efforts, and the total production was doubtless small, but it would be difficult to underestimate the importance of the attitude toward manufacturing that originated at this time. In a letter of Abigail Adams can be seen the way in which the Puritan Ethic was leading Americans to challenge the power not only of Parliament but also of economic forces hitherto regarded as inexorable. Abigail was writing to her husband, who was at the First Continental Congress, helping to frame the Continental Association for non-importation, non-exportation, and non-consumption:

If we expect to inherit the blessings of our Fathers, we should return a little more to their primitive Simplicity of Manners, and not sink into inglorious ease. We have too many high sounding words, and too few actions that correspond with them. I have spent one Sabbeth in Town since you left me. I saw no difference in respect to ornaments, etc. etc. but in the Country you must look for that virtue, of which you find but small Glimerings in the Metropolis. Indeed they have not the advantages, nor the resolution to encourage their own Manufactories which people in the country have. To the Mercantile part, tis considered as throwing away their own Bread; but they must retrench their expenses and be content with a small share of gain for they will find but few who will wear their Livery. As for me I will seek wool and flax and work willingly with my Hands, and indeed their is occasion for all our industry and economy.[20]

In 1774, when Abigail was writing, "manufacture" retained its primitive meaning of something made by hand, and making things by hand seemed a fitting occupation for frugal country people who had always exhibited more of the Puritan Ethic than high-living city folk. Abigail's espousal of manufactures, with its defiant rejection of dependence on the merchants of the city, marks a step away from the traditional notion that America because of its empty lands and scarcity of people was unsuited to manufactures and must therefore obtain them from the Old World. Through the non-importation movements the colonists discovered that manufacturing was a calling not beyond the capacities of a frugal, industrious people, however few in number, and that importation of British manufactures actually menaced frugality and industry. The result of the discovery was to make a connection with Britain seem neither wholly necessary nor wholly desirable, so that when the thought of independence at last came, it was greeted with less apprehension than it might otherwise have been.

Non-importation had produced in effect a trial run in economic self-sufficiency. The trial was inconclusive as a demonstration of American economic capacity, but it carried immense significance intellectually, for it obliged the colonists to think about the possibility of an economy that would not be colonial. At the same time it confirmed them in the notion that liberty was the companion not only of property but of frugality and industry, two virtues that in turn fostered manufactures. By invoking the Puritan Ethic in behalf of a protest movement, Americans had led themselves into affirmations of value in which can be seen the glimmerings of a future national economic policy.

While engaged in their campaign of patriotic frugality, Americans were also articulating the political principles that they thought should govern free countries and that should bar

[20] Oct. 16, 1774, in Butterfield, ed., *Adams Family Correspondence*, I, 173.

Parliament from taxing them. The front line of defense against Parliament was the ancient maxim that a man could not be taxed except by his own consent given in person or by his representative. The colonists believed this to be an acknowledged principle of free government, indelibly stamped on the British Constitution, and they wrote hundreds of pages affirming it. In those pages the Puritan Ethic was revealed at the very root of the constitutional principle when taxation without representation was condemned as an assault on every man's calling. To tax a man without his consent, Samuel Adams said, was "against the plain and obvious rule of equity, whereby the industrious man is intitled to the fruits of his industry."[21] And the New York Assembly referred to the Puritan Ethic when it told Parliament that the effect of the sugar and stamp taxes would be to "dispirit the People, abate their Industry, discourage Trade, introduce Discord, Poverty, and Slavery."[22] Slavery, of course, meant no liberty and no property, and without these men had no motive for frugality and industry. In other words, the New York protest was pointing out that uncontrolled Parliamentary taxation, like luxury and extravagance, was an attack not merely on property but on industry and frugality, for which liberty and property must be the expected rewards. With every protest that British taxation was reducing them to slavery, Americans reaffirmed their devotion to industry and frugality and their readiness to defy the British threat to them. Students of the American Revolution have often found it difficult to believe that the colonists were willing to fight about an abstract principle and have sometimes dismissed the constitutional arguments of the time as mere rhetoric. But the constitutional principle on which the colonists rested their case was not the product either of abstract political philosophy or of the needs of the moment. In the colonists' view, the principle of no taxation without representation was a means, hallowed by history, of protecting property

21 [*Boston Gazette,* Dec. 19, 1768] in Cushing, ed., *Writings of Samuel Adams,* I, 271.

22 E. S. Morgan, ed., *Prologue to Revolution: Sources and Documents on the Stamp Act Crisis, 1764–1766* (Chapel Hill, 1959), 13.

and of maintaining those virtues, associated with property, without which no people could be free. Through the rhetoric, if it may be called that, of the Puritan Ethic, the colonists reached behind the constitutional principle to the enduring human needs that had brought the principle into being.

We may perhaps understand better the urgency both of the constitutional argument and of the drive toward independence that it ultimately generated, if we observe the growing suspicion among the colonists that the British government had betrayed its own constitution and the values which that constitution protected. In an earlier generation the colonists had vied with one another in praising the government of England. Englishmen, they believed, had suffered again and again from invasion and tryanny, had each time recovered control of their government, and in the course of centuries had developed unparalleled constitutional safeguards to keep rulers true to their callings. The calling of a ruler, as the colonists and their Puritan forebears saw it, was like any other calling: it must serve the common good; it must be useful, productive; and it must be assiduously pursued. After the Glorious Revolution of 1688, Englishmen had reshaped their government into what seemed a nearly perfect instrument that blended monarchy, aristocracy, and democracy in a mixture designed to avoid the defects and secure the benefits of each. But something had gone wrong. The human capacity for corruption had transformed the balanced government of King, Lords, and Commons into a single-minded body of rulers bent on their own enrichment and heedless of the public good.

A principal means of corruption had been the multiplication of officeholders who served no useful purpose but fattened on the labors of those who did the country's work. Even before the dispute over taxation began, few colonists who undertook trips to England failed to make unflattering comparisons between the simplicity, frugality, and industry that prevailed in the colonies and the extravagance, luxury, idleness, drunkenness, poverty, and crime that they saw in the mother country. To Americans bred on the values of the Puritan Ethic, England seemed to have fallen prey to her own opulence, and the government shared heavily in the corruption. In England, the most powerful country in the world, the visitors found the people laboring under a heavy load of taxes, levied by a government that swarmed with functionless placeholders and pensioners. The cost of government in the colonies, as Professor Gipson has shown, was vastly lower than in England, with the per capita burden of taxation only a fraction of that which Englishmen bore.[23] And whatever the costs of maintaining the empire may have contributed to the British burden, it was clear that the English taxpayers supported a large band of men who lived well from offices that existed only to pay their holders. Even an American like George Croghan, who journeyed to London to promote dubious speculative schemes of his own, felt uncomfortable in the presence of English corruption: "I am Nott Sorry I Came hear," he wrote, "as it will Larn Me to be Contented on a Litle farm in amerrica. . . . I am Sick of London and harttily Tierd of the pride and pompe. . . ."[24]

In the 1760's Americans were given the opportunity to gain the perspective of a Croghan without the need for a trip abroad. The Townshend Acts called for a reorganization of the customs service with a new set of higher officials, who would perforce be paid out of the duties they extracted from the colonists. In the establishment of this American Board of Customs Commissioners, Americans saw the extension of England's corrupt system of officeholding to America. As Professor Dickerson has shown, the Commissioners were indeed corrupt.[25] They engaged in extensive "customs racketeering" and they were involved in many of the episodes that heightened the tension between England and the colonies: it was on their request that troops were sent to Boston; the Boston

[23] L. H. Gipson, *The British Empire before the American Revolution* . . . (New York, 1936–   ), X, 53–110; Gipson, *The Coming of the Revolution, 1763–1775* (New York, 1954), 116–61.

[24] Quoted in T. P. Abernethy, *Western Lands and the American Revolution* (New York, 1937), 24.

[25] O. M. Dickerson, *The Navigation Acts and the American Revolution* (Philadelphia, 1951), 208–65.

Massacre took place before their headquarters; the *Gaspée* was operating under their orders. But it was not merely the official actions of the Commissioners that offended Americans. Their very existence seemed to pose a threat both to the Puritan Ethic and to the conscientious, frugal kind of government that went with it. Hitherto colonial governments had been relatively free of the evils that had overtaken England. But now the horde of placeholders was descending on America.

From the time the Commissioners arrived in Boston in November 1767, the newspapers were filled with complaints that "there can be no such thing as common good or common cause where mens estates are ravaged at pleasure to lavish on parasitical minions."[26] Samuel Adams remarked that the Commissioners were "a useless and very expensive set of officers" and that they had power to appoint "as many officers under them as they please, for whose Support it is said they may sink the whole revenue."[27] American writers protested against the "legions of idle, lazy, and to say no worse, altogether useless customs house locusts, catterpillars, flies and lice."[28] They were "a parcel of dependant tools of arbitrary power, sent hither to enrich themselves and their Masters, on the Spoil of the honest and industrious of these colonies." [29] By 1774, when the debate between colonies and Parliament was moving into its final stages, town meetings could state it as an intolerable grievance "that so many unnecessary officers are supported by the earnings of honest industry, in a life of dissipation and ease; who, by being *properly* employed, might be useful members of society."[30]

The coming of the Customs Commissioners showed the colonists that the ocean barrier which had hitherto isolated them from the corruption of Britain was no longer adequate. Eventually, perhaps, Englishmen would again arise, turn out

26 *Boston Evening Post,* Nov. 30, 1767.

27 To Dennys De Berdt, May 14, 1768, in Cushing, ed., *Writings of Samuel Adams,* I, 216.

28 *Newport Mercury,* June 21, 1773.

29 *Ibid.,* July 13, 1772.

30 Resolves of Bristol, R.I., *ibid.,* March 21, 1774.

the scoundrels, and recall their government to its proper tasks. And Americans did not fail to support Englishmen like John Wilkes whom they thought to be working toward this end. But meanwhile they could not ignore the dangers on their own shores. There would henceforth be in their midst a growing enclave of men whose lives and values denied the Puritan Ethic; and there would be an increasing number of lucrative offices to tempt Americans to desert ancestral standards and join the ranks of the "parasitical minions." No American was sure that his countrymen would be able to resist the temptation. In 1766, after repeal of the Stamp Act, George Mason had advised the merchants of London that Americans were "not yet debauched by wealth, luxury, venality and corruption."[31] But who could say how long their virtue would withstand the closer subjection to British control that Whitehall seemed to be designing? Some Americans believed that the British were deliberately attempting to undermine the Puritan Ethic. In Boston Samuel Adams observed in 1771 that "the Conspirators against our Liberties are employing all their Influence to divide the people, . . . introducing Levity Luxury and Indolence and assuring them that if they are quiet the Ministry will alter their Measures."[32] And in 1772 Henry Marchant, a Rhode Island traveler in England, wrote to his friend Ezra Stiles: "You will often hear the following Language—Damn those Fellows we shall never do any Thing with Them till we root out that cursed puritanick Spirit—How is this to be done?—keep Soldiers amongst Them, not so much to awe Them, as to debauch their Morals—Toss off to them all the Toies and Baubles that genius can invent to weaken their Minds, fill Them with Pride and Vanity, and beget in them all possible Extravagance in Dress and Living, that They may be kept poor and made wretched. . . ."[33]

By the time the First Continental Congress came together in

[31] Morgan, *Prologue to Revolution*, 160.

[32] To Arthur Lee, Oct. 31, 1771, in Cushing, ed., *Writings of Samuel Adams*, II, 266–67.

[33] Quoted in E. S. Morgan, *The Gentle Puritan: A Life of Ezra Stiles, 1727–1795* (New Haven, 1962), 265.

1774, large numbers of leading Americans had come to identify Great Britain with vice and America with virtue, yet with the fearful recognition that virtue stands in perennial danger from the onslaughts of vice. Patrick Henry gave voice to the feeling when he denounced Joseph Galloway's plan for an inter-colonial American legislature that would stand between the colonies and Parliament. "We shall liberate our Constituents," he warned, "from a corrupt House of Commons, but thro[w] them into the Arms of an American Legislature that may be bribed by that Nation which avows in the Face of the World, that Bribery is a Part of her System of Government."[34] A gov-ernment that had succeeded in taxing seven million English-men (with the consent of their supposed representatives), to support an army of placeholders, would have no hesitation in using every means to corrupt the representatives of two and one half million Americans.

When the Second Congress met in 1775, Benjamin Franklin, fresh from London, could assure the members that their con-trast of England and America was justified. Writing back to Joseph Priestley, he said it would "scarce be credited in Britain, that men can be as diligent with us from zeal for the public good, as with you for thousands per annum. Such is the difference between uncorrupted new states, and corrupted old ones."[35] Thomas Jefferson drew the contrast even more bluntly in an answer rejecting Lord North's Conciliatory Proposal of February 20, 1775, which had suggested that Parliament could make provisions for the government of the colonies. "The provisions we have made," said Jefferson, "are such as please our selves, and are agreeable to our own circumstances; they answer the substantial purposes of government and of justice, and other purposes than these should not be answered. We do not mean that our people shall be burthened with oppressive taxes to provide sinecures for the idle or the wicked. . . ."[36]

[34] Sept. 28, 1774, in L. H. Butterfield *et al.*, eds., *Diary and Autobiogra-phy of John Adams* (Cambridge, Mass., 1961), II, 143.

[35] July 6, 1775, in E. C. Burnett, ed., *Letters of Members of the Con-tinental Congress* (Washington, 1921–36), I, 156.

[36] July 31, 1775, in Boyd, ed., *Jefferson Papers*, I, 232.

When Congress finally dissolved the political bands that had connected America with England, the act was rendered less painful by the colonial conviction that America and England were already separated as virtue is from vice. The British Constitution had foundered, and the British government had fallen into the hands of a luxurious and corrupt ruling class. There remained no way of preserving American virtue unless the connection with Britain was severed. The meaning of virtue in this context embraced somewhat more than the values of the Puritan Ethic, but those values were pre-eminent in it. In the eyes of many Americans the Revolution was a defense of industry and frugality, whether in rulers or people, from the assaults of British vice. It is unnecessary to assess the weight of the Puritan Ethic among the many factors that contributed to the Revolution. It is enough simply to recognize that the Puritan Ethic prepared the colonists, in their political as in their economic thinking, to consider the idea of independence.

III

Virtue, as everyone knew, was a fragile and, too often, fleeting possession. Even while defending it from the British, Americans worried about their own uneasy hold on it and eyed one another for signs of its departure. The war, of course, furnished the conditions of adversity in which virtue could be expected to flourish. On the day after Congress voted independence, John Adams wrote exultantly to Abigail of the difficulties ahead: "It may be the Will of Heaven that America shall suffer Calamities still more wasting and Distresses yet more dreadfull. If this is to be the Case, it will have this good Effect, at least: it will inspire Us with many Virtues, which We have not, and correct many Errors, Follies, and Vices, which threaten to disturb, dishonour, and destroy Us.—The Furnace of Affliction produces Refinement, in States as well as Individuals."[37] Thereafter, as afflictions came, Adams welcomed them

[37] July 3, 1776, in Butterfield, ed., *Adams Family Correspondence*, II, 28.

in good Puritan fashion. But the war did not prove a sufficient spur to virtue, and by the fall of 1776 Adams was already observing that "There is too much Corruption, even in this infant Age of our Republic. Virtue is not in Fashion. Vice is not infamous."[38] Sitting with the Congress in Philadelphia, he privately yearned for General Howe to capture the town, because the ensuing hardship "would cure Americans of their vicious and luxurious and effeminate Appetites, Passions and Habits, a more dangerous Army to American Liberty than Mr. Howes."[39]

Within a year or two Americans would begin to look back on 1775 and 1776 as a golden age, when vice had given way to heroic self-denial, and greed and corruption had not yet raised their heads. In Revolutionary America as in Puritan New England the virtues of the Puritan Ethic must be quickened by laments for their loss.

Many of these lamentations in the eighteenth century as in the seventeenth seem perfunctory—mere nostalgic ritual in which men purged their sins by confessing their inferiority to their fathers. But in the years after 1776 the laments were prompted by a genuine uneasiness among the revolutionists about their own worthiness for the role they had undertaken. In the agitation against Britain they had repeatedly told themselves that liberty could not live without virtue. Having cast off the threat posed to both liberty and virtue by a corrupt monarchy, they recognized that the republican governments they had created must depend for their success on the virtue, not of a king or of a few aristocrats, but of an entire people. Unless the virtue of Americans proved equal to its tasks, liberty would quickly give way once again to tyranny and perhaps a worse tyranny than that of George III.

As Americans faced the problems of independence, the possibility of failure did not seem remote. By recalling the values that had inspired the resistance to British taxation, they hoped to lend success to their venture in republican government. The

---

38 John to Abigail Adams, Sept. 22, 1776, *ibid.*, II, 131.
39 Same to same, Sept. 8, 1777, *ibid.*, II, 338. Cf. 169–70, 326.

Puritan Ethic thus continued to occupy their consciousness (and their letters, diaries, newspapers, and pamphlets) and to provide the framework within which alternatives were debated and sides taken.

Next to the task of defeating the British armies, perhaps the most urgent problem that confronted the new nation was to prove its nationality, for no one was certain that independent Americans would be able to get on with one another. Before the Revolution there had been many predictions, both European and American, that if independence were achieved it would be followed by bloody civil wars among the states, which would eventually fall prostrate before some foreign invader. Americans in the eighteenth century were not without divisions, but they did manage to stay together and did not engage in civil war until nearly a century later. One reason was the Puritan Ethic. While it generated conflicts among them, it also furnished them with common values that set bounds to conflict and helped to make an American nation possible.

In the period after 1776 perhaps the most immediate threat to the American union was the possibility that the secession of the United States from Great Britain would be followed by a secession of the lower Mississippi and Ohio valleys from the United States. The gravity of the threat, which ended with the fiasco of the Burr Conspiracy, is difficult to assess, but few historians would deny that real friction between East and West existed.

The role of the Puritan Ethic in the conflict was characteristic: each side tended to see the other as deficient in the same virtues. To westerners the eastern-dominated governments seemed to be in the grip of speculators and merchants determined to satisfy their own avarice by sacrificing the interests of the industrious farmers of the West. To easterners, or at least to some easterners, the West seemed to be filling up with shiftless adventurers, as lazy and lawless and unconcerned with the values of the Puritan Ethic as were the native Indians. Such men were unworthy of a share in government and must be restrained in their restless hunt for land and furs; they must be made to settle down and build civilized communities where industry and frugality would thrive.

The effects of these attitudes cannot be domonstrated at length here, but may be suggested by the views of a key figure, John Jay. As early as 1779, the French Ambassador, Conrad Alexandre Gérard, had found Jay one of the most reasonable members of Congress, that is, one of the members most ready to fall in with the Ambassador's instructions to discourage American expansion. Jay belonged to a group which suggested that Spain ought to close the Mississippi to American navigation in order to keep the settlers of the West "from living in a half-savage condition." Presumably the group reasoned that the settlers were mostly fur traders; if they were prevented from trading their furs through New Orleans, they might settle down to farming and thus achieve "an attachment to property and industry."[40] Whatever the line of reasoning, the attitude toward the West is clear, and Jay obliged the French Ambassador by volunteering the opinion that the United States was already too large.[41]

In 1786 Jay offered similar opinions to Jefferson, suggesting that settlement of the West should be more gradual, that Americans should be prevented from pitching their tents "through the Wilderness in a great Variety of Places, far distant from each other, and from those Advantages of Education, Civilization, Law, and Government which compact Settlements and Neighbourhood afford."[42] It is difficult to believe that Jay was unaffected by this attitude in the negotiations he was carrying on with the Spanish envoy Gardoqui over the right of the United States to navigate the Mississippi.

[40] John J. Meng, ed., *Despatches and Instructions of Conrad Alexandre Gérard* . . . (Baltimore, 1939), 531. Gérard reported of this group in Feb. 1779, 'qu'ils desiroient fortement que Sa Majesté Catholique tint la clef du Mississippi de sorte que personne n'entrat du Mississippi dans l'Ocean ni de l'Ocean dans ce fleuve; mais qu'il falloit du Commerce aux peuplades dont il s'agit; que par là seulement on pourroit les empêcher de demeurer à demi Sauvages en les attachant à la propriété et à l'industrie."

[41] *Ibid.*, 433–34, 494.

[42] Dec. 14, 1786, in Boyd, ed., *Jefferson Papers*, X, 599.

When Jay presented Congress with a treaty in which the United States agreed to forgo navigation of the Mississippi in return for commercial concessions in Spain, it seemed, to westerners at least, that the United States Secretary for Foreign Affairs was willing to sacrifice their interests in favor of his merchant friends in the East.

Fortunately the conflict was not a lasting one. The advance wave of uncouth fur traders and adventurers who worried John Jay occupied only a brief moment in the history of any part of the West. The tens of thousands of men who entered Kentucky and Tennessee in the 1780's came to farm the rich lands, and they carried the values of the Puritan Ethic with them. As this fact became apparent, conflict subsided. Throughout American history the wild West was perpetually turning into a new East, complete with industrious inhabitants, spurred by adversity, and pursuing their callings with an assiduity that the next generation would lament as lost.

Another sectional conflict was not so transitory. The South was not in the process of becoming northern or the North southern. And to an astute observer like James Madison their differing interests were already discernible in the 1780's as the primary source of friction among Americans. The difference arose, he believed, "principally from the effects of their having or not having slaves."[43]

The bearing of the Puritan Ethic on slavery, as on many other institutions, was complex and ambivalent. It heightened the conflict between those who did and those who did not have slaves. But it also, for a time at least, set limits to the conflict by offering a common ground on which both sides could agree in deploring the institution.

The Puritans themselves had not hesitated to enslave Indian captives or to sell and buy slaves. At the opening of the Revolution no state prohibited slavery. But the institution

43 In Convention, June 30, 1787, in C. C. Tansill, ed., *Documents Illustrative of the Formation of the Union of the American States* (Washington, 1927), 310.

obviously violated the precepts of the Puritan Ethic: it deprived men of the fruits of their labor and thus removed a primary motive for industry and frugality. As soon as Americans began complaining of Parliament's assault on their liberty and property, it was difficult not to see the inconsistency of continuing to hold slaves. "I wish most sincerely," Abigail Adams wrote to her husband in 1774, "there was not a Slave in the province. It allways appeard a most iniquitous Scheme to me—fight ourselfs for what we are daily robbing and plundering from those who have as good a right to freedom as we have."[44] Newspaper articles everywhere made the same point. As a result, slavery was gradually abolished in the northern states (where it was not important in the economy), and the self-righteousness with which New Englanders already regarded their southern countrymen was thereby heightened.

Although the South failed to abolish slavery, southerners like northerners recognized the threat it posed to the values that all Americans held. Partly as a result of that recognition, more slaves were freed by voluntary manumission in the South than by legal and constitutional abolition in the North. There were other reasons for hostility to slavery in both North and South, including fear of insurrection, humanitarianism, and apprehension of the wrath of God; but a predominant reason, in the South at least, was the evil effect of slavery on the industry and frugality of both master and slave, but especially of the master.

A perhaps extreme example of this argument, divested of all considerations of justice and humanity, appeared in a Virginia newspaper in 1767. The author (who signed himself "Philanthropos"!) proposed to abolish slavery in Virginia by having the government lay a prohibitory duty on importation and then purchase one tenth of everyone's slaves every year. The purchase price would be recovered by selling the slaves in the West Indies. Philanthropos acknowledged that slaves were "used with more barbarity" in the West Indies than in

[44] Sept. 22, 1774, in Butterfield, ed., *Adams Family Correspondence*, I, 162.

Virginia but offered them the consolation "that this sacrifice of themselves will put a quicker period to a miserable life." It would not do to emancipate them and leave them in Virginia, because they would probably "attempt to arrive at our possessions by force, rather than wait the tedious operation of labour, industry and time." But unless slavery was abolished in Virginia, the industry and frugality of the free population would expire. As it was, said Philanthropos, when a man got a slave or two, he sat back and stopped working. Promising young men failed to take up productive occupations because they could get jobs as overseers. By selling off their slaves in the West Indies, Virginians would get the money to import white indentured servants and would encourage "our own common people, who would no longer be diverted from industry by the prospect of overseers places, to [enter] agriculture and arts."[45]

Few opponents of slavery were so callous, but even the most humane stressed the effect of slavery on masters and the problems of instilling the values of industry in emancipated slaves. Thomas Jefferson hated slavery, but he hated idleness equally, and he would not have been willing to abolish slavery without making arrangements to preserve the useful activity it exacted from its victims. He had heard of one group of Virginia slaves who had been freed by their Quaker owners and kept as tenants on the land. The results had been unsatisfactory, because the ex-slaves had lacked the habits of industry and "chose to steal from their neighbors rather than work." Jefferson had plans to free his own slaves (after he freed himself from his creditors) by a gradual system which provided means for educating the Negroes into habits of industry.[46] But Jefferson never put his scheme into practice. He and most other southerners continued to hold slaves, and slavery steadily eroded the honor accorded work among southerners.

During the Revolutionary epoch, however, the erosion had not yet proceeded far enough to alienate North from South.

[45] Reprinted in *Pennsylvania Chronicle*, Aug. 31–Sept. 7, 1767. The Virginia paper in which it originally appeared has not been found.

[46] To Edward Bancroft, Jan. 26, 1788, in Boyd, ed., *Jefferson Papers*, XIV, 492.

Until well into the nineteenth century southerners continued to deplore the effects of slavery on the industry and frugality at least of the whites. Until the North began to demand immediate abolition and the South began to defend slavery as a permanent blessing, leaders of the two sections could find a good deal of room for agreement in the shared values of the Puritan Ethic.

The fact that Americans of different sections could remain united came as something of a surprise. Even more surprising, so surprising that for a long time few could believe it, was the fact that party divisions in politics, instead of hindering, actually helped the cause of union. Parties or "factions" had been everywhere denounced in the eighteenth century. When men disagreed on political issues, each side was likely to accuse the other of being a party. Advocates of any measure preceded their arguments by disclaiming adherence to a party. And the last thing that the architects of the American national government wanted or anticipated was that it would fall into the hands of parties. But that of course is precisely what happened, and the result proved to be a blessing.

The unexpected success of the American party system has been the subject of continuous comment and congratulation among historians and political scientists ever since. Success, it seems clear, has depended in large part on the absence of any clear ideological difference between the major parties. It would be difficult, for example, for any but the most experienced historian, if presented with the Republican and Democratic platforms of the past hundred years, to distinguish one from the other. Our political disputes are peaceful, because both parties espouse similar principles and objectives and neither feels itself severely threatened by the other. And yet in any given issue or election neither side has difficulty in identifying friends and enemies. The members of any party recognize their own kind.

This situation has prevailed in American national politics from the outset. In the Continental Congress and in the first Congresses under the new Constitution, political divisions were unorganized. In the Continental Congress, partly because of rotation in office, groupings were transitory. But one finds the same absence of ideological difference and the same recognition by political partisans of their own kind. In the absence of party organization, one can see in these early divisions, even more clearly than in later ones, the forces that led some men to join one side and others another.[47] If we examine the men on each side, together with their avowed principles and their application of those principles, if we examine the way a man regarded men on his own side and men on the other side, we will discover, I believe, that the Puritan Ethic, in this period at least, helped both to create political divisions and to limit them.

The first serious division in national politics after independence occurred in 1778 and 1779 over the conduct of the American envoy to France, Silas Deane; and the men who voted together in the divisions on that question often voted together on other seemingly unrelated matters. On each side, in other words, a kind of party was formed. The question at issue was whether Deane had used public funds and public office for private gain, as was charged by another American agent abroad, Arthur Lee. When challenged by Congress, Deane was unable to produce vouchers to account for his expenditures, but he consistently maintained that the money had been spent on legitimate public business; and in the private papers that have survived he never admitted, even to himself, that he had done anything wrong.

Although the facts in the Deane case will probably never be fully known, we know now a good deal more about him than the members of Congress did.[48] We know, for example, that his

[47] A work of major importance is Herbert James Henderson, *Party Politics in the Continental Congress* (New York, 1974). I am indebted to Professor Henderson for permitting me to see an early version of it in manuscript.

[48] The complexity of the problems involved can be appreciated by anyone who reads the *Deane Papers*, published by the New-York Historical Society in its *Collections* for 1886–1890. Important aspects of the case are presented in Thomas P. Abernethy, "Commercial Activities of Silas Deane in France," *American Historical Review*, XXXIX (1933–34), 477–85; Samuel

close associate, Edward Bancroft, was a double agent. We know that Deane did engage in private speculation while in public office. But we still do not know that his transactions were any more dubious than those of, say, Robert Morris, who also mingled public and private funds and by so doing emerged as the financier of the Revolution. The members of Congress in 1778 and 1779, knowing even less than we do, were obliged to decide whether to honor Silas Deane's accounts. In a series of votes on questions relating to this issue the members had to make up their minds with very little to go on. Under the circumstances, it would not be surprising if they lined up according to the way in which Silas Deane struck them as a man. Those who found him to be their sort of person would take one side; those who distrusted that sort of person would take the other side.

What sort of person, then, was Silas Deane? He was, to begin with, an able man. He made a good impression at the First Continental Congress, and when Connecticut dropped him from its delegation, Congress sent him to France. In France he was indubitably successful in securing the supplies that made possible the success of the American armies at Saratoga. After Congress dismissed him and refused to honor his accounts, Deane became disillusioned with the patriot cause, and in a series of letters to friends in Connecticut, unfortunately intercepted by the British, he argued that the war and the French alliance had corrupted his countrymen and that independence would consequently prove a curse instead of a blessing. In his native Connecticut, he said, he had seen "thousands of industrious youth forced from the plough and other useful, homely occupations, and prematurely destroyed by the diseases, wants, and sufferings of a military life, whilst the survivors, by exchanging their plain morals and honest industry for the habits of idleness and vice, appeared more

---

F. Bemis, "British Secret Service and the French-American Alliance," *ibid.*, XXIX (1923–24), 474–95; and Julian P. Boyd, "Silas Deane: Death by a Kindly Teacher of Treason?" *William and Mary Quarterly*, 3rd ser., XVI (1959), 165–87, 319–42, 515–50.

likely to burthen than to benefit their country hereafter."[49]
Silas Deane could avow his attachments to the values of the
Puritan Ethic as ardently as any man.

But avowing the values was not quite the same as exemplifying them, and Deane as a person exhibited none of the
moral austerity that ardent practitioners of the Puritan Ethic
demanded. John Adams, always sensitive in these matters, was
Deane's successor in the American mission to France. There he
observed with distate that Deane had taken extravagant lodg-
ings in Paris in addition to his quarters with Benjamin Franklin at Passy.[50] Adams, though he always found Franklin's
company trying, preferred to put up with it rather than cause
the United States extra expense. Adams later recalled Deane
as "a person of a plausible readiness and Volubility with his
Tongue and his Pen, much addicted to Ostentation and Expence in Dress and Living but without any deliberate forecast
or reflection or solidarity of Judgment, or real Information."[51]
Deane, on the other hand, found Adams absurdly spartan.
"This man," he wrote, "who may have read much, appears
to have retained nothing, except law knowledge and the
fierce and haughty manners of the Lacedemonians and first
Romans. These he has adopted as a perfect model to form a
modern republican by."[52] If Adams could have read the criti-
cism, he would have taken it as a tribute.

Adams, of course, was not a member of Congress when the
Deane case was under debate, but Deane's characterization of
Adams could as aptly be applied to the three delegates who
led the fight against Deane: Samuel Adams of Massachusetts,
Richard Henry Lee of Virginia, and Henry Laurens of South
Carolina.

Samuel Adams thought of the Revolution as a holy war to
save America from British corruption, and corruption to
Adams meant luxury, extravagance, and avarice. During the
non-importation crusade he had worried about such weak-

---

[49] To Jesse Root, May 20, 1781, in *Deane Papers*, IV, 350.

[50] April 1778, in Butterfield, ed., *Diary and Autobiography of John
Adams*, IV, 42.

[51] Nov.–Dec. 1775, *ibid.*, III, 340.

[52] To John Jay, Nov. 1780, in *Deane Papers*, IV, 262.

nesses in the American merchants; and after independence merchants still failed to live up to the standards he expected of Americans. In 1778, detecting a spirit of avarice in Boston, he remarked, "but it rages only among the few, because perhaps, the few only are concerned at present in trade."[53] Even a little avarice was too much, however, for Adams, who had visions of Boston as the Sparta of America. Writing from Philadelphia to a Boston friend, he expressed concern about reports that the city had become exceedingly gay in appearance. "I would fain hope," he said, "this is confind to Strangers. Luxury and Extravagance are in my opinion totally destructive of those Virtues which are necessary for the Preservation of the Liberty and Happiness of the People. Is it true that the Review of the Boston Militia was closd with an expensive Entertainment? If it was, and the Example is followed by the Country, I hope I shall be excusd when I venture to pledge myself, that the Militia of that State will never be put on such a Footing as to become formidable to its Enemies."[54]

Richard Henry Lee, a brother of the man who first accused Deane, was a Virginia gentleman planter but not so strange an ally for Samuel Adams as one might suppose. The two had been in correspondence even before the First Continental Congress, and there they had sided together from the beginning. Although Lee was a slaveowner, he had spoken out against slavery (condemning it for its ill effect on industriousness), and by 1779 he was contemplating retirement to Massachusetts. "The hasty, unpersevering, aristocratic genius of the south," he confessed, "suits not my disposition, and is inconsistent with my ideas of what must constitute social happiness and security."[55] Lee who was an Anglican, never carried out his intention of retiring to Massachusetts and probably would not have been happy if he had, but he sometimes must have struck his contemporaries as a New Englander manqué. The French Ambassador, Gérard, not surprisingly mistook him for a Presbyterian, for he had, according to Gérard, "the

[53] To Francis Lee [?], 1778, in Cushing, ed., *Writings of Samuel Adams,* IV, 19.

[54] To Samuel Savage, Oct. 6, 1778, *ibid.,* IV, 67–68.

[55] Burnett, ed., *Letters of Members,* II, 155.

severity of manners, and the gravity that is natural to Presbyterians."[56]

Lee had begun his attacks on political corruption in 1764 by sniffing out a scandal in the Virginia government: the Speaker of the House of Burgesses, John Robinson, who was also Treasurer, had been lending vast amounts in public funds to his political friends, and his friends included some of the best families in Virginia. The people involved were able to hush things up, but they did not forgive Lee for demanding an investigation.[57] The Deane affair, then, was not the first time he had caught men in high office with their fingers in the public till.

Henry Laurens, like Lee, was an Anglican, but the description of him by a fellow South Carolinian, David Ramsay, who knew him well, makes Laurens, too, sound like a Puritan: "In the performance of his religious duties Mr. Laurens was strict and exemplary. The emergency was great which kept him from church either forenoon or afternoon, and very great indeed which kept him from his regular monthly communion. With the bible he was intimately acquainted. Its doctrines he firmly believed, its precepts and history he admired, and was much in the habit of quoting and applying portions of it to present occurrences. He not only read the scriptures diligently to his family, but made all his children read them also. His family bible contained in his own hand-writing several of his remarks on passing providences." Ramsay also tells us that Laurens frowned on cardplaying and gambling. On some occasions in Charleston society when he could not avoid playing cards without being rude, he promptly paid if he lost, "but uniformly refused to receive what he won, esteeming it wrong to take any man's money without giving an equivalent."[58]

[56] ". . . la sévérité des moeurs, et la gravité naturelle aux Presbytériens." Meng, ed., *Despatches of Gérard*, 569.

[57] Burton J. Hendrick, *The Lees of Virginia: Biography of a Family* (Boston, 1935), 101–5; David J. Mays, *Edmund Pendleton, 1721–1803: A Biography* (Cambridge, Mass., 1952), I, 174–208.

[58] David Ramsay, *The History of South Carolina from its first Settlement in 1670 to the Year 1808* (Charleston, 1809), II, 484, 485.

Laurens had himself been a merchant and a very methodical and assiduous one. After making a fortune, he transferred his activities from trade to planting. He seldom slept more than four hours a day, and he had a low opinion of gentlemen of leisure. Like Richard Henry Lee he had had a brush with corruption in high places earlier in his career when the customs officers in Charleston seized a ship of his on a flimsy pretext. They had offered to release the ship in return for a bribe. Laurens had indignantly refused, and the officers, in collusion with a judge of the Admiralty Court, had succeeded in having the ship condemned and sold. Laurens had then written and published an account of the whole affair, including the attempt to shake him down.[59]

It was this episode that converted Laurens from staunch support of British authority to a deep suspicion of British corruption. But avarice among his own countrymen perturbed him even more. At the time when the Deane case came up, Laurens was serving as president of the Continental Congress. He had already denounced the "sacrilegious Robberies of public Money" by congressmen and military officers carrying on private trade in army supplies.[60] A little later he observed that many members of Congress, doubtless because they were themselves engaged in such practices, were ready to defend them, so that "he must be a pitiful rogue indeed, who, when detected, or suspected, meets not with powerful advocates among those, who in the present corrupt time, ought to exert all their powers in defence and support of these friend-plundered, much injured, and I was almost going to say, sinking States."[61]

Although Laurens was a merchant, he was so shocked by the activities of other merchants in and out of Congress that he wrote in despair in 1779: "Reduce us all to poverty and cut off or wisely restrict that bane of patriotism, Commerce, and we

[59] David D. Wallace, *The Life of Henry Laurens* . . . (New York, 1915); Dickerson, *Navigation Acts*, 224–31.

[60] Laurens to Rawlins Lowndes, May 17, 1778, in Burnett, ed., *Letters of Members*, III, 248.

[61] Laurens to John Houstoun, Aug. 27 [1778], *ibid.*, III, 385.

shall soon become Patriots, but how hard is it for a rich or covetous Man to enter heartily into the Kingdom of Patriotism?"[62] When Congress voted what Laurens considered too high salaries for the secretaries of its ministry abroad and elected Laurens's son to one of these positions, Laurens protested and informed his son that "men who are sincerely devoted to the service of their Country will not accept of Salaries which will tend to distress it."[63]

It is impossible to examine here the rank and file of Deane's opponents, but perhaps enough has been said to suggest what sort of person disliked Deane—persons who exhibited a certain austerity in their daily lives, persons who were shocked by profiteering, persons to whom the public good was the ultimate end and object of every calling, persons, in short, whose lives were most visibly affected by the Puritan Ethic. In such persons Silas Deane's ostentatious gentility aroused immediate suspicions. If a man exhibited so little of the austerity demanded by the Puritan Ethic, it was reasonable to suppose that he would also disregard its injunctions to seek the public good.

It will come as no surprise that Deane's supporters were men more like himself. A principal supporter, of course, was Robert Morris, who had engaged deeply in trading enterprises with Deane but whose commercial empire extended throughout the country. At the outset of Deane's mission to France, Morris had directed him in both his private and his public investments and had advised him that "there never has been so fair an oppertunity of making a large Fortune. . . ."[64] At the time of the Deane affair, Morris was not a member of Congress, but he remained in Philadelphia, served in the Pennsylvania Assembly, and helped to marshal support for Deane. Deane's other defenders, like his opponents, were too numerous to bear examination in detail here, but they included men from the same states as his principal opponents.

In Massachusetts John Hancock was a Deane man, and it

[62] Laurens to William Livingston, April 19 [1779], *ibid.*, IV, 163.
[63] H. Laurens to John Laurens, Oct. 5, 1779, *ibid.*, IV, 467.
[64] From Robert Morris, Aug. 11, 1776, in *Deane Papers*, I, 176.

was Hancock who had provided the expensive entertainment for the militia which so disturbed Samuel Adams. Indeed Hancock, when inaugurated as Governor of Massachusetts in 1780, scandalized Adams by sponsoring a whole series of balls and parties. By introducing such "Scenes of Dissipation and Folly" Adams believed that Hancock endangered public virtue, and when virtue departed, liberty would accompany it. Adams accordingly considered Hancock a peril to the republic, as dangerous as the British.[65]

In Virginia Deane's supporters included most of the congressional delegates, apart from the Lees. Benjamin Harrison's position can be anticipated from John Adams's characterization of him at the Second Continental Congress as "an indolent, luxurious, heavy Gentleman," and as "another Sir John Falstaff, excepting in his Larcenies and Robberies, his Conversation disgusting to every Man of Delicacy or decorum, Obscaene, profane, impious, perpetually ridiculing the Bible, calling it the Worst Book in the World. . . ."[66] In Congress Harrison associated frequently with Hancock. He was also engaged in business with Robert Morris. When he got his son made Deputy Paymaster General of the Southern District, the son made a secret agreement with Morris to charge a premium of 2 percent on any bills that either drew on the other in connection with public business.[67]

Carter Braxton, another supporter of Deane from Virginia, was discovered in 1778 to have made a dubious deal with Morris and in 1779 was censured by Congress for sponsoring a privateer which captured a Portuguese vessel, an act that amounted to piracy, since the United States was not at war with Portugal and in fact was seeking Portuguese trade.[68] Braxton had been one of the many Virginians involved in the

[65] Cushing, ed., *Writings of Samuel Adams*, IV, 208, 210, 227–30, 236–38, 241–42, 244–48; John C. Miller, *Sam Adams: Pioneer in Propaganda* (Boston, 1936), 359–69.

[66] Feb., March 1776, in Butterfield, ed., *Diary and Autobiography of John Adams*, III, 367, 371.

[67] Abernethy, *Western Lands*, 159–60.

[68] *Ibid.*, 215, 232.

Robinson scandal.[69] The Lees tried to exclude such men from representing Virginia in Congress by securing passage in the Virginia legislature of a law requiring delegates to swear that they were not engaged and would not engage in trade.[70] But the delegates who took the oath evidently interpreted their business dealings as something other than trade.

From South Carolina Deane's advocate was William Henry Drayton, a man with whom Henry Laurens regularly disagreed. Their different characters were significantly revealed in an insignificant episode, when Drayton in 1779 urged Congress to authorize the celebration of Independence Day by an elaborate display of fireworks. In what Laurens called "a funny declamation," Drayton praised the Olympic games and other festivities by which nations celebrated their nativity. Laurens, outraged by the extravagance of celebrations in general, answered that "the Olympic Games of Greece and other fooleries brought on the desolation of Greece." When Drayton won approval for his motion and pointed out that the Olympic games "were calculated for improving bodily strength, to make men athletic and robust," Laurens was left to reflect in his diary, "Is drinking Madeira Wine from 5 to 9 o'clock, then sallying out to gaze at fire works, and afterwards returning to Wine again, calculated to make men athletic and robust?"[71]

Two years earlier on the first anniversary of independence, Congress had also celebrated and there had also been a dissenter, William Williams of Connecticut, who wrote on July 5, 1777, to his friend Governor Trumbull: "Yesterday was in my opinion poorly spent in celebrating the anniversary of the Declaration of Independence . . . a great expenditure of Liquor, Powder etc. took up the Day, and of candles thro the City good part of the night."[72] By an interesting coincidence, William Williams was also an early opponent of Silas Deane.

---

[69] Mays, *Pendleton*, I, 180, 359.

[70] From Meriwether Smith, July 6, 1779, in Boyd, ed., *Jefferson Papers*, III, 28–29, 29n.

[71] Laurens, Notes, July 2, 1779, Burnett, ed., *Letters of Members*, IV, 293–94.

[72] *Ibid.*, II, 401.

He had opposed Deane's election as a delegate to Congress; he had warned his friend Samuel Adams, as early as July 30, 1774, before the first Congress met, that Deane would be likely to place private interests above patriotism; and he had finally secured Deane's dismissal from the Connecticut delegation in 1775. Williams's own record in the Revolution, like Laurens's, was one of financial sacrifice.[73]

It would be impossible to prove conclusively that all the opponents of Silas Deane were frugal, industrious, and devoted to the common good or that all his advocates were addicted to trade, speculation, and profiteering. Men on both sides proclaimed their belief in the same values, but it seems likely that men like Adams, Lee, and Laurens recognized one another as kindred spirits and that men like Morris, Harrison, and Braxton did the same.[74] In the Continental Congress the turnover of delegates (required by the Articles of Confederation) prevented the formation of any durable parties, but in 1779 the groups that formed over the Deane issue tended to act together also in other divisions, such as the dispute over half pay for army officers and the dispute over war aims. In the latter dispute, for example, the French Ambassador found the friends of Deane far more amenable than the Adams-Lee-Laurens group, many of whom felt a sense of shame that the United States had been unable to fight its own battles without French financial and military assistance.[75]

The party divisions of 1778–79 seem to indicate that although most Americans made adherence to the Puritan Ethic

[73] Oscar Zeichner, *Connecticut's Years of Controversy, 1750–1776* (Chapel Hill, 1949), 322.

[74] Other active opponents of Deane included William Whipple of New Hampshire, James Lovell of Massachusetts, Roger Sherman of Connecticut, Nathaniel Scudder of New Jersey, and James Searle and William Shippen of Pennsylvania. Other advocates of Deane included Gouverneur Morris and John Jay of New York, Cyrus Griffin and Meriwether Smith of Virginia, William Carmichael of Maryland, and Henry Wynkoop of Pennsylvania.

[75] The Solidity of the division is perhaps exaggerated in the extended reports on it by Gérard in Meng, ed., *Despatches of Gérard*, esp. 429–918, *passim*. On the half-pay issue R. H. Lee parted from his anti-Deane allies.

an article of faith, some Americans were far more assiduous than others in exemplifying it. Since such men were confined to no particular section, and since men active in national politics could recognize their own kind from whatever section, political divisions in the early years of the republic actually brought Americans from all over the country into working harmony within a single group. And parties, instead of destroying the union, became a means of holding it together.

Recent studies have shown that there was no continuity in the political divisions of the 1770's, 1780's, and 1790's, by demonstrating that the split between Federalists and Republicans in the 1790's cannot be traced to the preceding splits between reluctant and ardent revolutionaries of 1776 or between Federalists and Antifederalists of 1789. The continuity that a previous generation of historians had seen in the political history of these years has thus proved specious. It is tempting, however, to suggest that there may have been a form of continuity in American political history hitherto unnoticed, a continuity based on the attitudes we have been exploring. Although the divisions of 1778–79 did not endure, Americans of succeeding years continued to show differing degrees of attachment to the values of the Puritan Ethic. By the time when national political parties were organized in the 1790's, a good many other factors were involved in attracting men to one side or the other, far too many to permit discussion here. But the Puritan Ethic remained a constant ingredient, molding the style of American politics not only in the 1790's but long afterwards. Men on both sides, and seemingly the whole population, continued to proclaim their devotion to it by mourning its decline, and each side regularly accused the other of being deficient in it. It served as a weapon for political conflict but also as a tether which kept parties from straying too far apart. It deserves perhaps to be considered as one of the major reasons why American party battles have generally remained rhetorical and American national government has endured as a workable government.

IV

As the Puritan Ethic helped to give shape to national politics, so too it helped to shape national policy, especially in the economic sphere. Before 1776 the economic policy of the American colonies had been made for them in London: they had been discouraged from manufacturing, barred from certain channels of trade, and encouraged to exploit the natural resources of the continent, especially its land. After 1776 the independent states were free to adopt, singly or collectively, any policy that suited them. At first the exigencies of the war against England directed every measure; but as the fighting subsided, Americans began to consider the economic alternatives open to them.

There appeared to be three possible kinds of activity: agriculture, manufacturing, and commerce. Of these, agriculture and commerce had hitherto dominated the American scene. Americans, in accepting the place assigned them under the British Navigation Acts, had seen the force of their own environment operating in the same direction as British policy: as long as the continent had an abundance of unoccupied land and a scarcity of labor, it seemed unlikely that its inhabitants could profitably engage in manufacturing. The non-importation agreements, as we have seen, had done much to dispel this opinion in America; and the war that followed, by interdicting trade in some regions and hindering it in others, gave a further spur to manufactures. By the time peace came, numerous observers were able to point out fallacies in the supposition that manufacturing was not economically feasible in the United States. From England, Richard Price reminded Americans that their country contained such a variety of soils and climates that it was capable of "producing not only every *necessary*, but every *convenience* of life," and Americans were quick to agree.[76] They acknowledged that their population was

[76] Richard Price, *Obeservations on the Importance of the American Revolution* . . . (London, 1785), 75. Cf. *New Haven Gazette and Connecticut Magazine*, Nov. 16, 23, 1786; *American Mercury* (Hartford), Aug. 13, 1787.

small by comparison with Europe's and the numbers skilled in manufacturing even smaller. But they now discovered reasons why this deficiency was no insuperable handicap. People without regular employment, women and children for example, could be put to useful work in manufacturing. More-over, if Americans turned to manufactures, many skilled arti-sans of the Old World, losing their New World customers, would move to America in order to regain them. Immigrants would come in large numbers anyhow, attracted by the bless-ings of republican liberty. The scarcity of labor might be over-come not only by immigration but also by the already explo-sive native birthrate and by labor-saving machinery and by water and steam power.[77]

A few men like Thomas Jefferson continued to think manu-facturing neither feasible nor desirable for Americans, but the economic vicissitudes of the postwar years subdued the voices of such men to a whisper. No one suggested that the country should abandon its major commitment to agriculture in favor of manufacturing, but it became a commonplace that too many Americans were engaged in commerce and that the moral, economic, and political welfare of the United States demanded a greater attention to manufacturing. The profiteer-ing of merchants during the war had kept the old suspicions of that calling very much alive, so that long before the fight-ing stopped, people were worried about the effects of an unrestrained commerce on the independent United States. A Yale student reflected the mood in a declamation offered in July 1778. If the country indulged too freely in commerce, he warned, the result would be "Luxury with its train of the blackest vices, which will debase our manliness of sentiment, and spread a general dissolution of manners thro the Con-

[77] Hugh Williamson, *Letters from Sylvius to the Freemen Inhabitants of the United States* . . . (New York, 1787); Tench Coxe: *An Address to an Assembly of the Friends of American Manufactures* . . . (Philadelphia, 1787); *An Enquiry into the Principles on which a commercial system for the United States of America should be founded* . . . (Philadelphia, 1787); and *Observations on the Agriculture, Manufactures and Commerce of the United States* . . . (New York, 1789).

tinent. This extensive Commerce is the most direct method to ruin our country, and we may affirm that we shall exist as an empire but a short space, unless it can be circumscribed within narrow limits."[78]

Within a year or two of the war's end the country seemed to be lurching down this very road to ruin. As soon as the peace treaty was signed, American merchants rushed to offer Americans the familiar British goods which they had done without for nearly a decade. The British gladly supplied the market, extending a liberal credit, and the result was a flood of British textiles and hardware in every state. As credit extended from merchant to tradesman to farmer and planter, Americans were caught up in an orgy of buying. But at the same time Britain barred American ships from her West Indies possessions, where American cattle, lumber, and foodstuffs had enjoyed a prime market. The British could now buy these articles in the United States at their own prices and carry them in their own ships, depriving the American merchant and farmer alike of accustomed profits. Hard cash was rapidly drained off: debts grew to alarming proportions; and the buying boom turned to a sharp depression.[79]

Casting about for a remedy, some states turned to the old expedient of paper money. But to many Americans this was a cure worse than the disease and no real cure anyhow. The root of the trouble, they told themselves, was their own frivolity. Newspapers and pamphlets from one end of the continent to the other lamented the lost virtues that had inspired resistance to tyranny a few short years before. While Rome had enjoyed a republican simplicity for centuries, the United States seemed to have sunk into luxury and decay almost as soon as born. And who indulged this weakness, who coaxed Americans into this wild extravagance? It was the merchants. Shelves bulging with oversupplies of ribbons, laces, and yard goods, the mer-

[78] Declamation, July 18, 1778, Yale University Archives, New Haven, Conn.

[79] This picture of the economic history of the 1780's seems to have been universally accepted at the time. A typical statement is in Coxe, *Observations*, 59–64.

chants outdid themselves in appealing to every gullible woman and every foolish fop to buy. There was an oversupply, it seemed, not merely of ribbons and laces but of merchants, a breed of men, according to Hugh Williamson of North Carolina, "too lazy to plow, or labour at any other calling."[80] "What can we promise ourselves," asked another writer, "if we still pursue the same extensive trade? What, but total destruction to our manners, and the entire loss of our virtue?"[81]

The basic remedy in the 1780's as in the 1760's and 1770's, must be frugality. The laments over luxury were a summons to Americans to tighten their belts, as they had done before in the face of adversity. And once again they linked frugality with non-importation and with manufacturing for themselves, but this time with an enlarged appreciation of what manufacturing might mean to the country. In earlier campaigns they had told themselves that an industrious, frugal people would manufacture for themselves. Now, chastened by the results of their failure to carry on, they were ready to believe that manufacturing, if firmly established in the United States, would promote the very virtues that had fostered it. "Manufactures will promote industry, and industry contributes to health, virtue, riches and population."[82] And even if the riches produced by manufacturing might eventually sap the virtues that begot them, such riches would somehow not be quite as corrupting as the wealth that arose from trade and speculation: "the evils resulting from opulence in a nation whose inhabitants are habituated to industry in their childhood, will never be so predominant as in those nations, whose riches are spontaneously produced without labour or care. . . ."[83]

As the link between manufactures and virtue was recalled and enlarged, so was the link between manufactures and liberty. For it finally dawned on Americans that manufacturing might be as necessary in the maintenance of their inde-

80 Williamson, *Letters from Sylvius*, 30.
81 *The American Museum*, I (Feb. 1787), 124.
82 *American Mercury*, Aug. 13, 1787.
83 *New Haven Gazette and Connecticut Magazine*, Nov. 23, 1786.

pendence as it had been in the fight to achieve independence. "America must adopt [a] new policy," David Ramsay insisted in 1785, "or she never will be independent in reality. We must import less and attend more to agriculture and manufactures."[84] It was now possible to see a new significance in England's old restraints on colonial manufacturing. Why had she prevented Americans from "working up those materials that God and nature have given us?" The answer was clear to a Maryland writer: because England knew "it was the only way to our real independence, and to render the habitable parts of our country truly valuable. What countries are the most flourishing and most powerful in the world? Manufacturing countries. It is not hills, mountains, woods, and rivers that constitute the true riches of a country. It is the number of industrious mechanic and manufacturing as well as agriculturing inhabitants. That a country composed of agricultivators and shepherds is not so valuable as one wherein a just proportion of the people attend to arts and manufactures, is known to every politician in Europe: And America will never feel her importance and dignity, until she alters her present system of trade, so ruinous to the interests, to the morals, and to the reputation of her citizens."[85]

Britain's extension of credit to American merchants, it now seemed, was only part of a perfidious plan to undermine through trade the independence she had acknowledged by treaty. Samuel Adams had once detected a British plan to destroy American liberty by introducing luxury and levity among the people. Having been thwarted in 1776, the British were now on the verge of success. As a South Carolina writer charged, they had let loose, "as from Pandora's box, a ruinous luxury, speculation, and extravagance, vitiated our taste, corrupted our manners, plunged the whole state into a private debt, never before equalled, and thro' the means of their trade, luxury, influence, and good things, brought the Republic into

[84] R. L. Brunhouse, ed., *David Ramsay, 1749–1815: Selections from His Writings*, American Philosophical Society, *Transactions*, LV, Pt. 4 (1965), 87.

[85] *American Museum*, I (Feb. 1787), 124–25.

a dilemma, an example of which has not before happened in the world."[86] From France, where he was serving as ambassador, Thomas Jefferson could see that Britain by her liberal credits had put the whole United States in the same economic thralldom in which her merchants had held (and still held) the Virginia tobacco planters. From economic thralldom back to political thralldom was only a step. Unless the United States could break the grip, her experiment in independence was over.

Jefferson, while joining in the hymns to frugality (he thought extravagance a "more baneful evil than toryism was during the war"),[87] had a peculiar prejudice against manufacturing and hoped to break the British grip and achieve economic independence by gaining new commerical treaties with other countries.[88] But few of his countrymen shared his prejudice. In every state they told themselves to manufacture. Even if it cost more to make a coat or a pair of shoes or a plow or a gun in America, the price of foreign imports was the loss of independence. "No man," warned Hugh Williamson, drawing upon another precept of the Puritan Ethic, "is to say that a thing may be good for individuals which is not good for the public, or that our citizens may thrive by cheap bargains, while the nation is ruined by them." Considered in the light of the national interest, "every domestic manufacture is cheaper than a foreign one, for this plain reason, by the first nothing is lost to the country, by the other the whole value is lost—it is carried away never to return."[89]

Williamson, like many others, welcomed the economic depression as the kind of adversity that brings its own cure. Poverty might induce Americans of necessity to manufacture

---

[86] [Anonymous], *A Few Salutary Hints, pointing out the Policy and Consequences of Admitting British Subjects to Engross our Trade and Become our Citizens* (Charleston printed, New York reprinted, 1786), 4.

[87] To John Page, May 4, 1786, in Boyd, ed., *Jefferson Papers*, IX, 445.

[88] These views are scattered throughout Jefferson's letters during his stay in France. See Boyd, ed., *Jefferson Papers*, VIII–XV. For a typical statement see letter to Thomas Pleasants, May 8, 1786, *ibid.*, IX, 472–73.

[89] Williamson, *Letters from Sylvius*, 13–14.

for themselves. Societies for the promotion of arts and manufactures sprang up everywhere, as they had in the 1760's and 1770's, and in Boston there was even a new non-importation agreement.[90] But Americans as an independent nation were no longer confined to such informal and extralegal methods. To bring pressure on the British and encourage domestic manufactures, the states could now levy duties and prohibitions against foreign importations, and several did so. But the uncoordinated actions of individual states in penalizing foreign trade did not break the British grip on the American market, did not end the drainage of specie, and did not lead Britain to restore trading privileges in the West Indies. Instead they became an unexpected source of bitterness and disunion. When states tried individually to regulate commerce, they often failed to discern the harmful repercussions of their measures in other states. As John Sullivan confessed concerning the New Hampshire law, "it was a blow aimed at Britain but wounds us and our friends."[91]

The advocates of frugality and manufacturing did not conclude from such failures that trade needed no regulation or that it could not be regulated. "If we Americans do not choose to regulate it," one of them warned, "it will regulate us, till we have not a farthing left in our land. . . . unless we shortly regulate and correct the abuses of our trade by lopping off its useless branches, and establishing manufactures, we shall be corrected, perhaps even to our very destruction."[92] Even Thomas Jefferson, who had been impressed by Adam Smith's advocacy of free trade, thought that Smith's policy could not be adopted unilaterally.[93] As long as the

90 *American Mercury*, Nov. 18, 1786.

91 From John Sullivan, March 4, 1786, in Boyd, ed., *Jefferson Papers*, IX, 314.

92 *American Museum*, I (March 1787), 213.

93 To G. K. van Hogendorp, Oct. 13, 1785, in Boyd, ed., *Jefferson Papers*, VIII, 633. While Smith argued for free trade, he based his arguments on a new conception of the wealth of nations that stressed the achievement of maximum productivity. With this conception and with Smith's palpable hostility to merchants and their efforts to influence policy, the Americans could readily agree.

other nations of the world continued to regulate trade, the United States could not survive without doing likewise. What the failure of individual state regulation showed was not that regulation was wrong but that it must be nationwide. As James Madison wrote to Jefferson in March 1786, "The States are every day giving proofs that seperate regulations are more likely to set them by the ears, than to attain the common object."[94]

At the time of the Townshend duties the foundering of the non-importation agreements (after the merchants of one colony gave way) had impressed upon Americans the importance of union. In the 1780's the failure of state regulation of trade taught the same lesson. This time, however, the merchants, almost to a man, were strong advocates of united action, that is to say, of giving to the central government the authority to make trade regulations binding on all the states. Their object, of course, was the enlargement of their trade by more effective retaliation against British trade restrictions on it. Other Americans, especially in the South, were wary of erecting a government with powers tailored to the needs of merchants. But in this case, as so often in successful political movements, the momentary goals of a powerful group of men coincided with the goals of other men who had larger things in view. The support that the merchants gave the movement for a stronger central government has often blinded us to the far-reaching aims of men like Madison and Hamilton who, as the latter put it, thought "continentally." What they wanted was to transform the still colonial economy of the United States by directing the industry and productivity of its citizens toward a balanced self-sufficiency that would assure the economic independence of the nation. The country, they knew, would remain predominantly agricultural for some years to come. They also knew that it could support its own merchant class, as it had done under British rule. But they agreed with David Ramsay that to attain true independence the United States

94 *Ibid.*, IX, 334.

must import less and somehow find a way to give manufacturing a place beside commerce and agriculture. When they demanded a national regulation of trade, continental-minded Americans had in view as much the restraint as the encouragement of trade, in particular the restraint of imports that might hamper the development of American manufacturing. Unlike the merchants, they did not want to strike merely at British commerce in favor of American, but to strike at all commerce (American included) that stood in the way of the economic independence of the United States.

The balanced economy they hoped to achieve by means of trade regulation would not be a northern economy or a southern economy but an American economy, of the kind described some decades later by Henry Clay. Although different branches of it might predominate in different parts of the country, the possibility of integrating them into a harmonious whole did not seem visionary in 1789. Southerners already acknowledged that New Englanders would excel in manufacturing. The climate, the compact settlements, the absence of slavery all favored them. But it was pointed out that the New Englanders, as they turned their efforts to manufactures, would buy raw materials and foodstuffs from the South. National-minded southerners like Madison even spoke up for a national navigation act to confine American trade to American vessels, though they knew that in shipbuilding and commerce as in manufactures the New Englanders would surpass them.[95] Manufacturing, commerce, and agriculture were all necessary to an independent nation, and all three might need encouragement and protection, not only from foreign sources but from each other. After the postwar buying spree and the resulting depression, it needed no demonstration that commerce, if unregulated, could bring down the whole economy. And Tench Coxe (who argued strongly for restraining commerce in favor

---

[95] Jan. 22, 1786, Nov. 14, 1785, *ibid.*, IX, 198, 203–4; Williamson, *Letters from Sylvius, passim; A Few Salutary Hints, passim;* St. George Tucker, *Reflections on the Policy and Necessity of Encouraging the Commerce of the Citizens of the United States of America . . .* (Richmond, 1785), *passim.*

of manufactures) expressed the larger concern for economic coordination when he warned that trade regulations must be phrased with great care, so as not to injure the various agricultural activities which occupied the bulk of the people throughout the country.[96] Not everyone who supported national regulation was moved by a large view of the national interest. As merchants looked for better trading opportunities, farmers looked for higher prices and would-be manufacturers for protection. But because national regulation could offer something to everyone, and because the appeal of the Puritan Ethic could be harnessed to it, men who did see its larger implications for national independence were able to enlist powerful support behind it.

There were, of course, many forces working simultaneously toward the establishment of an effective national government in the 1780's, and the most important was the Americans' continuing search for a way to make life, liberty, and property secure. By declaring independence they had gained permanent freedom from Parliamentary taxation, but political independence did not of itself bring the security they sought. What was needed, it gradually became clear, was a national economic policy that would enable a frugal, industrious people to enjoy the fruits of their labor, a policy that would bring economic as well as political independence. From the time of the first non-importation agreements Americans had been groping toward such a policy. Long before the country had a national government capable of executing it, the outlines of that policy were visible, and the national government of 1789 was created, in part at least, in order to carry it out. Americans had come to believe that only an independent national economy could guarantee the political independence that they had declared in 1776, and that only an independent national economy could preserve the virtue, the industry, frugality, and simplicity that they had sought to protect from the luxury and corruption of Great Britain. By 1787 it had become clear that none of these objectives could be attained without a national government

[96] Coxe, *An Enquiry into the Principles, passim.*

empowered to control trade—and through trade all other parts of the national economy.

It is altogether fitting that the united states, which first acted together as a government when the Continental Congress undertook the non-importation, non-exportation, non-consumption Association of 1774, gained a permanent effective government when Americans again felt an urgent need to control trade. There was in each case an immediate objective, to bring pressure on the British, and in each case a larger objective, to build American economic and moral strength. As the Constitutional Convention was drafting its great document, Tench Coxe expressed a hope which many members of that body cherished equally with the members of the First Continental Congress, that the encouragement of manufacturing would "lead us once more into the paths of virtue by restoring frugality and industry, those potent antidotes to the vices of mankind and will give us real independence by rescuing us from the tyranny of foreign fashions, and the destructive torrent of luxury."[97] Patriotism and the Puritan Ethic marched hand in hand from 1764 to 1789.

The vicissitudes of the new national government in carrying out a national economic policy form another story, and one full of ironies. Alexander Hamilton, the brilliant executor of the policy, had scarcely a grain of the Puritan Ethic in him and did not hesitate to enroll the merchant class in his schemes. But Hamilton, for purely economic and patriotic reasons, favored direct encouragement of manufactures by the national government; and in this his merchant allies helped to defeat him. Thomas Jefferson, devoted to the values of the Puritan Ethic but prejudiced against manufactures, fought against governmental support of them, yet as President of the United States he adopted the measures that turned the country decisively toward manufacturing.

The Puritan Ethic did not die with the eighteenth century.

[97] Coxe, *An Address to Friends of Manufactures*, 29–30. Coxe was not a member of the Convention. He was addressing, in Philadelphia, a group "convened for the purpose of establishing a Society for the Encouragement of Manufactures and the Useful Arts."

Throughout our history it has been there, though it has continued to be in the process of expiring. One student of the Jacksonian period has concluded that politics in the 1830's and 1840's was dominated by an appeal for restoration of the frugality and simplicity which men of that generation thought had prevailed in the preceding one. The most popular analysis of American society after the Second World War was a lament for the loss of inner-directedness (read simplicity, industry, frugality) which had been replaced by other-directedness (read luxury, extravagance). The Puritan Ethic has always been known by its epitaphs. Perhaps it is not quite dead yet.

CHAPTER V

SLAVERY AND FREEDOM
The American Paradox

❖❖❖❖❖❖❖❖❖❖❖❖❖❖❖❖❖❖❖❖❖❖❖❖❖

The English settlement of North America began in Virginia. A study of American attitudes toward work had to begin there and in sixteenth-century England, where the experience and expectations of the first settlers were formed. It was a long reach from sixteenth-century England and seventeenth-century Virginia to the American Revolution, and along the way lay the settlement of a dozen more colonies. I hoped to consider all the settlements and from there make my way back to the Revolution with new insights. But historical investigations have a way of redirecting the investigator. In the history of Virginia, and especially in a study focused on attitudes toward work, one must sooner or later confront the problem of slavery.

By the time my historian's progress reached the landing at Jamestown, slavery had become a major concern of American historians, and my investigation was doubtless affected by that concern as well as by the more general concern with race relations that has occupied Americans since the 1960s. The development of Virginia society and the role of slavery in that development proved such engrossing problems and so difficult to make sense of that they gradually usurped the place of the *larger study I had originally intended. The part played by Virginians in the Revolution was, besides, so large that one might hope to find in Virginia some clues to the meaning of what was emerging for me as the central paradox of American history: the simultaneous growth of slavery and of the devotion to freedom that animated the leaders of the Revolution. My efforts to understand the paradox, even within the confines of Virginia, ultimately required a larger book than this to relate, but I first tried to adumbrate the elements of the problem in the essay that follows.**

AMERICAN historians interested in tracing the rise of liberty, democracy, and the common man have been challenged in the past two decades by other historians, interested in tracing the history of oppression, exploitation, and racism. The challenge has been salutary, because it has made us examine more directly than historians have hitherto been willing to do the role of slavery in our early history. Colonial historians, in particular, when writing about the origin and development of American institutions have found it possible until recently to deal with slavery as an exception to everything they had to say. I am speaking about myself but also about most of my generation. We owe a debt of gratitude to those who have insisted that slavery was something more than an exception, that one fifth of the American population at the time of the Revolution is too many people to be treated as an exception.[1]

We shall not have met the challenge simply by studying the history of that one fifth, fruitful as such studies may be, urgent as they may be. Nor shall we have met the challenge if we merely execute the familiar maneuver of turning our old inter-

---

* The paper was delivered as the presidential address of the Organization of American Historians at Washington, D.C., April 6, 1972, and was first published in the *Journal of American History*, LIX (June, 1972), 5–29. The book has been published: *American Slavery—American Freedom: The Ordeal of Colonial Virginia* (New York, 1975).

[1] Particularly Staughton Lynd, *Class Conflict, Slavery, and the United States Constitution: Ten Essays* (Indianapolis, 1967).

pretations on their heads. The temptation is already apparent to argue that slavery and oppression were the dominant features of American history and that efforts to advance liberty and equality were the exception, indeed no more than a device to divert the masses while their chains were being fastened. To dismiss the rise of liberty and equality in American history as a mere sham is not only to ignore hard facts, it is also to evade the problem presented by those facts. The rise of liberty and equality in this country was accompanied by the rise of slavery. That two such contradictory developments were taking place simultaneously over a long period of our history, from the seventeenth century to the nineteenth, is the central paradox of American history.

The challenge, for a colonial historian at least, is to explain how a people could have developed the dedication to human liberty and dignity exhibited by the leaders of the American Revolution and at the same time have developed and maintained a system of labor that denied human liberty and dignity every hour of the day.

The paradox is evident at many levels if we care to see it. Think, for a moment, of the traditional American insistence on freedom of the seas. "Free ships make free goods" was the cardinal doctrine of American foreign policy in the Revolutionary era. But the goods for which the United States demanded freedom were produced in very large measure by slave labor. The irony is more than semantic. American reliance on slave labor must be viewed in the context of the American struggle for a separate and equal station among the nations of the earth. At the time the colonists announced their claim to that station they had neither the arms nor the ships to make the claim good. They desperately needed the assistance of other countries, especially France, and their single most valuable product with which to purchase assistance was tobacco, produced mainly by slave labor. So largely did that crop figure in American foreign relations that one historian has referred to the activities of France in supporting the Americans as "King Tobacco Diplomacy," a reminder that the position of the United States in the world depended not only in 1776 but during the span of a long lifetime thereafter on slave labor.[2] To a very large degree it may be said that Americans bought their independence with slave labor.

The paradox is sharpened if we think of the state where most of the tobacco came from. Virginia at the time of the first United States census in 1790 had 40 percent of the slaves in the entire United States. And Virginia produced the most eloquent spokesmen for freedom and equality in the entire United States: George Washington, James Madison, and, above all, Thomas Jefferson. They were all slaveholders and remained so throughout their lives. In recent years we have been shown in painful detail the contrast between Jefferson's pronouncements in favor of republican liberty and his complicity in denying the benefits of that liberty to blacks.[3] It has been tempting to dismiss Jefferson and the whole Virginia dynasty as hypocrites. But to do so is to deprive the term "hypocrisy" of useful meaning. If hypocrisy means, as I think it does, deliberately to affirm a principle without believing it, then hypocrisy requires a rare clarity of mind combined with an unscrupulous intention to deceive. To attribute such an intention, even to attribute such clarity of mind in the matter, to Jefferson, Madison, or Washington is once again to evade the challenge. What we need to explain is how such men could have arrived at beliefs and actions so full of contradiction.

Put the challenge another way: how did England, a country priding itself on the liberty of its citizens, produce colonies where most of the inhabitants enjoyed still greater liberty, greater opportunties, greater control over their own lives than most men in the mother country, while the remainder, one

---

[2] Curtis P. Nettels, *The Emergence of a National Economy 1775–1815* (New York, 1962), 19. See also Merrill Jensen, "The American Revolution and American Agriculture," *Agricultural History*, XLIII (Jan. 1969), 107–24.

[3] William Cohen, "Thomas Jefferson and the Problem of Slavery," *Journal of American History*, LVI (Dec. 1969), 503–26; D. B. Davis, *Was Thomas Jefferson an Authentic Enemy of Slavery?* (Oxford, 1970); Winthrop D. Jordan, *White over Black: American Attitudes toward the Negro, 1550–1812* (Chapel Hill, 1968), 429–81.

fifth of the total, were deprived of virtually all liberty, all opportunities, all control over their own lives? We may admit that the Englishmen who colonized America and their revolutionary descendants were racists, that consciously or unconsciously they believed liberties and rights should be confined to persons of a light complexion. When we have said as much, even when we have probed the depths of racial prejudice, we will not have fully accounted for the paradox. Racism was surely an essential element in it, but I should like to suggest another element, that I believe to have influenced the development of both slavery and freedom as we have known them in the United States.

I

Let us begin with Jefferson, the slaveholding spokesman of freedom. Could there have been anything in the kind of freedom he cherished that would have made him acquiesce, however reluctantly, in the slavery of so many Americans? The answer, I think, is yes. The freedom that Jefferson spoke for was not a gift to be conferred by governments, which he mistrusted at best. It was a freedom that sprang from the independence of the individual. The man who depended on another for his living could never be truly free. We may seek a clue to Jefferson's enigmatic posture toward slavery in his attitude toward those who enjoyed a seeming freedom without the independence needed to sustain it. For such persons Jefferson harbored a profound distrust, which found expression in two phobias that crop up from time to time in his writings.

The first was a passionate aversion to debt. Although the entire colonial economy of Virginia depended on the willingness of planters to go into debt and of British merchants to extend credit, although Jefferson himself was a debtor all his adult life—or perhaps because he was a debtor—he hated debt and hated anything that made him a debtor. He hated it because it limited his freedom of action. He could not, for example, have freed his slaves so long as he was in debt. Or so at least he told himself. But it was the impediment not simply to their freedom but to his own that bothered him. "I am miserable," he wrote, "till I shall owe not a shilling. . . ."[4]

The fact that he had so much company in his misery only added to it. His Declaration of Independence for the United States was mocked by the hold that British merchants retained over American debtors, including himself.[5] His hostility to Alexander Hamilton was rooted in his recognition that Hamilton's pro-British foreign policy would tighten the hold of British creditors, while his domestic policy would place the government in the debt of a class of native American creditors, whose power might become equally pernicious.

Though Jefferson's concern with the perniciousness of debt was almost obsessive, it was nevertheless altogether in keeping with the ideas of republican liberty that he shared with his countrymen. The trouble with debt was that by undermining the independence of the debtor it threatened republican liberty. Whenever debt brought a man under another's power, he lost more than his own freedom of action. He also weakened the capacity of his country to survive as a republic. It was an axiom of current political thought that republican government required a body of free, independent, property-owning citizens.[6] A nation of men, each of whom owned enough property

---

[4] Julian P. Boyd, ed., *The Papers of Thomas Jefferson* (18 vols., Princeton, 1950–), X, 615. For other expressions of Thomas Jefferson's aversion to debt and distrust of credit, both private and public, see *ibid.*, II, 275–76, VIII, 398–99, 632–33, IX, 217–18, 472–73, X, 304–5, XI, 472, 633, 636, 640, XII, 385–86.

[5] Jefferson's career as ambassador to France was occupied very largely by unsuccessful efforts to break the hold of British creditors on American commerce.

[6] See Caroline Robbins, *The Eighteenth-Century Commonwealthman: Studies in the Transmission, Development and Circumstance of English Liberal Thought from the Restoration of Charles II until the War with the Thirteen Colonies* (Cambridge, Mass., 1959); J. G. A. Pocock, "Machiavelli, Harrington, and English Political Ideologies in the Eighteenth Century," *William and Mary Quarterly*, XXII (Oct. 1965), 549–83.

to support his family, could be a republic. It would follow that a nation of debtors, who had lost their property or mortgaged it to creditors, was ripe for tyranny. Jefferson accordingly favored every means of keeping men out of debt and keeping property widely distributed. He insisted on the abolition of primogeniture and entail; he declared that the earth belonged to the living and should not be kept from them by the debts or credits of the dead; he would have given fifty acres of land to every American who did not have it—all because he believed the citizens of a republic must be free from the control of other men and that they could be free only if they were economically free by virtue of owning land on which to support themselves.[7]

If Jefferson felt so passionately about the bondage of the debtor, it is not surprising that he should also have sensed a danger to the republic from another class of men who, like debtors, were nominally free but whose independence was illusory. Jefferson's second phobia was his distrust of the landless urban workman who labored in manufactures. In Jefferson's view, he was a free man in name only. Jefferson's hostility to artificers is well known and is generally attributed to his romantic preference for the rural life. But both his distrust for artificers and his idealization of small landholders as "the most precious part of a state" rested on his concern for individual independence as the basis of freedom. Farmers made the best citizens because they were "the most vigorous, the most independant, the most virtuous. . . ." Artificers, on the other hand, were dependent on "the casualties and caprice of customers." If work was scarce, they had no land to fall back on for a living. In their dependence lay the danger. "Dependance," Jefferson argued, "begets subservience and venality, suffocates the germ of virtue, and prepares fit tools for the designs of ambition." Because artificers could lay claim to freedom without the independence to go with it, they were

[7] Boyd, ed., *Papers of Thomas Jefferson*, I, 344, 352, 362, 560, VIII, 681–82.

"the instruments by which the liberties of a country are generally overturned."[8]

II

In Jefferson's distrust of artificers we begin to get a glimpse of the limits—and limits not dictated by racism—that defined the republican vision of the eighteenth century. For Jefferson was by no means unique among republicans in his distrust of the landless laborer. Such a distrust was a necessary corollary of the widespread eighteenth-century insistence on the independent, property-holding individual as the only bulwark of liberty, an insistence originating in James Harrington's republican political philosophy and a guiding principle of American colonial politics, whether in the aristocratic South Carolina assembly or in the democratic New England town.[9] Americans both before and after 1776 learned their republican lessons from the seventeenth- and eighteenth-century British commonwealthmen; and the commonwealthmen were uninhibited in their contempt for the masses who did not have the propertied independence required of proper republicans.

John Locke, the classic explicator of the right of revolution for the protection of liberty, did not think about extending that right to the landless poor. Instead, he concocted a scheme of compulsory labor for them and their children. The children were to begin at the age of three in public institutions, called working schools because the only subject taught would be work (spinning and knitting). They would be paid in bread

8 *Ibid.*, VIII, 426, 682; Thomas Jefferson, *Notes on the State of Virginia*, William Peden, ed. (Chapel Hill, 1955), 165. Jefferson seems to have overlooked the dependence of Virginia's farmers on the casualties and caprice of the tobacco market.

9 See Robbins, *The Eighteenth-Century Commonwealthman*; Pocock, "Machiavelli, Harrington, and English Political Ideologies,' 549–83; Michael Zuckerman, "The Social Context of Democracy in Massachusetts," *William and Mary Quarterly*, XXV (Oct. 1968), 523–44; Robert M. Weir, " 'The Harmony We Were Famous For': An Interpretation of Pre-Revolutionary South Carolina Politics," *ibid.*, XXVI (Oct. 1969), 473–501.

and water and grow up "inured to work." Meanwhile the mothers, thus relieved of the care of their offspring, could go to work beside their fathers and husbands. If they could not find regular employment, then they too could be sent to the working school.[10]

It requires some refinement of mind to discern precisely how this version of women's liberation from child care differed from outright slavery. And many of Locke's intellectual successors, while denouncing slavery in the abstract, openly preferred slavery to freedom for the lower ranks of laborers. Adam Ferguson, whose works were widely read in America, attributed the overthrow of the Roman republic, in part at least, to the emancipation of slaves, who "increased, by their numbers and their vices, the weight of that dreg, which, in great and prosperous cities, ever sinks, by the tendency of vice and misconduct to the lowest condition."[11]

That people in the lowest condition, the dregs of society, generally arrived at that position through their own vice and misconduct, whether in ancient Rome or modern Britain, was an unexamined article of faith among eighteenth-century republicans. And the vice that was thought to afflict the lower ranks most severely was idleness. The eighteenth century's preferred cure for idleness lay in the religious and ethical doctrines which R. H. Tawney described as the New Medicine for Poverty, the doctrines in which Max Weber discerned the origins of the spirit of capitalism. But in every society a stubborn mass of men and women refused the medicine. For such persons the commonwealthmen did not hesitate to prescribe slavery. Thus Francis Hutcheson, who could argue eloquently against the enslavement of Africans, also argued that perpetual slavery should be "the ordinary punishment of such idle vagrants as, after proper admonitions and tryals of

10 C. B. Macpherson, *The Political Theory of Possessive Individualism* (Oxford, 1962), 221–24; H. R. Fox Bourne, *The Life of John Locke* (2 vols., London, 1876), II, 377–90.

11 Adam Ferguson, *The History of the Progress and Termination of the Roman Republic* (5 vols., Edinburgh, 1799), I, 384. See also Adam Ferguson, *An Essay on the History of Civil Society* (London, 1768), 309–11.

temporary servitude, cannot be engaged to support themselves and their families by any useful labours."[12] James Burgh, whose *Political Disquisitions* earned the praises of many American revolutionists, proposed a set of press gangs "to seize all idle and disorderly persons, who have been three times complained of before a magistrate, and to set them to work during a certain time, for the benefit of great trading, or manufacturing companies, &c."[13]

The most comprehensive proposal came from Andrew Fletcher of Saltoun. Jefferson hailed in Fletcher a patriot whose political principles were those "in vigour at the epoch of the American emigration [from England]. Our ancestors brought them here, and they needed little strengthening to make us what we are. . . ."[14] Fletcher, like other common-wealthmen, was a champion of liberty, but he was also a champion of slavery. He attacked the Christian church not only for having promoted the abolition of slavery in ancient times but also for having perpetuated the idleness of the freed-men thus turned loose on society. The church by setting up hospitals and almshouses had enabled men through the succeeding centuries to live without work. As a result, Fletcher argued, his native Scotland was burdened with 200,000 idle rogues, who roamed the country, drinking, cursing, fighting, robbing, and murdering. For a remedy he proposed that they all be made slaves to men of property. To the argument that their masters might abuse them, he answered in words which

[12] Francis Hutcheson, *A System of Moral Philosophy* (2 vols., London, 1755), II, 202; David B. Davis, *The Problem of Slavery in Western Culture* (Ithaca, 1966), 374–78. I am indebted to David B. Davis for several valuable suggestions.

[13] James Burgh, *Political Disquisitions; or, An ENQUIRY into public Errors, Defects, and Abuses* . . . (3 vols., London, 1774–75), III, 220–21. See the proposal of Bishop George Berkeley that "sturdy beggars should . . . be seized and made slaves to the public for a certain term of years." Quoted in R. H. Tawney, *Religion and the Rise of Capitalism: A Historical Essay* (New York, 1926), 270.

[14] E. Millicent Sowerby, ed., *Catalogue of the Library of Thomas Jefferson* (5 vols., Washington, 1952–59), I, 192.

might have come a century and a half later from a George
Fitzhugh: that this would be against the master's own interest,
"That the most brutal man will not use his beast ill only out
of a humour; and that if such Inconveniences do sometimes
fall out, it proceeds, for the most part, from the perverseness
of the Servant."[15]

In spite of Jefferson's tribute to Fletcher, there is no reason
to suppose that he endorsed Fletcher's proposal. But he did
share Fletcher's distrust of men who were free in name while
their empty bellies made them thieves, threatening the property
of honest men, or else made them slaves in fact to anyone who
would feed them. Jefferson's own solution for the kind of situation described by Fletcher was given in a famous letter to
Madison, prompted by the spectacle Jefferson encountered in
France in the 1780s, where a handful of noblemen had engrossed huge tracts of land on which to hunt game, while
hordes of the poor went without work and without bread.
Jefferson's proposal, characteristically phrased in terms of
natural right, was for the poor to appropriate the uncultivated
lands of the nobility. And he drew for the United States his
usual lesson of the need to keep land widely distributed
among the people.[16]

Madison's answer, which is less well known than Jefferson's
letter, raised the question whether it was possible to eliminate
the idle poor in any country as fully populated as France.
Spread the land among them in good republican fashion and
there would still be, Madison thought, "a great surplus of inhabitants, a greater by far than will be employed in cloathing
both themselves and those who feed them. . . ." In spite of
those occupied in trades and as mariners, soldiers, and so on,
there would remain a mass of men without work. "A certain
degree of misery," Madison concluded, "seems inseparable

15 Andrew Fletcher, *Two Discourses concerning the Affairs of Scotland;
Written in the Year 1698* (Edinburgh, 1698). See second discourse (separately
paged), 1–33, especially 16.

16 Boyd, ed., *Papers of Thomas Jefferson*, VIII, 681–83.

from a high degree of populousness."[17] He did not, however, go on to propose, as Fletcher had done, that the miserable and idle poor be reduced to slavery.

The situation contemplated by Madison and confronted by Fletcher was not irrelevant to those who were planning the future of the American republic. In a country where population grew by geometric progression, it was not too early to think about a time when there might be vast numbers of landless poor, when there might be those mobs in great cities that Jefferson feared as sores on the body politic. In the United States as Jefferson and Madison knew it, the urban labor force as yet posed no threat, because it was small; and the agricultural labor force was, for the most part, already enslaved. In Revolutionary America, among men who spent their lives working for other men rather than working for themselves, slaves probably constituted a majority.[18] In Virginia they constituted a large majority.[19] If Jefferson and Madison, not to mention Washington, were unhappy about that fact and yet did nothing to alter it, they may have been restrained, in part at least, by thoughts of the role that might be played in the United States by a large mass of free laborers.

When Jefferson contemplated the abolition of slavery, he found it inconceivable that the freed slaves should be allowed to remain in the country.[20] In this attitude he was probably moved by his or his countrymen's racial prejudice. But he may also have had in mind the possibility that when slaves ceased to be slaves, they would become instead a half million idle poor, who would create the same problems for the United States that the idle poor of Europe did for their states. The

---

[17] *Ibid.*, IX, 659–60.

[18] Jackson Turner Main, *The Social Structure of Revolutionary America* (Princeton, 1965), 271.

[19] In 1755, Virginia had 43,329 white tithables and 60,078 black. Tithables included white men over sixteen years of age and black men and women over sixteen. In the census of 1790, Virginia had 292,717 slaves and 110,936 white males over sixteen, out of a total population of 747,680. Evarts B. Green and Virginia D. Harrington, *American Population before the Federal Census of 1790* (New York, 1932), 150–55.

[20] Jefferson, *Notes on the State of Virginia*, 138.

slave, accustomed to compulsory labor, would not work to support himself when the compulsion was removed. This was a commonplace among Virginia planters before the creation of the republic and long after. "If you free the slaves," wrote Landon Carter, two days after the Declaration of Independence, "you must send them out of the country or they must steal for their support."[21]

Jefferson's plan for freeing his own slaves (never carried out) included an interim educational period in which they would have been half taught, half compelled to support themselves on rented land; for without guidance and preparation for self-support, he believed, slaves could not be expected to become fit members of a republican society.[22] And St. George Tucker, who drafted detailed plans for freeing Virginia's slaves, worried about "the possibility of their becoming idle, dissipated, and finally a numerous banditti, instead of turning their attention to industry and labour." He therefore included in his plans a provision for compelling the labor of the freedmen on an annual basis. "For we must not lose sight of this important consideration," he said, "that these people must be *bound* to labour, if they do not *voluntarily* engage therein. . . . In absolving them from the yoke of slavery, we must not forget the interests of society. Those interests require the exertions of every individual in some mode or other; and those who have not wherewith to support themselves honestly without corporal labour, whatever be their complexion, ought to be compelled to labour."[23]

It is plain that Tucker, the would-be emancipator, distrusted the idle poor regardless of color. And it seems probable that the Revolutionary champions of liberty who acquiesced in the continued slavery of black labor did so not only because of racial prejudice but also because they shared with Tucker a

21 Jack P. Greene, ed., *The Diary of Colonel Landon Carter of Sabine Hall, 1752–1778* (2 vols., Charlottesville, 1965), II, 1055.

22 Boyd, ed., *Papers of Thomas Jefferson*, XIV, 492–93.

23 St. George Tucker, *A Dissertation on Slavery with a Proposal for the Gradual Abolition of It, in the State of Virginia* (Philadelphia, 1796). See also Jordan, *White over Black*, 555–60.

distrust of the poor that was inherent in eighteenth-century conceptions of republican liberty. Their historical guidebooks had made them fear to enlarge the free labor force.

III

That fear, I believe, had a second point of origin in the experience of the American colonists, and especially of Virginians, during the preceding century and a half. If we turn now to the previous history of Virginia's labor force, we may find, I think, some further clues to the distrust of free labor among Revolutionary republicans and to the paradoxical rise of slavery and freedom together in colonial America.

The story properly begins in England with the burst of population growth there that sent the number of Englishmen from perhaps three million in 1500 to four and one-half million by 1650.[24] The increase did not occur in response to any corresponding growth in the capacity of the island's economy to support its people. And the result was precisely that misery which Madison pointed out to Jefferson as the consequence of "a high degree of populousness." Sixteenth-century England knew the same kind of unemployment and poverty that Jefferson witnessed in eighteenth-century France and Fletcher in seventeenth-century Scotland. Alarming numbers of idle and hungry men drifted about the country looking for work or plunder. The government did what it could to make men of means hire them, but it also adopted increasingly severe measures against their wandering, their thieving, their roistering, and indeed their very existence. Whom the workhouses and prisons could not swallow the gallows would have to, or perhaps the army. When England had military expeditions to conduct abroad, every parish packed off its most unwanted inhabitants to the almost certain death that awaited them from the diseases of the camp.[25]

[24] Joan Thirsk, ed., *The Agrarian History of England and Wales*, vol. IV: *1500–1640* (Cambridge, England, 1967), 531.

[25] See Edmund S. Morgan, "The Labor Problem at Jamestown, 1607–18," *American Historical Review*, 76 (June 1971), 595–611, esp. 600–606.

As the mass of idle rogues and beggars grew and increasingly threatened the peace of England, the efforts to cope with them increasingly threatened the liberties of Englishmen. Englishmen prided themselves on a "gentle government,"[26] a government that had been releasing its subjects from old forms of bondage and endowing them with new liberties, making the "rights of Englishmen" a phrase to conjure with. But there was nothing gentle about the government's treatment of the poor; and as more Englishmen became poor, other Englishmen had less to be proud of. Thoughtful men could see an obvious solution: get the surplus Englishmen out of England. Send them to the New World, where there were limitless opportunities for work. There they would redeem themselves, enrich the mother country, and spread English liberty abroad.

The great publicist for this program was Richard Hakluyt. His *Principall Navigations, Voiages and Discoveries of the English nation*[27] was not merely the narrative of voyages by Englishmen around the globe, but a powerful suggestion that the world ought to be English or at least ought to be ruled by Englishmen. Hakluyt's was a dream of empire, but of benevolent empire, in which England would confer the blessings of her own free government on the less fortunate peoples of the world. It is doubtless true that Englishmen, along with other Europeans, were already imbued with prejudice against men of darker complexions than their own. And it is also true that the principal beneficiaries of Hakluyt's empire would be Englishmen. But Hakluyt's dream cannot be dismissed as mere hypocrisy any more than Jefferson's affirmation of human equality can be so dismissed. Hakluyt's compassion for the poor and oppressed was not confined to the English poor, and in Francis Drake's exploits in the Caribbean Hakluyt saw, not a thinly disguised form of piracy, but a model for English liberation of men of all colors who labored under the tyranny of the Spaniard.

[26] This is Richard Hakluyt's phrase. See E. G. R. Taylor, ed., *The Original Writings & Correspondence of the Two Richard Hakluyts* (2 vols., London, 1935), I, 142.

[27] Richard Hakluyt, *The Principall Navigations, Voiages and Discoveries of the English nation* . . . (London, 1589).

Drake had gone ashore at Panama in 1572 and made friends with an extraordinary band of runaway Negro slaves. "Cimarrons" they were called, and they lived a free and hardy life in the wilderness, periodically raiding the Spanish settlements to carry off more of their people. They discovered in Drake a man who hated the Spanish as much as they did and who had the arms and men to mount a stronger attack than they could manage by themselves. Drake wanted Spanish gold, and the Cimarrons wanted Spanish iron for tools. They both wanted Spanish deaths. The alliance was a natural one and apparently untroubled by racial prejudice. Together the English and the Cimarrons robbed the mule train carrying the annual supply of Peruvian treasure across the isthmus. And before Drake sailed for England with his loot, he arranged for future meetings.[28] When Hakluyt heard of this alliance, he concocted his first colonizing proposal, a scheme for seizing the Straits of Magellan and transporting Cimarrons there, along with surplus Englishmen. The straits would be a strategic strong point for England's world empire, since they controlled the route from Atlantic to Pacific. Despite the severe climate of the place, the Cimarrons and their English friends would all live warmly together, clad in English woolens, "well lodged and by our nation made free from the tyrannous Spanyard, and quietly and courteously governed by our nation."[29]

The scheme for a colony in the Straits of Magellan never worked out, but Hakluyt's vision endured, of liberated natives and surplus Englishmen, courteously governed in English colonies around the world. Sir Walter Raleigh caught the vision. He dreamt of wresting the treasure of the Incas from the Spaniard by allying with the Indians of Guiana and sending Englishmen to live with them, lead them in rebellion against Spain, and govern them in the English manner.[30]

[28] The whole story of this extraordinary episode is to be found in I. A. Wright, ed., *Documents concerning English Voyages to the Spanish Main 1569–1580* (London, 1932).

[29] Taylor, ed., *Original Writings & Correspondence*, I, 139–46.

[30] Walter Raleigh, *The Discoverie of the large and bewtiful Empire of Guiana*, V. T. Harlow, ed. (London, 1928), 138–49; V. T. Harlow, ed.,

Raleigh also dreamt of a similar colony in the country he named Virginia. Hakluyt helped him plan it.[31] And Drake stood ready to supply Negroes and Indians, liberated from Spanish tyranny in the Caribbean, to help the enterprise.[32]

Virginia from the beginning was conceived not only as a haven for England's suffering poor, but as a spearhead of English liberty in an oppressed world. That was the dream; but when it began to materialize at Roanoke Island in 1585, something went wrong. Drake did his part by liberating Spanish Caribbean slaves, and carrying to Roanoke those who wished to join him.[33] But the English settlers whom Raleigh sent there proved unworthy of the role assigned them. By the time Drake arrived they had shown themselves less than courteous to the Indians on whose assistance they depended. The first group of settlers murdered the chief who befriended them, and then gave up and ran for home aboard Drake's returning ships. The second group simply disappeared, presumably killed by the Indians.[34]

What was lost in this famous lost colony was more than the band of colonists who have never been traced. What was also lost and never quite recovered in subsequent ventures was the dream of Englishman and Indian living side by side in peace and liberty. When the English finally planted a perma-

---

Ralegh's Last Voyage: Being an account drawn out of contemporary letters and relations . . . (London, 1932), 44–45.

[31] Taylor, ed., *Original Writings & Correspondence*, II, 211–377, esp. 318.

[32] Irene A. Wright, trans. and ed., *Further English Voyages to Spanish America, 1583–1594: Documents from the Archives of the Indies at Seville* . . . (London, 1951), lviii, lxiii, lxiv, 37, 52, 54, 55, 159, 172, 173, 181, 188–89, 204–6.

[33] The Spanish reported that "Although their masters were willing to ransom them the English would not give them up except when the slaves themselves desired to go." *Ibid.*, 159. On Walter Raleigh's later expedition to Guiana, the Spanish noted that the English told the natives "that they did not desire to make them slaves, but only to be their friends; promising to bring them great quantities of hatchets and knives, and especially if they drove the Spaniards out of their territories." Harlow, ed., *Ralegh's Last Voyage*, 179.

[34] David Beers Quinn, ed., *The Roanoke Voyages 1584–1590* (2 vols., London, 1955).

nent colony at Jamestown they came as conquerors, and their government was far from gentle. The Indians willing to endure it were too few in numbers and too broken in spirit to play a significant part in the settlement.

Without their help, Virginia offered a bleak alternative to the workhouse or the gallows for the first English poor who were transported there. During the first two decades of the colony's existence, most of the arriving immigrants found precious little English liberty in Virginia.[35] But by the 1630s the colony seemed to be working out, at least in part, as its first planners had hoped. Impoverished Englishmen were arriving every year in large numbers, engaged to serve the existing planters for a term of years, with the prospect of setting up their own households a few years later. The settlers were spreading up Virginia's great rivers, carving out plantations, living comfortably from their corn fields and from the cattle they ranged in the forests, and at the same time earning perhaps ten or twelve pounds a year per man from the tobacco they planted. A representative legislative assembly secured the traditional liberties of Englishmen and enabled a larger proportion of the population to participate in their own government than had ever been the case in England. The colony even began to look a little like the cosmopolitan haven of liberty that Hakluyt had first envisaged. Men of all countries appeared there: French, Spanish, Dutch, Turkish, Portuguese, and African.[36] Virginia took them in and began to make Englishmen out of them.

It seems clear that most of the Africans, perhaps all of them,

[35] Morgan, "The Labor Problem at Jamestown, 1607–18," 595–611; Edmund S. Morgan, "The First American Boom: Virginia 1618 to 1630," *William and Mary Quarterly*, XXVIII (April 1971), 169–98.

[36] There are no reliable records of immigration, but the presence of persons of these nationalities is evident from county court records, where all but the Dutch are commonly identified by name, such as "James the Scotchman," or "Cursory the Turk." The Dutch seem to have anglicized their names at once and are difficult to identify except where the records disclose their naturalization. The two counties for which the most complete records survive for the 1640s and 1650s are Accomack-Northampton and Lower Norfolk. Microfilms are in the Virginia State Library, Richmond.

came as slaves, a status that had become obsolete in England, while it was becoming the expected condition of Africans outside Africa and of a good many inside.[37] It is equally clear that a substantial number of Virginia's Negroes were free or became free. And all of them, whether servant, slave, or free, enjoyed most of the same rights and duties as other Virginians. There is no evidence during the period before 1660 that they were subjected to a more severe discipline than other servants. They could sue and be sued in court. They did penance in the parish church for having illegitimate children. They earned money of their own, bought and sold and raised cattle of their own. Sometimes they bought their own freedom. In other cases, masters bequeathed them not only freedom but land, cattle, and houses.[38] Northampton, the only county for which full records exist, had at least ten free Negro households by 1668.[39]

As Negroes took their place in the community, they learned English ways, including even the truculence toward authority that has always been associated with the rights of Englishmen. Tony Longo, a free Negro of Northampton, when served a

[37] Because the surviving records are so fragmentary, there has been a great deal of controversy about the status of the first Negroes in Virginia. What the records do make clear is that not all were slaves and that not all were free. See Jordan, *White over Black*, 71–82.

[38] For examples, see Northampton County Court Records, Deeds, Wills, etc., Book III, f.83, Book V, ff.38, 54, 60, 102, 117–19; York County Court Records, Deeds, Orders, Wills, etc., no. 1, ff.232–34; Surry County Court Records, Deeds, Wills, etc., no. 1, f.349; Henrico County Court Records, Deeds and Wills 1677–1692, f.139.

[39] This fact has been arrived at by comparing the names of householders on the annual list of tithables with casual identifications of persons as Negroes in the court records. The names of householders so identified for 1668, the peak year during the period for which the lists survive (1662–1677) were: Bastian Cane, Bashaw Ferdinando, John Francisco, Susan Grace, William Harman, Philip Mongum, Francis Pane, Manuel Rodriggus, Thomas Rodriggus, and King Tony. The total number of households in the county in 1668 was 177; total number of tithables 406; total number of tithable free Negroes 17; total number of tithable unfree Negroes 42. Thus nearly 29 percent of tithable Negroes and probably of all Negroes were free; and about 14.5 percent of all tithables were Negroes.

warrant to appear as a witness in court, responded with a scatological opinion of warrants, called the man who served it an idle rascal, and told him to go about his business. The man offered to go with him at any time before a justice of the peace so that his evidence could be recorded. He would go with him at night, tomorrow, the next day, next week, any time. But Longo was busy getting in his corn. He dismissed all pleas with a "Well, well, Ile goe when my Corne is in," and refused to receive the warrant.[40]

The judges understandably found this to be contempt of court; but it was the kind of contempt that free Englishmen often showed to authority, and it was combined with a devotion to work that English moralists were doing their best to inculcate more widely in England. As England had absorbed people of every nationality over the centuries and turned them into Englishmen, Virginia's Englishmen were absorbing their own share of foreigners, including Negroes, and seemed to be successfully molding a New World community on the English model.

IV

But a closer look will show that the situation was not quite so promising as at first it seems. It is well known that Virginia in its first fifteen or twenty years killed off most of the men who went there. It is less well known that it continued to do so. If my estimate of the volume of immigration is anywhere near correct, Virginia must have been a death trap for at least another fifteen years and probably for twenty or twenty-five. In 1625 the population stood at 1,300 or 1,400; in 1640 it was about 8,000.[41] In the fifteen years between those dates at least

40 Northampton Deeds, Wills, etc., Book V, 54–60 (Nov. 1, 1654).

41 The figure for 1625 derives from the census for that year, which gives 1,210 persons, but probably missed about 10 percent of the population. Morgan, "The First American Boom," 170n–71n. The figure for 1640 is derived from legislation limiting tobacco production per person in 1639–40. The legislation is summarized in a manuscript belonging to Jefferson,

15,000 persons must have come to the colony.[42] If so, 15,000 immigrants increased the population by less than 7,000. There is no evidence of a large return migration. It seems probable that the death rate throughout this period was comparable only to that found in Europe during the peak years of a plague. Virginia, in other words, was absorbing England's surplus laborers mainly by killing them. The success of those who survived and rose from servant to planter must be attributed partly to the fact that so few did survive.

After 1640, when the diseases responsible for the high death rate began to decline and the population began a quick rise, it became increasingly difficult for an indigent immigrant to pull himself up in the world. The population probably passed

---

printed in William Waller Hening, *The Statutes at Large; Being a Collection of All the Laws of Virginia, from the First Session of the Legislature, in the Year 1619* (13 vols., New York, 1823), I, 224–25, 228. The full text is in "Acts of the General Assembly, Jan. 6, 1639–40," *William and Mary Quarterly*, IV (Jan. 1924), 17–35, and "Acts of the General Assembly, Jan. 6, 1639–40," *ibid.* (July 1924), 159–62. The assembly calculated that a levy of four pounds of tobacco per tithable would yield 18,584 pounds, implying 4,646 tithables (men over sixteen). It also calculated that a limitation of planting to 170 pounds per poll would yield 1,300,000, implying 7,647 polls. Evidently the latter figure is for the whole population, as is evident also from Hening, *Statutes*, I, 228.

42 In the year 1635, the only year for which such records exist, 2,010 persons embarked for Virginia from London alone. See John Camden Hotten, ed., *The Original Lists of Persons of Quality . . .* (London, 1874), 35–145. For other years casual estimates survive. In February 1627/8 Francis West said that 1,000 had been "lately received." Colonial Office Group, Class 1, Piece 4, folio 109 (Public Record Office, London). Hereafter cited CO 1/4, f.109. In February 1633/4 Governor John Harvey said that "this yeares newcomers" had been 1,200. *Virginia Magazine of History and Biography*, VIII (1900–1901), 155. Captain Thomas Yong reported in July 1634 that 1,500 had arrived "this yeare." Yong to Sir Tobie Matthew, July 13, 1634, "Aspinwall Papers," *Massachusetts Historical Society Collections*, IX (1871), 110. In May 1635, Samuel Mathews said that 2,000 had arrived "this yeare." Mathews to?, May 25, 1635, "The Mutiny in Virginia, 1635," *Virginia Magazine of History and Biography*, I (April 1894), 417. And in March 1636, John West said that 1,606 persons had arrived "this yeare." West to Commissioners for Plantations, March 28, 1636, "Virginia in 1636," *ibid.*, IX (July 1901), 37.

25,000 by 1662,[43] hardly what Madison would have called a high degree of populousness. Yet the rapid rise brought serious trouble for Virginia. It brought the engrossment of tidewater land in thousands and tens of thousands of acres by speculators, who recognized that the demand would rise.[44] It brought a huge expansion of tobacco production, which helped to depress the price of tobacco and the earnings of the men who planted it.[45] It brought efforts by planters to prolong the terms of servants, since they were now living longer and therefore had a longer expectancy of usefulness.[46]

It would, in fact, be difficult to asses all the consequences of the increased longevity; but for our purposes one development was crucial, and that was the appearance in Virginia of a growing number of freemen who had served their terms but who were now unable to afford land of their own except on

[43] The official count of tithables for 1662 was 11,838. Clarendon Papers, 82 (Bodleian Library, Oxford). The ratio of titables to total population by this time was probably about one to two. (In 1625 it was 1 to 1.5; in 1699 it was 1 to 2.7.) Since the official count was almost certainly below the actuality, a total population of roughly 25,000 seems probable. All population figures for seventeenth-century Virginia should be treated as rough estimates.

[44] Evidence of the engrossment of lands after 1660 will be found in CO 1/39, f.196; CO 1/40, f.23; CO 1/48, f.48; CO 5/1309, numbers 5, 9, and 23; Sloane Papers, 1008, ff.334–35 (British Museum, London). A recent count of headrights in patents issued for land in Virginia shows 82,000 headrights claimed in the years from 1635 to 1700. Of these nearly 47,000 or 57 percent (equivalent to 2,350,000 acres) were claimed in the twenty-five years after 1650. W. F. Craven, *White, Red, and Black: The Seventeenth-Century Virginian* (Charlottesville, 1971), 14–16.

[45] No continuous set of figures for Virginia's tobacco exports in the seventeenth century can now be obtained. The available figures for English imports of American tobacco (which was mostly Virginian) are in United States Bureau of the Census, *Historical Statistics of the United States, Colonial Times to 1957* (Washington, D.C., 1960), series Z 238–240, p. 766. They show for 1672 a total of 17,559,000 pounds. In 1631 the figure had been 272,300 pounds. Tobacco crops varied heavily from year to year. Prices are almost as difficult to obtain now as volume. Those for 1667–75 are estimated from London prices current in Warren Billings, "Virginia's Deploured Condition, 1660–1676: The Coming of Bacon's Rebellion" (doctoral dissertation, Northern Illinois University, 1969), 155–59.

[46] See below.

the frontiers or in the interior. In years when tobacco prices were especially low or crops especially poor, men who had been just scraping by were obliged to go back to work for their larger neighbors simply in order to stay alive. By 1676 it was estimated that one fourth of Virginia's freemen were without land of their own.[47] And in the same year Francis Moryson, a member of the governor's council, explained the term "freedmen" as used in Virginia to mean "persons without house and land," implying that this was now the normal condition of servants who had attained freedom.[48]

Some of them resigned themselves to working for wages; others preferred a meager living on dangerous frontier land or a hand-to-mouth existence, roaming from one county to another, renting a bit of land here, squatting on some there, dodging the tax collector, drinking, quarreling, stealing hogs, and enticing servants to run away with them.

The presence of this growing class of poverty-stricken Virginians was not a little frightening to the planters who had made it to the top or who had arrived in the colony already at the top, with ample supplies of servants and capital. They were caught in a dilemma. They wanted the immigrants who kept pouring in every year. Indeed they needed them and prized them the more as they lived longer. But as more and more turned free each year, Virginia seemed to have inherited the problem that she was helping England to solve. Virginia, complained Nicholas Spencer, secretary of the colony, was "a sinke to drayen England of her filth and scum."[49]

The men who worried the upper crust looked even more dangerous in Virginia than they had in England. They were, to begin with, young, because it was young persons that the planters wanted for work in the fields; and the young have always seemed impatient of control by their elders and superiors, if not downright rebellious. They were also pre-

[47] Thomas Ludwell and Robert Smith to the king, June 18, 1676, vol. LXXVII, f. 128, Coventry Papers Longleat House, American Council of Learned Societies British Mss. project, reel 63 (Library of Congress).

[48] *Ibid.*, 204–5.

[49] Nicholas Spencer to Lord Culpeper, Aug. 6, 1676, *ibid.*, 170. See also CO 1/49, f.107.

dominantly single men. Because the planters did not think women, or at least English women, fit for work in the fields, men outnumbered women among immigrants by three or four to one throughout the century.[50] Consequently most of the freedmen had no wife or family to tame their wilder impulses and serve as hostages to the respectable world.

Finally, what made these wild young men particularly dangerous was that they were armed and had to be armed. Life in Virginia required guns. The plantations were exposed to attack from Indians by land and from privateers and petty-thieving pirates by sea.[51] Whenever England was at war with the French or the Dutch, the settlers had to be ready to defend themselves. In 1667 the Dutch in a single raid captured twenty merchant ships in the James River, together with the English warship that was supposed to be defending them; and in 1673 they captured eleven more. On these occasions Governor William Berkeley gathered the planters in arms and at least prevented the enemy from making a landing. But while he stood off the Dutch he worried about the ragged crew at his back. Of the able-bodied men in the colony he estimated that "at least one third are Single freedmen (whose Labour will hardly maintaine them) or men much in debt, both which wee may reasonably expect upon any Small advantage the Enemy may gaine upon us, wold revolt to them in hopes of bettering their Condicion by Shareing the Plunder of the Country with them."[52]

---

[50] The figures are derived from a sampling of the names of persons for whom headrights were claimed in land patents. Patent Books I–IX (Virginia State Library, Richmond). Wyndham B. Blanton found 17,350 women and 75,884 men in "a prolonged search of the patent books and other records of the times . . . ," a ratio of 1 woman to 4.4 men. Wyndham B. Blanton, "Epidemics, Real and Imaginary, and Other Factors Influencing Seventeenth Century Virginia's Population," *Bulletin of the History of Medicine*, XXXI (Sept.–Oct. 1957), 462. See also Craven, *White, Red, and Black*, 26–27.

[51] Pirates were particularly troublesome in the 1680s and 1690s. See CO 1/48, f.71; CO 1/51, f.340; CO 1/52, f.54; CO 1/55, ff.105–6; CO 1/57, f.300; CO 5/1311, no. 10.

[52] CO 1/30, ff.114–15.

Berkeley's fears were justified. Three years later, sparked not by a Dutch invasion but by an Indian attack, rebellion swept Virginia. It began almost as Berkeley had predicted, when a group of volunteer Indian fighters turned from a fruitless expedition against the Indians to attack their rulers. Bacon's Rebellion was the largest popular rising in the colonies before the American Revolution. Sooner or later nearly everyone in Virginia got in on it, but it began in the frontier counties of Henrico and New Kent, among men whom the governor and his friends consistently characterized as rabble.[53] As it spread eastward, it turned out that there were rabble everywhere, and Berkeley understandably raised his estimate of their numbers. "How miserable that man is," he exclaimed, "that Governes a People wher six parts of seaven at least are Poore Endebted Discontented and Armed."[54]

Virginia's poor had reason to be envious and angry against the men who owned the land and imported the servants and ran the government. But the rebellion produced no real program of reform, no ideology, not even any revolutionary slogans. It was a search for plunder, not for principles. And when the rebels had redistributed whatever wealth they could lay their hands on, the rebellion subsided almost as quickly as it had begun.

It had been a shattering experience, however, for Virginia's first families. They had seen each other fall in with the rebels in order to save their skins or their possessions or even to share in the plunder. When it was over, they eyed one another distrustfully, on the lookout for any new Bacons in their midst, who might be tempted to lead the still restive rabble on more plundering expeditions. When William Byrd and Laurence Smith proposed to solve the problems of defense against the Indians by establishing semi-independent buffer settlements on the upper reaches of the rivers, in each of which they would engage to keep fifty men in arms, the assembly at first reacted favorably. But it quickly occurred to the governor

---

[53] CO 1/37, ff.35–40.
[54] Vol. LXXVII, 144–46, Coventry Papers.

and council that this would in fact mean gathering a crowd of Virginia's wild bachelors and furnishing them with an abundant supply of arms and ammunition. Byrd had himself led such a crowd in at least one plundering foray during the rebellion. To put him or anyone else in charge of a large and permanent gang of armed men was to invite them to descend again on the people whom they were supposed to be protecting.[55]

The nervousness of those who had property worth plundering continued throughout the century, spurred in 1682 by the tobacco-cutting riots in which men roved about destroying crops in the fields, in the desperate hope of producing a shortage that would raise the price of the leaf.[56] And periodically in nearby Maryland and North Carolina, where the same conditions existed as in Virginia, there were tumults that threatened to spread to Virginia.[57]

As Virginia thus acquired a social problem analogous to England's own, the colony began to deal with it as England had done, by restricting the liberties of those who did not have the proper badge of freedom, namely, the property that government was supposed to protect. One way was to extend the terms of service for servants entering the colony without indentures. Formerly they had served until twenty-one; now the age was advanced to twenty-four.[58] There had always been laws requiring them to serve extra time for running away; now the laws added corporal punishment and, in order to make habitual offenders more readily recognizable, specified that their hair be cropped.[59] New laws restricted the movement of servants on the highways and also increased the amount of extra time to be served for running away. In addition to serv-

---

[55] Hening, *Statutes*, II, 448–54; CO 1/42, f.178; CO 1/43, f.29; CO 1/44, f.398; CO 1/47, ff.258–60, 267; CO 1/48, f.46; vol. LXXVIII, 378–81, 386–87, 398–99, Coventry Papers.

[56] CO 1/48 *passim*.

[57] CO 1/43, ff.359–65; CO 1/44, ff.10–62; CO 1/47, f.261; CO 1/48, ff.87–96, 100–102, 185; CO 5/1305, no. 43; CO 5/1309, no. 74.

[58] Hening, *Statutes*, II, 113–14, 240.

[59] *Ibid.*, II, 266, 278.

ing two days for every day's absence, the captured runaway was now frequently required to compensate by labor for the loss to the crop that he had failed to tend and for the cost of his apprehension, including rewards paid for his capture.[60] A three weeks' holiday might result in a year's extra service.[61] If a servant struck his master, he was to serve another year.[62] For killing a hog he had to serve the owner a year and the informer another year. Since the owner of the hog, and the owner of the servant, and the informer were frequently the same man, and since a hog was worth at best less than one tenth the hire of a servant for a year, the law was very profitable to masters. One Lancaster master was awarded six years' extra service from a servant who killed three of his hogs, worth about thirty shillings.[63]

The effect of these measures was to keep servants for as long as possible from gaining their freedom, especially the kind of servants who were most likely to cause trouble. At the same time the engrossment of land was driving many back to servitude after a brief taste of freedom. Freedmen who engaged to work for wages by so doing became servants again, subject to to most of the same restrictions as other servants.

Nevertheless, in spite of all the legal and economic pressures to keep men in service, the ranks of the freedmen grew, and so did poverty and discontent. To prevent the wild bachelors from gaining an influence in the government, the assembly in 1670 limited voting to landholders and householders.[64] But to disfranchise the growing mass of single freemen was not to

60 *Ibid.*, II, 116–17, 273–74, 277–78.

61 For example, James Gray, absent twenty-two days, was required to serve fifteen months extra. Order Book 1666–1680, p. 163, Lancaster County Court Records.

62 Hening, *Statutes*, II, 118.

63 Order Book 1666–1680, p. 142, Lancaster County Court Records.

64 Hening, *Statutes*, II, 280. It had been found, the preamble to the law said, that such persons "haveing little interest in the country doe oftner make tumults at the election to the disturbance of his majesties peace, then by their discretions in their votes provide for the conservasion thereof, by makeing choyce of persons fitly qualifyed for the discharge of soe great a trust. . . ."

deprive them of the weapons they had wielded so effectively under Nathaniel Bacon. It is questionable how far Virginia could safely have continued along this course, meeting discontent with repression and manning her plantations with annual importations of servants who would later add to the unruly ranks of the free. To be sure, the men at the bottom might have had both land and liberty, as the settlers of some other colonies did, if Virginia's frontier had been safe from Indians, or if the men at the top had been willing to forgo some of their profits and to give up some of the lands they had engrossed. The English government itself made efforts to break up the great holdings that had helped to create the problem.[65] But it is unlikely that the policy makers in Whitehall would have contended long against the successful.

In any case they did not have to. There was another solution, which allowed Virginia's magnates to keep their lands, yet arrested the discontent and the repression of other Englishmen, a solution which strengthened the rights of Englishmen and nourished that attachment to liberty which came to fruition in the Revolutionary generation of Virginia statesmen. But the solution put an end to the process of turning Africans into Englishmen. The rights of Englishmen were preserved by destroying the rights of Africans.

V

I do not mean to argue that Virginians deliberately turned to African Negro slavery as a means of preserving and extending the rights of Englishmen. Winthrop Jordan has suggested that slavery came to Virginia as an unthinking decision.[66] We might go further and say that it came without a decision. It came automatically as Virginians bought the cheapest labor they could get. Once Virginia's heavy mortality ceased, an investment in slave labor was much more profitable

[65] CO 1/39 f.196; CO 1/48, f.48; CO 5/1309,, nos. 5, 9, 23; CO 5/1310, no. 83.

[66] Jordan, *White over Black*, 44–98.

than an investment in free labor; and the planters bought slaves as rapidly as traders made them available. In the last years of the seventeenth century they bought them in such numbers that slaves probably already constituted a majority or nearly a majority of the labor force by 1700.[67] The demand was so great that traders for a time found a better market in Virginia than in Jamaica or Barbados.[68] But the social benefits of an enslaved labor force, even if not consciously sought or recognized at the time by the men who bought the slaves, were larger than the economic benefits. The increase in the importation of slaves was matched by a decrease in the importation of indentured servants and consequently a decrease in the dangerous number of new freedmen who annually emerged seeking a place in society that they would be unable to achieve.[69]

If Africans had been unavailable, it would probably have proved impossible to devise a way to keep a continuing supply of English immigrants in their place. There was a limit beyond which the abridgment of English liberties would have resulted not merely in rebellion but in protests from England and in the cutting off of the supply of further servants. At the time of Bacon's Rebellion the English commission of investigation had shown more sympathy with the rebels than with the well-to-do planters who had engrossed Virginia's lands. To have attempted the enslavement of English-born laborers would have caused more disorder than it cured. But

[67] In 1700 they constituted half of the labor force (persons working for other men) in Surry County, the only county in which it is possible to ascertain the numbers. Robert Wheeler, "Social Transition in the Virginia Tidewater, 1650–1720: The Laboring Household as an Index," paper delivered at the Organization of American Historians' meeting, New Orleans, April 15, 1971. Surry County was on the south side of the James, one of the least wealthy regions of Virginia. See E. S. Morgan, *American Slavery —American Freedom*, 227–30, 418–31.

[68] See the letters of the Royal African Company to its ship captains, Oct. 23, 1701; Dec. 2, 1701; Dec. 7, 1704; Dec. 21, 1704; Jan. 25, 1704/5, T70/58 (Public Record Office, London).

[69] Abbot Emerson Smith, *Colonists in Bondage: White Servitude and Convict Labor in America 1607–1776* (Chapel Hill, 1947), 335. See also Thomas J. Wertenbaker, *The Planters of Colonial Virginia* (Princeton, 1922), 130–31, 134–35; Craven, *White, Red, and Black*, 17.

to keep as slaves black men who arrived in that condition *was* possible and apparently regarded as plain common sense.

The attitude of English officials was well expressed by the attorney who reviewed for the Privy Council the slave codes established in Barbados in 1679. He found the laws of Barbados to be well designed for the good of His Majesty's subjects there, for, he said, "although Negros in that Island are punishable in a different and more severe manner than other Subjects are for Offences of the like nature; yet I humbly conceive that the Laws there concerning Negros are reasonable Laws, for by reason of their numbers they become dangerous, and being a bruitish sort of People and reckoned as goods and chattels in that Island, it is of necessity or at least convenient to have Laws for the Government of them different from the Laws of England, to prevent the great mischief that otherwise may happen to the Planters and Inhabitants in that Island."[70] In Virginia too it seemed convenient and reasonable to have different laws for black and white. As the number of slaves increased, the assembly passed laws that carried forward with much greater severity the trend already under way in the colony's labor laws. But the new severity was reserved for people without white skin. The laws specifically exonerated the master who accidentally beat his slave to death, but they placed new limitations on his punishment of "Christian white servants."[71]

Virginians worried about the risk of having in their midst a body of men who had every reason to hate them.[72] The fear of

[70] CO 1/45, f.138.

[71] Hening, *Statutes*, II, 481–82, 492–93; III, 86–88, 102–3, 179–80, 333–35, 447–62.

[72] For example, see William Byrd II to the Earl of Egmont, July 12, 1736, in Elizabeth Donnan, ed., *Documents Illustrative of the History of the Slave Trade to America* (4 vols., Washington, 1930–35), IV, 131–32. But compare Byrd's letter to Peter Beckford, Dec. 6, 1735, "Letters of the Byrd Family," *Virginia Magazine of History and Biography*, XXXVI (April 1928), 121–23, in which he specifically denies any danger. The Virginia assembly at various times laid duties on the importation of slaves. See Donnan, ed., *Documents Illustrative of the History of the Slave Trade*, IV, 66–67, 86–88, 91–94, 102–17, 121–31, 132–42. The purpose of some of

a slave insurrection hung over them for nearly two centuries. But the danger from slaves actually proved to be less than that which the colony had faced from its restive and armed freedmen. Slaves had none of the rising expectations that so often produce human discontent. No one had told them that they had rights. They had been nurtured in heathen societies where they had lost their freedom; their children would be nurtured in a Christian society and never know freedom.

Moreover, slaves were less troubled by the sexual imbalance that helped to make Virginia's free laborers so restless. In an enslaved labor force women could be required to make tobacco just as the men did; and they also made children, who in a few years would be an asset to their master. From the beginning, therefore, traders imported women in a much higher ratio to men than was the case among English servants,[73] and the level of discontent was correspondingly reduced. Virginians did not doubt that discontent would remain, but it could be repressed by methods that would not have been considered reasonable, convenient, or even safe if applied to Englishmen. Slaves could

---

the acts was to discourage imports, but apparently the motive was to redress the colony's balance of trade after a period during which the planters had purchased far more than they could pay for. See also Wertenbaker, *The Planters of Colonial Virginia,* 129.

[73] The Swiss traveler Francis Ludwig Michel noted in 1702 that "Both sexes are usually bought, which increase afterwards." William J. Hinke, trans. and ed., "Report of the Journey of Francis Louis Michel from Berne Switzerland to Virginia, October 2, (1) 1701–December 1, 1702: Part II," *Virginia Magazine of History and Biography,* XXIV (April 1916), 116. A sampling of the names identifiable by sex, for whom headrights were claimed in land patents in the 1680s and 1690s, shows a much higher ratio of women to men among blacks than among whites. For example, in the years 1695–99 (Patent Book 9) I count 818 white men and 276 white women, 376 black men and 220 black women (but compare Craven, *White, Red, and Black,* 99–100). In Northampton County in 1677, among seventy-five black tithables there were thirty-six men, thirty-eight women, and one person whose sex cannot be determined. In Surry County in 1703, among 211 black tithables there were 132 men, seventy-four women, and five persons whose sex cannot be determined. These are the only counties where the records yield such information. Northampton County Court Records, Order Book 10, 189–91; Surry County Court Records, Deeds, Wills, etc., No. 5, part 2, 287–90.

be deprived of opportunities for association and rebellion. They could be kept unarmed and unorganized. They could be subjected to savage punishments by their owners without fear of legal reprisals. And since their color disclosed their probable status, the rest of society could keep close watch on them. It is scarcely surprising that no slave insurrection in American history approached Bacon's Rebellion in its extent or in its success.

Nor is it surprising that Virginia's freedmen never again posed a threat to society. Though in later years slavery was condemned because it was thought to compete with free labor, in the beginning it reduced by so much the number of freedmen who would otherwise have competed with each other. When the annual increment of freedmen fell off, the number that remained could more easily find an independent place in society, especially as the danger of Indian attack diminished and made settlement safer at the heads of the rivers or on the Carolina frontier. There might still remain a number of irredeemable, idle, and unruly freedmen, particularly among the convicts whom England exported to the colonies. But the numbers were small enough so that they could be dealt with by the old expedient of drafting them for military expeditions.[74] The way was thus made easier for the remaining freedmen to

---

[74] Virginia disposed of so many this way in the campaign against Cartagena in 1741 that a few years later the colony was unable to scrape up any more for another expedition. Fairfax Harrison, "When the Convicts Came," *Virginia Magazine of History and Biography*, XXX (July 1922), 250–60, esp. 256–57; John W. Shy, "A New Look at Colonial Militia," *William and Mary Quarterly*, XX (April 1963), 175–85. In 1736, Virginia had shipped another batch of unwanted freedmen to Georgia because of a rumored attack by the Spanish. Byrd II to Lord Egmont, July 1736, "Letters of the Byrd Family," *Virginia Magazine of History and Biography*, XXXVI (July 1928), 216–17. Observations by an English traveler who embarked on the same ship suggest that they did not go willingly: "our Lading consisted of all the Scum of Virginia, who had been recruited for the Service of Georgia, and who were ready at every Turn to mutiny, whilst they belch'd out the most shocking Oaths, wishing Destruction to the Vessel and every Thing in her." "Observations in Several Voyages and Travels in America in the Year 1736," *William and Mary Quarterly*, XV (April 1907), 224.

acquire property, maybe acquire a slave or two of their own, and join with their superiors in the enjoyment of those English liberties that differentiated them from their black laborers.

A free society divided between large landholders and small was much less riven by antagonisms than one divided between landholders and landless, masterless men. With the freedman's expectations, sobriety, and status restored, he was no longer a man to be feared. That fact, together with the presence of a growing mass of alien slaves, tended to draw the white settlers closer together and to reduce the importance of the class difference between yeoman farmer and large plantation owner.[75]

The seventeenth century has sometimes been thought of as the day of the yeoman farmer in Virginia; but in many ways a stronger case can be made for the eighteenth century as the time when the yeoman farmer came into his own, because slavery relieved the small man of the pressures that had been reducing him to continued servitude. Such an interpretation conforms to the political development of the colony. During the seventeenth century the royally appointed governor's council, composed of the largest property owners in the colony, had been the most powerful governing body. But as the tide of slavery rose between 1680 and 1720, Virginia moved toward a government in which the yeoman farmer had a larger share. In spite of the rise of Virginia's great families on the black tide, the power of the council declined; and the elective House of Burgesses became the dominant organ of government. Its members nurtured a closer relationship with their yeoman constituency than had earlier been the case.[76] And in its chambers Virginians developed the ideas they so fervently asserted in the Revolution: ideas about taxation, representation, and the rights of Englishmen, and ideas agout the prerogatives and powers and sacred calling of the independent, property-holding yeoman farmer—commonwealth ideas.

[75] Compare Lyon G. Tyler, "Virginians Voting in the Colonial Period," *William and Mary Quarterly*, VI (July 1897), 7–13.

[76] John C. Rainbolt, "The Alteration in the Relationship between Leadership and Constituents in Virginia, 1660 to 1720," *William and Mary Quarterly*, XXVII (July 1970), 411–34.

In the eighteenth century, because they were no longer threatened by a dangerous free laboring class, Virginians could afford these ideas, whereas in Berkely's time they could not. Berkeley himself was obsessed with the experience of the English civil wars and the danger of rebellion. He despised and feared the New Englanders for their asociation with the Puritans who had made England, however briefly, a commonwealth.[77] He was proud that Virginia, unlike New England, had no free schools and no printing press, because books and schools bred heresy and sedition.[78] He must have taken satisfaction in the fact that when his people did rebel against him under Bacon, they generated no republican ideas, no philosophy of rebellion or of human rights. Yet a century later, without benefit of rebellions, Virginians had learned republican lessons, had introduced schools and printing presses, and were as ready as New Englanders to recite the aphorisms of the commonwealthmen.

It was slavery, I suggest, more than any other single factor, that had made the difference, slavery that enabled Virginia to nourish representative government in a plantation society, slavery that transformed the Virginia of Governor Berkeley to the Virginia of Jefferson, slavery that made the Virginians dare to speak a political language that magnified the rights of freemen, and slavery, therefore, that brought Virginians into the same commonwealth political tradition with New Englanders. The very institution that was to divide North and South after the Revolution may have made possible their union in a republican government.

Thus began the American paradox of slavery and freedom, intertwined and interdependent, the rights of Englishmen supported on the wrongs of Africans. The American Revolution only made the contradictions more glaring, as the slaveholding colonists proclaimed to a candid world the rights not simply of Englishmen but of all men. To explain the origin of the con-

[77] William Berkeley to Richard Nicolls, May 20, 1666, May 4, 1667, Additional Mss. 28,218, ff.14–17 (British Museum, London).

[78] Hening, *Statutes,* II, 517.

tradictions, if the explanation I have suggested is valid, does not eliminate them or make them less ugly. But it may enable us to understand a little better the strength of the ties that bound freedom to slavery, even in so noble a mind as Jefferson's. And it may perhaps make us wonder about the ties that bind more devious tyrannies to our own freedoms and give us still today our own American paradox.

CHAPTER VI

CONFLICT AND CONSENSUS

✦✦✦✦✦✦✦✦✦✦✦✦✦✦✦✦✦✦✦✦✦✦✦✦✦

Historical understanding of the Revolution has proceeded in a series of reactions, one generation of historians emphasizing problems and espousing views that the previous generation seemed to neglect or reject. One may see the process as simply a seesaw from one side to the other and back again, from a Whiggish, pro-American view to a Toryish, pro-English view, back to a pro-American one, and so on. But actually the movement has not been so simple or so futile. The successive reactions have carried us to new levels of perception. The so-called consensus historians could scarcely have reached their own understanding of the Revolution without attention to the discoveries of the progressive historians who emphasized the internal conflicts of the Revolution. Similarly, New Left historians, while returning to themes of conflict, have also built on the work of those with whom they disagree.

Since the time needed to produce a historian is a good deal less than a lifespan, a lively dialogue has been possible among generations of scholars. As it proceeds, the question of conflict versus consensus will doubtless be left behind as no longer a profitable approach to understanding. But that has not yet *happened, and it seemed to me worthwhile to re-examine the whole question of consensus and conflict during the Revolutionary era in the light of what I had learned in studying freedom and slavery in Virginia. The following essay is the result.**

DURING the past fifteen or twenty years a division has emerged among historians of the American Revolution, a division between those who emphasize the consensus achieved by the revolting colonists and those who emphasize conflicts among them. The division has excited attention and has perhaps been exaggerated because of the special position occupied by the Revolution in our national consciousness. As the noises of the approaching bicentennial grow louder, it is scarcely necessary to point out that most Americans, including historians, seem to think the Revolution was a good thing. If any episode in our past is enshrined in our consciousness, this is it. By consequence any group or cause that can affiliate itself with the Revolution may hope to have some goodness rub off on it. As an example, some of us can remember vividly the campaign of the 1930s to make the Revolution and its Founding Fathers rise to the support of Stalinism. Under the slogan "Communism is twentieth-century Americanism," Washington, Jefferson, and Franklin were enrolled posthumously in the popular front. We have similarly had, long since, Catholic interpretations of the Revolution and Calvinist interpretations, Massachusetts interpretations and Virginia interpretations, and a host of others, each somehow concerned with reflecting American Revolutionary glory on Catholicism or Calvinism, on Massachusetts or Virginia, or whatever.

The alacrity with which the current division among scholars has been recognized, if not promoted, I believe, lies in this sanctifying power of the Revolution and its Founding Fathers. Those who contend that the Revolution bore few marks of

* The essay was presented at a symposium sponsored by the Institute of Early American History at Williamsburg, Virginia, March 12, 1971. It was first published in S. G. Kurtz and J. H. Hutson, eds., *Essays on the American Revolution* (Chapel Hill, 1973), 289–309.

social conflict or social upheaval seem to be denying the blessing of the Founding Fathers to present-day struggles against the establishment, while those who emphasize conflicts seem to be suggesting that conflicts, or at least conflicts against an upper class or established system, are sponsored by the Founding Fathers, consecrated in the fires at Valley Forge. No such power attaches to other episodes in our history. The New Deal, for example, has not achieved sanctifying power in the national memory. Hence no one would think to classify as conservative those historians who deny that the New Deal achieved or aimed at radical social change. But to say that the Revolution did not achieve or aim at radical social change and lacked the conflicts that generally accompany such change is taken as a denial that radical social change is a good thing. Hence those who give the Founding Fathers failing grades as social revolutionaries are greeted, sometimes to their astonishment, as conservative.

But conservative and radical are relative terms, and so are consensus and conflict; and relative terms, if I may be allowed to follow for a moment the logic of Peter Ramus, can be understood only in relation to each other. Those impressed by the achievement of consensus among the revolutionists can scarcely hope to understand the nature of that consensus without understanding the conflicts that had to be overcome or repressed in order to arrive at it. Nor can those who emphasize conflict gauge the force of the movements they examine without considering the kind of consensus that later grew out of those movements or that succeeded in subduing them. Therefore, in attempting to assess the meaning of the American Revolution, it may be worthwhile to survey the various points of consensus and conflict that can be discerned in the Revolutionary period, to weigh their effect on the Revolution, and then to examine the kind of consensus that emerged at the end, even if that consensus is thought to be no more than a sullen acquiescence in the measures of a ruling class.

I

The type of internal conflict that historians have most eagerly searched for among Americans of the Revolutionary period is class conflict. The search is handicapped by a problem of identification. With the struggle of the colonies against the mother country dominating the scene, how does one distinguish a class conflict within that larger conflict?

Not by the side a man chose to support. Although the first historians of the loyalists did assume that they represented an upper if not a ruling class, subsequent investigations have revealed that loyalists, like patriots, were drawn from all classes. That a man sided with the mother country or against her tells us little about his social position. Although it seems altogether likely on the latest evidence that a larger percentage of the well-to-do could be found among the loyalists than among the revolutionists, the Revolution cut sharply across nearly all previous divisions, whether regional, ethnic, religious, or class. It was not a conflict in which one side was predominantly upper class and the other predominantly lower class.

If, then, we look only at one side, at the Americans who supported the Revolution, or who did not oppose it, can we there find that lower-class rebels were bent on the overthrow or reduction of ruling-class rebels? A moment's reflection on the nature of the Revolutionary War may moderate our expectations. The Revolutionary effort against Great Britain tended to suppress or encompass social conflicts. Where it did not, where hostility between social groups rose to a level of intensity approximating that of the conflict with the mother country, one group or the other would be likely to join with the loyalists. Some merchants in New York City, for example, felt that the local Revolutionary leaders threatened their interests more than the mother country did; and similarly some tenant farmers of the Hudson Valley felt more bitter toward their patriot landlords than they did toward king and Parliament. But these men, whether merchants or tenants, by joining the loyalist side deprived themselves of a part in any contest about who should rule at home. Loyalism in this way tended to absorb social groups that felt endangered or oppressed by the Revolutionary party. It operated as a safety valve to remove from the American side men who felt a high degree of social discontent. Or to change the figure, it drew off men at either end of the political spectrum, reducing the range of disagreements. It removed from the scene the intransigents, of whatever persuasion, who might have prevented the achievement of consensus.

Disputes did occur, of course, among those who remained on the Revolutionary side, but the extraordinary social mobility characteristic of eighteenth-century American society usually prevented such disputes from hardening along class lines. Although recent statistical samplings point to a narrowing of economic opportunity in the latter half of the eighteenth century, Americans still enjoyed an upward mobility unknown in other societies. In a land of rising men a political group formed along lower-class lines had little prospect of endurance.

The Revolution probably increased social mobility temporarily both upward and downward, ruining the fortunes of many established families and opening opportunities for speedy ascent by daring upstarts. This very mobility engendered, as it always has, political disputes, but seldom along class lines. An American who had moved up from the lower ranks carried with him the expectation of sharing with those who had already arrived the offices of government traditionally exercised by the economically and socially successful. If he found himself excluded, he could call upon a wide electorate of his former equals but present inferiors to help him achieve the kind of office that they, no less than he, considered proper for successful men. But the fact that the lower ranks were involved in the contest should not obscure the fact that the contest itself was generally a struggle for office and power between members of an upper class: the new against the established. We must be wary of seeing such struggles, like Patrick Henry's successful bid for power in Virginia, as a rising of the oppressed against their masters.

I do not mean to argue that hostility between classes did not exist at all among those who supported the Revolution or that it cannot be discerned or recognized. In the anti-rent riots of 1766, for example, New York tenant farmers expressed a hostility to their landlords that was not entirely absorbed by loyalism after 1775. More than one scholar has found clear expressions of class conflict in the conduct of the war and of politics in Revolutionary New York. But in assessing class conflict as a Revolutionary force, we shall be hard pressed to find many instances outside New York in which antagonism rose to the level of actual fighting or even to openly expressed hostility of the kind that might be expected to lead to fighting.

American social structure was so fluid that to talk about social classes at all in most colonies or states requires the use of very loose economic categories such as rich, poor, and middle class, or contemporary designations like "the better sort" or "the poorer sort," or occupational categories like merchant, planter, lawyer, farmer, artisan, and seaman. Americans were no less skilled than other peoples in measuring the degree of deference due to each of their neighbors for the host of reasons and prejudices that confer honor or contempt on the members of any community. But such distinctions were local, seldom negotiable beyond the neighborhood where a man was known, and not always easy to discern even there.

Nevertheless, one absolute, clearly defined, and easily recognized division did exist, that between freeman and slave. Half a million Americans, perhaps a fifth of the total population, were slaves, and slavery is so direct an assault by one group of men on another that it can properly be considered as a form of class conflict in itself. In the American Revolution, however, slaves were unable to mount any serious uprising against their masters. Although the armies of both sides sooner or later made use of slaves and gave some of them freedom for their services, neither side provided the help necessary for large-scale insurrection. Both felt more need to woo masters than slaves. Perhaps the possibility of insurrection was even lessened by the few efforts of the British to promote it. When Lord Dunmore invited the slaves of Virginia to desert their masters and join his forces, he probably drew off many of the bolder individuals, leaving behind those who were less likely to rise in revolt later. Again loyalism tended to absorb men who might otherwise have directed their energies more radically against a local ruling class.

That the American Revolution did not produce an uprising of the group in colonial society that was most visibly and legally oppressed, and oppressed with the explicit or tacit approval of the rest of the society, is itself an instructive comment on the nature of social conflict and consensus during the Revolution.

The absence of any massive revolt, white or black, may perhaps be put in perspective if we compare the labor force of the Revolutionary period with that of a century earlier, when Bacon's Rebellion had terrorized the first families of Virginia. In the seventeenth century as in the eighteenth the greater part of the colonial labor force, that is, of men who worked for other men, was concentrated in the South and especially in Virginia. In 1676, when Bacon's Rebellion occurred, the laborers were mostly imported servants, English, Irish, Scottish, or Welsh, whose terms of service generally expired when they reached the age of twenty-four. They were imported at the rate of eight hundred to a thousand or perhaps as many as fifteen hundred or two thousand annually; they were mostly male, and they had come in expectation of a better life once their terms of service were up.

For a variety of reasons, in the ten or fifteen years before 1676, Virginia underwent a depression that severely curtailed the opportunities for a newly freed servant to make his way in the world. Tobacco prices were low. Land in the settled areas had been taken up in large quantities by earlier comers, and men either had to rent land at prices that left no room for profit or else they had to move to the frontiers, where Indians mounted guerrilla attacks on them. The officers of government lived high on the hog in spite of depression, by levying high taxes and voting each other generous fees, salaries, and sinecures. The result was the presence of a clearly distinguishable privileged class and a clearly distinguishable lower class, composed not merely of servants who made tobacco for their betters but of former servants who were trying to make it for themselves. These freedmen were likely to be single. They were likely to be without land of their own. But they were not likely to be without guns, especially those who had moved, as many had, to the frontier.

As early as 1673 Governor Berkeley recognized the dangers of this situation. At least one-third of Virginia's militia, he estimated, were single freedmen, who would have nothing to lose by turning their arms against their superiors for the sake of plunder. Three years later, goaded by Indian raids, they did it. Bacon's Rebellion swept across Virginia, starting among the penniless pioneers of the frontier counties and gathering momentum from the adherence of other men who had nothing to lose in a free-for-all scramble for the accumulated wealth of the privileged few. In the midst of it Berkeley wrote to England, understandably raising his estimate of the numbers of the disaffected. "How miserable that man is," he complained, "that Governes a People wher six parts of seaven at least are Poore Endebted Discontented and Armed."

A hundred years later the situation had changed radically in at least one important respect. In the South, where a large labor force still furnished the way to wealth for plantation owners, the laborers were not continually emerging into the status of independent, poverty-stricken, discontented freemen trying to make a start against heavy odds. By the middle of the eighteenth century the majority of the entire labor force in the plantation colonies was held in permanent slavery. The development of slavery is perhaps the key to the consensus that prevailed in colonial America, for slavery meant the substitution of a helpless, closely guarded lower class for a dangerous, armed lower class that would fight if exploited too ruthlessly. The slave had more reason to revolt than the servant or the new freedman. But he was less able to. He had no hope, no rising expectations, and no arms. On top of that he was black. His status in the community was proclaimed by his color and maintained by a tyranny in which white men of all ranks and regions consented and approved. The consensus on which colonial society rested was a racist consensus.

Had the southern plantations not shifted from free to slave labor, had the planters continued to import masses of indentured servants and continued to pour them into their own and other colonies a few years later as indigent freedmen, then the picture of social mobility in the colonial period and of class conflict in the Revolution might have been quite different. The Minutemen of 1775 might have been truly a rabble in arms, ready to turn from fighting the British to fighting their well-to-do neighbors, just as Bacon's men turned from fighting the Indians to fighting Berkeley and his crew. But in the century between 1676 and 1776 the growth of slavery had curbed the growth of a free, depressed lower class and correspondingly magnified the social and economic opportunities of whites. It is perhaps the greatest irony of a Revolution fought in the name of freedom, a Revolution that indeed advanced the cause of freedom throughout the world, that the men who carried it out were able to unite against British oppression because they had so completely and successfully oppressed the largest segment of their own laboring population.

To be sure, there were those among the revolutionists who felt uncomfortable about rebelling against what they chose to call the threat of slavery, while they themselves held some 20 percent of their own population in slavery. But such feelings were translated into legal action only in states where slaves were few in number. Those were not the states where an enslaved labor force grew the country's principal exports. And if northerners freed their own slaves, they did not propose at this time to free their neighbors'. The racial consensus on which colonial society had rested was shaken a little but not broken by the Revolution.

There of course continued to be indentured servants and servants who worked for wages both in the plantation colonies and in the North. But the great majority of men who worked for other men were probably the slaves of the plantation colonies. The growing economy, in spite of periodic depressions

like that of the 1670s, could absorb the number of indentured
servants who turned free each year and could offer most of
them an independent and comfortable if not affluent existence
on the land. Only a small minority fell permanently into the
servant class, like some of the sailors whom Jesse Lemisch has
described, and even they reacted more visibly, violently, and
vociferously against iniquities of the British government than
against whatever oppression was visited upon them by their
compatriots.

In sum, the evidence of Revolutionary class conflict is scanty,
and for good reason. With a majority of laborers in chains and
with the most discontented freemen venting their discontent in
loyalism, the struggle over who should rule at home was unlikely to bear many of the marks of class conflict. Class conflict
was indubitably present, but it did not surface with an effective
intensity until a later day, after the Revolution had built a
consensus that could both nourish and contain it, and after
social, political, and economic change had produced greater
provocations to it.

II

Let us turn now to another kind of conflict that was more in-
tense and also, I believe, more significant for the Revolution. If
we examine the occasions when Americans fought with one
another or came very close to fighting between 1763 and 1789,
excluding battles between loyalists and patriots, we find a
number of episodes, all of them involving men who had moved
from the older coastal regions into the interior: the march of
the Paxton Boys against Philadelphia, the Regulator movement in the Carolinas with its Battle of Alamance, the activities of the Green Mountain Boys in Vermont, the skirmishes of
Pennamite and Yankee in the Wyoming Valley of Pennsylvania, and Shays's Rebellion in Massachusetts. However diverse in immediate cause and attendant circumstance, these
conflicts had one thing in common: they were all manifesta-
tions of the discontent of western settlers or settlers on new

lands against governments dominated by or subservient to the interests of older or eastern regions.

Americans of the Revolutionary period were less successful in repressing sectional conflicts than conflicts arising from class or race. Though this fact is obvious and though the westward movement has received its full share of attention, historians considering the Revolution as a social movement have not always borne in mind two conspicuous conditions of life in eighteenth-century America, conditions that lay at the root of East-West conflict: first, the extraordinary rate of population growth and, second, the abundance of land, unoccupied or only thinly occupied by the native Indians.

Although the rate of population growth in the colonies varied a good deal from place to place and from year to year, the over-all long-range trend is clear. The total population of the thirteen colonies that participated in the Revolution more than doubled every twenty-five years during the eighteenth century. Beginning at about 250,000 in 1700, it rose to over 5,000,000 by 1800. As we learn more about the role of population growth in history, it may ultimately appear that the most significant social fact about America in the eighteenth century was this fearful growth, unlike anything that had been known in Europe in recorded history. Every twenty-five years the colonies had to absorb numbers equal to their total population. The result by the last quarter of the eighteenth century was explosive emigration out of the older settled regions into the West. Consider the westward thrust into the Kentucky-Tennessee area alone: the population there could scarcely have amounted to 10,000 in 1781; by 1790 it had soared to 110,000. If we note that this migration over the mountains in the 1780s by itself dwarfed the so-called Great Migration over the ocean in the 1630s, when probably no more than 50,000 left England for all parts of the New World, if we note also that migration was simultaneously occurring into other western areas, then we may begin to appreciate the magnitude of a western factor in the Revolutionary period.

The westward population explosion probably relieved the East from social conflicts that might have arisen from overcrowding; but it generated other conflicts potentially as dangerous. It set rival groups of speculators into contests for control of the richest western lands, contests that drew in and corrupted state governments and the national government. And it created a bloc of Americans who by moving west acquired different needs and interests from eastern Americans, but who by the same move lost their political ability to make their needs heard or attended to. People moved west so rapidly that even with the best of intentions a government could scarcely have kept up with them in furnishing the town or parish or county organization that formed the units of representation in the legislature. Because representation did not keep up with the expansion of population into new territory, governments remained under the domination of easterners and frequently neglected the needs of westerners. Even where representation was fairly proportioned, the location of the legislature subjected it to eastern influences that could bring it into serious conflict with the West.

Eastern insensitivity to western needs was the source of the Paxton incident, as it had been in part of Bacon's Rebellion. The prime western need in the early years of a settlement was to cope with the Indians, who gathered to attack the invaders of their land. Indian raids were no longer part of life in the East. The very existence of westerners furnished a buffer zone to easterners, enabling them to view the rights and wrongs of the situation with an objectivity that westerners could not achieve or afford. We need not assume that the Paxton Boys were righteous. Benjamin Franklin called them "Christian White Savages," and the epithet was deserved. They were armed thugs, terrorists, murderers; but they were also westerners, and as westerners they had grievances against an eastern-dominated legislature that spent its time arguing about who would pay the bills while it neglected the defense of the frontier.

The Regulator movement represents another phase of the same East-West conflict: the eastern-dominated governments of South Carolina and North Carolina failed to extend the machinery of law enforcement into the West as rapidly as the needs of the settlers required, and so the West took the law in its own hands. In Shays's Rebellion the Shaysites, who also called themselves Regulators, hoped to gain by direct action what the government in Boston had denied them. The Pennamite-Yankee conflict and the activities of the Green Mountain Boys offer a variation on the theme. In these cases two colonial governments, representing different speculative interests, were engaged in a contest for western lands, and the actual settlers fought with each other. The significance of the frontier in early American history, if we may borrow that phrase, was that it kept Americans in conflict. Movement of the exploding population into new lands was continually generating new communities with interests differing from those of the older communities that retained, or at least claimed, control over them.

This kind of internal conflict among Americans was far more visible during the Revolutionary period than was class conflict. Although there were overtones of class conflict in any contest between established eastern interests and the interests of pioneer western farmers, the contest was primarily geographical, created by the problem of stretching the social and political apparatus that bound one group of people to another in the expanding American universe.

That this form of conflict produced more active hostility in the Revolutionary period will seem no more than natural if we view the Revolution itself from the same perspective. The English colonies in America stood to England in the way that the western parts of the colonies stood to the eastern parts, but with even stronger grievances and correspondingly stronger hostility. The institutions that England devised for her overseas emigrants in the wake of the Great Migration were even more inadequate by 1776 than the institutions that they had devised for themselves. While many colonial legislatures had too few representatives from their western areas, Parliament, which could legislate for all the colonies, had not a single representative from them. When the colonists cried out that Parliament without American representatives knew nothing about their needs and had no right to tax them, they spoke to England in the voice of westerners speaking to easterners. In the Declaration of Independence they announced that the social and political bonds that tied them to an eastern government were severed. The American Revolution was itself a revolt of settlers in a new land against a government that by its location and composition could not be properly acquainted with their needs and could not keep up with their growth.

After 1776, in seeking to sustain the new nation they had just proclaimed themselves to be, the Americans had to contain the very force that had impelled their revolt against the mother country. If the colonies could secede from England, the West could secede from the East for the same reasons. The danger was aggravated by the fact that slavery and loyalism, which helped to lower tension between classes, perversely heightened tension between East and West. Since slavery did not move westward as rapidly as freedom, the much higher concentration of slaves in the East served to emphasize the difference in sectional interests. And since loyalism had as much appeal for disaffected regions as for disaffected individuals, it could become a catastrophic ingredient in sectional conflicts. If an entire region became sufficiently hostile to a government dominated by easterners, it might choose to rejoin the mother country. The result, as in the defection of individuals or groups, might be a greater harmony among those remaining. But the defection of a whole region could have jeopardized the viability of the union; and a consensus formed by the secession of all dissident elements would scarcely deserve the name.

The British were not slow to recognize the advantages for them of sectional conflict and kept hoping for it after the war was over. In violation of the treaty they clung to their northwest trading posts, flirted with the disgruntled leaders of Vermont, and made plans for detaching the whole Northwest. Nor was Britain the only recourse for discontented westerners: Spain had eyes on the whole Southwest. She came uncomfortably close to detaching Kentucky when the Spanish minister maneuvered the Continental Congress into what appeared to westerners as a gross display of eastern indifference to western interests. If Congress had actually ratified the Jay-

Gardoqui Treaty, with its seeming recognition of Spanish control of the Mississippi, the Americans who marched across the mountains into Kentucky and Tennessee in the 1780s might well have marched right into the arms of Spain.

In sum, while class conflict tended to be muted during the Revolutionary period by social mobility among whites, by the enslavement of blacks, and by loyalism, sectional conflict was aggravated. The gravest form of sectional conflict was East-West, but it was not the only form. The greater North-South conflict had already cast its ominous shadow in congressional voting alignments, in the uneasiness of both northerners and southerners over the continuance of slavery, and in steps taken toward abolition of slavery in the North, but not in the South. The most farsighted Americans sensed already that North-South differences as well as East-West differences might one day lead to secession. Indeed in the late 1780s so many sectional disagreements were festering that men who had led their states to a united independence fifteen years earlier now predicted the breakup of the American nation.

III

We know that it did not break up. What, then, other than the superior wisdom of the Founding Fathers, prevented the breakup? What sort of consensus enabled Americans to contain not only the immediate threats to their union perceived in the 1780s but also the threats that grew with time from sectional and class conflict? The question in some measure answers itself. The Americans did achieve nationality during the Revolutionary period, and nationalism has proved to be the most powerful, if the least understood, social force of modern times. In the shrinking world of the twentieth century it has often been a sinister force, confining the vision of its devotees to a single country when they should be looking at the entire globe. But for Americans of the Revolutionary period the world was expanding instead of shrinking, and nationalism exerted a cohesive influence among the people of the several states, stretching instead of confining their political horizons. Even Jefferson, whose state loyalties proved particularly strong, urged his fellow Virginians to send their best young men to Congress, so that they could acquire the continental vision early. That vision extended not merely up and down the Atlantic seaboard but westward to the areas where Americans were moving so rapidly in the 1780s. It scarcely occurred to Jefferson that the United States might not one day reach to the Pacific and indeed occupy the whole of North America, and perhaps the Caribbean and South America too. If not everyone felt this way, there were enough who did to give American nationalism an expansive quality and to make her statesmen conscious of the need to retain the westward migrants within the national community.

Nationalism was in itself the strongest force binding Americans of the Revolutionary generation together. Devotion to the nation helped to keep both sides in any conflict on speaking terms, helped to make disagreements negotiable within the framework of national politics, and even made possible the creation of a new and stronger framework in 1787 when the old one proved unsatisfactory. But nationalism was not the only force disposing Americans to bury their conflicts. The racial consensus of colonial times, though challenged and diminished, still prevailed and helped to keep the North-South conflict from coming to center stage. The revolutionists were not prepared to allow the issue of freedom for blacks to threaten the union of whites. By the consent of white Americans the American labor force, concentrated in the South, remained for the most part in slavery, outside the arena where American quarrels and conflicts were expected to take place. Contending factions, whether of class, region, or party, were agreed in not seeking or expecting the participation of men in chains.

The exclusion of most laborers meant that the participants on both sides of any conflict were men who possessed formidable powers, powers that were carefully withheld from slaves. Both sides could negotiate from strength and demand compromise. Although repression might be an effective mode of dealing with discontent or insubordination from slaves, it did not recommend itself as a way of handling men who had the means to fight back either politically or, if necessary, with force. Unlike the peasants of the Old World, Americans, or at least those Americans without black skin, possessed two palpable sources of power: most of them owned the land on which they lived, and a very large number of them owned guns. Land gave them economic and political power; and guns, we may as well admit, gave them firepower.

In the events that led up to the Revolution, England had failed to recognize the strength that these two kinds of power gave to her colonists. The colonists themselves knew at first hand that the ownership of land enabled a man to bid defiance to those who had traditionally controlled society through control of its lands. They had developed a society in which deference to birth and wealth was tempered by constant reminders to the rich and wellborn that their authority rested on the consent of ordinary property owners. Most adult male Americans owned property and could vote for the men who made the laws that affected their property. If they generally voted for a local bigwig, a man who held more property than they did, they did not hestitate to dump him if he neglected their interests. Similarly, within the legislative assemblies lesser men bowed to the leadership of bigger ones. As Robert Zemsky has shown, social status counted for more than seniority in at least one colonial assembly. But when the leaders of the assembly brought in a bill that looked oppressive to the back-benchers, they voted it down and even substituted impromptu measures of their own from the floor.

What alarmed Americans about taxation by Parliament was that they could not vote it down. The program that seemed so conventional and so reasonable from the standpoint of Whitehall appeared to the Americans as a threat to the power that enabled them to direct their own lives. If a legislature to which they elected no member could take their property in taxes, that legislature could ultimately take all their property and reduce them to the impotence of which they had such visible examples in the slaves at their feet. It was consensus on this point that enabled the colonies to unite so suddenly and so successfully againt Parliamentary taxation. The American reaction to Parliamentary taxation seemed to England too hysterical and wicked to be genuine, and her statesmen failed to deal with it adequately, partly because they failed to recognize its existence.

The British failed also to recognize the existence of American firepower. It would perhaps be an exaggeration to say that most Americans had guns and knew how to use them. But it seems likely that nowhere else in the world at the time was there a population so well armed as the Americans. Governor Berkeley had perceived and experienced the implications of this fact in 1676, and as early as 1691 William Blathwayt, the English auditor general for the colonies, who was more conversant in colonial affairs than any other Englishman of the time, recorded with admiration the familiarity of the colonists with guns. "There is no Custom more generally to be observed among the young Virginians," he noted, "than that they all learn to keep and use a gun with a Marvellous dexterity as soon as ever they have strength enough to lift it to their heads." Had Lord North been as keenly aware as Blathwayt of the skills thus acquired he and George III might not have underestimated so badly the American capacity for resistance.

In order to maintain themselves as a single nation, Americans had to recognize the economic power and firepower that Britain ignored. By the time of the Revolution the proportion of the population owning land in the East may have been somewhat reduced from what it had been fifty or a hundred years earlier, but the westerner by definition was a man who had broken out of the limited acreage of the East. Whether or not he held a secure title, he knew how to make his living from the land and to make life uncomfortable for anyone who tried to stop him. And he was even more likely than the easterner to be armed. The westerner in our history has always been a man with a gun. Eastern-dominated governments simply did not have sufficient power of their own in the long run to impose on the West conditions that armed westerners would not agree to, any more than the Continental Congress could have imposed its edicts on the states, as some members proposed, by the use of military force. American nationalism was obliged to start with the assumption that the population was armed and that no group within it, slaves excepted, could be pushed very hard in any direction it did not want to go.

With a population already equalized to a large degree by firepower and economic power, the United States began its independence appropriately with the declaration that all men are created equal. The immediate purpose was to affirm the equality of England's transatlantic colonists with Englishmen in England, who were taxed only by their elected representatives. But the simplicity of the declaration of equality endowed it with a resonance that was momentous for the whole subsequent history of the nation whose existence it announced.

It could not have been predicted at the time that this would become a national creed. The men who adopted the declaration in 1776 would scarcely have been unanimous if they had been obliged to state precisely what they meant by "created equal." Many of them, including the author of the phrase, held slaves. If the preceding analysis is correct, the fact that they were able to unite at all depended in part on their denial of equality to black Americans. Even when applied only to white Americans, the meaning of equality was hardly as self-evident as Congress declared the proposition itself to be. The equality promulgated by the Congress at Philadelphia had no power to dissolve at once the conflicts and tensions in American society. Westerners were obliged for several years to flirt with Spain and England, while eastern speculators, many of them in Congress, quarreled over the profits they hoped to gain from western settlement if the West could be kept under eastern domination. James Madison tried in vain to secure a guarantee in the federal Constitution of the equality of western states. Instead the principle was precariously acknowledged only as a result of a shady bargain during the last weeks of the expiring Continental Congress.

But acknowledged it was in the end. The Northwest Ordinance, by stipulating that western states should be admitted to the union on equal terms with the existing states, saved the nation from future attempts to make subordinate colonists out of its western emigrants. As the revolutionists gradually became aware of the implications of the creed to which they had committed themselves, they also whittled down, albeit even more gradually, the inequities in their laws governing religion, representation, and inheritance. And as the social structure of the nation changed in subsequent generations, Americans probed further into the meaning of equality.

It has generally taken more than the chanting of the creed to bring about the social justice that it promises. Our history is not the chronicle of steady and continuous application of the principle of equality to match the continuous expansion of the population. The reluctance of easterners to grant equal rights to westerners was prophetic of later contests. Those who have claimed the benefits of equality in America have usually had to press their own claims against stubborn opposition. Men with power over other men have often affirmed their dedication to the principle while denying it by their actions, masters denying it to slaves, employers to workmen, natives to immigrants, whites to blacks, men to women.

Is it fair, then, to call this a point of consensus? Was it not mere rhetoric? Perhaps, if by rhetoric is meant the terms on which men can agree to speak together. An alternative rhetoric and an alternative social creed prevailed before the Revolution both in America and Europe and continued to prevail in most of Europe. That creed also offered a way to consensus, but of a quite different sort. It affirmed divine sanction for a social hierarchy in which every man knew his place and was expected to keep it. The old creed was designed to suppress the aspirations of lower classes, to make them content with their lot. Redress of grievances was not impossible, if superiors failed in their acknowledged obligations to inferiors; but the likelihood was much greater that oppression would go unchecked and that resentment would build into an explosive, revolutionary situation before redress could be obtained. The American Revolution itself was brought on by a British minister who had rejected what he called "the absurd opinion that all men are equal." That absurd opinion became the basis of the American consensus that grew out of the Revolution.

It may indeed seem an absurd sort of consensus that rests upon an invitation to conflict. The creed of equality did not give men equality, but invited them to claim it, invited them, not to know their place and keep it, but to seek and demand a better place. Yet the conflicts resulting from such demands have generally, though not always, stopped short of large-scale violence and have generally eventuated in a greater degree of actual equality. After each side has felt out the other's strengths and weaknesses, some bargain, some equivalent to a Northwest Ordinance, is agreed upon, leaving demands not quite fulfilled, leaving the most radical still discontented with remaining inequalities, but keeping the nation still committed to the creed of equality and bound to move, if haltingly, in the direction it signals.

While the creed invites resistance by the oppressed, it also enjoins accommodation by the oppressor. If it is mere rhetoric, it is a rhetoric that has kept conservatism in America on the defensive. The power that the consensus of equality has wielded over the minds of Americans ever since the Revolution is in fact nowhere more clearly exhibited than in the posture it has imposed on conservatism. To Europeans it may seem odd for conservatism to be garbed in the language of human equality, but conservatives in America quickly learned that this was the only acceptable dress in which they could appear in public. In order to argue for special privilege in the United States it was necessary to show—and it sometimes required considerable legerdemain—that special privilege was somehow the outcome of equality or a device to protect equality. John Adams, for example, contended that Americans should reserve a special place in their governments for the rich, the talented, and the wellborn, on the grounds that it was necessary to isolate and thus ostracize and disarm these dangerous men in order to preserve equality. A century later William Graham Sumner argued against every kind of social legislation on the grounds that all Americans were created equal, so that every American who attained wealth and position had done so by his own efforts and therefore deserved to keep what he had earned, while the poor equally deserved their poverty. To aid the poor would threaten equality.

If these arguments today seem ludicrous, it is because conservatism in the United States has often been reduced to the ludicrous by the national commitment to equality. A conservatism based on a more congenial premise can make little headway. When the South, long after the Revolution, attempted to defend slavery on another premise, the attempt generated the greatest crisis American nationality has faced. The resulting conflict did not really destroy the racial consensus among whites and did not achieve equality for Negroes, but it did destroy slavery and it did preserve the national commitment to equality. That commitment is gradually eroding racism. And it continues to serve the oppressed, both black and white, in their efforts to attain what the nation has promised them, just as it also serves to keep most of the oppressed from totally rejecting a society that admits their right to an equal treatment not yet received.

If, then, the American Revolution produced a consensus among the victorious Americans, it was not a static consensus but one with the genius to serve changing times and needs. It was a consensus that invited conflicts and still invites them, a consensus peculiarly adapted to a growing people, a people on the move both geographically and socially. It could not have contained, but it did not produce, the kind of conflict that gaves Charles I his Cromwell. It made instead for a society where a Hamilton had his Jefferson, a Hoover his Roosevelt, and a Nixon—might profit by their example. If this be conservatism, it is radicals who have made the most of it.

CHAPTER VII

CHALLENGE
AND RESPONSE
Reflections on the Bicentennial

❖❖❖❖❖❖❖❖❖❖❖❖❖❖❖❖❖❖❖❖❖❖

The bicentennial has given us all reason to think again about the Revolution. But our response to the occasion has been disappointing. Our commemorative ceremonies with their self-congratulatory pronouncements have been calculated more for complacency than for reappraisal, either of the Revolution or of ourselves. And the filiopietism so evident in our celebratory rhetoric makes a strange contrast to the temper of the men who cast off their mother country to venture down untried paths.

The revolutionists thought a great deal about posterity, and they also thought a great deal about history. They saw themselves at a crucial point in the evolution of human society, at a point where it might be possible to hold on to what was best from the past without being tied to its mistakes. They thought hard about what kind of people they were and what kind of people they might become. And they would scarcely have been happy had they known that their descendants two hundred years later would be so preoccupied with celebration and so little with cerebration. In thinking about the Revolution on its anniversary, I have tried to look again at some of the developments dealt with earlier in these pages. I have attempted in this essay to place them in the context of their innovative daring; for if the Revolution deserves to be celebrated, it is because the men who made it dared to reject what had hitherto been taken for granted.*

IT CAN hardly have escaped the attention of anyone today who reads a newspaper or magazine or who turns on a television set that we have recently begun to celebrate the bicentennial of the American Revolution. The celebration fairly assaults us with medals and medallions, pewter mugs and porcelain plates, bicentennial burgers and John Hancock hot dogs, not to mention lectures by college professors. Since everyone seems bent on celebration, it would be natural to suppose that we all know what it is we are celebrating. And perhaps many of us do. But historians, I think, are not quite so sure as other people. Although it is their business to know about what happened two hundred years ago, I think you might get some widely different answers if you asked a number of them what we are celebrating.

For that matter, if you could ask the men and women who took part in the Revolution, you might get some pretty puzzling answers from them too. John Adams, who took as active a part in it as anyone, once declared that the American Revolution was all over before the Revolutionary War began. "The Revolution," he said, "was in the minds and hearts of the people."[1] The war and the Declaration of Independence were simply the 'outward results of the American colonists' having lost confidence in the government of England and turned their hearts away from England's king. But John Adams's good friend, Benjamin Rush, a Philadelphia physician who also lived through the events and felt his own mind and heart shaped by them, had a different view. He thought

---

* The essay was delivered as a lecture on the Goodyear Fellowship at the Foxcroft School, Middleburg, Virginia, Dec. 4, 1975. It has not previously been published.

1 John Adams, *Works*, C. F. Adams, ed. (Boston, 1856), X, 282.

the Declaration of Independence and the war with England were only the beginning of the Revolution. The "war is over," he said in 1787, "but this is far from being the case with the American Revolution. On the contrary, nothing but the first act of the great drama is closed."[2]

What, then, was the Revolution? And how could two men like Rush and Adams disagree so sharply about it that one thought it was over before the war began and the other thought it had scarcely begun when the war was over? We are almost obliged to conclude that the two men must have been talking about different things. Either that or else one or the other must have been badly confused. And if we look at a broader range of men, those who met in the continental congresses which directed the Revolution, we find contradictions in their collective behavior too. In the first intercolonial congress directed against British taxation, the Stamp Act Congress of 1765, the members took pains in their formal declaration to affirm their abiding loyalty to the king of England.[3] The Continental Congress that met in 1774 to protest against the Coercive Acts made the same affirmations; and a year later, after the fighting had begun at Lexington and Concord, they continued to disavow any desire for independence. In their "declaration on taking up arms," in 1775, drafted by none other than Thomas Jefferson, they expressly stated to the British "that we mean not to dissolve that union which has so long and so happily subsisted between us."[4] But in a little more than a year Jefferson was drafting a declaration of independence to dissolve that long and happy union. And once the declaration was adopted, Americans became as adamant about independence as they had previously been insistent on loyalty. By 1778, England was ready to give them everything they had asked for, short of independence, and sent a peace

[2] D. F. Hawke, *Benjamin Rush: Revolutionary Gadfly* (Indianapolis, 1971), 341.

[3] E. S. Morgan, *Prologue to Revolution: Sources and Documents on the Stamp Act Crisis, 1764–1766* (Chapel Hill, 1959), 62, 64.

[4] Julian Boyd, ed., *The Papers of Thomas Jefferson* (Princeton, 1950–   ), I, 197, 202, 217.

mission to make the offer, but the Americans scarcely gave the offer a hearing. They were now bent on independence, and nothing less would satisfy them.

It would thus seem that the American Revolution *was* a different thing before 1776 than it became after 1776. And indeed revolutions have a way of changing drastically in their ends and objectives once they get under way. Neither the French Revolution nor the Russian Revolution wound up with the results that their original progenitors had aimed at. And while the American Revolution, unlike those revolutions, retained much the same set of leaders throughout its course, the leaders themselves changed and grew in ways that few of them could have anticipated when the quarrel with England began. What started as a protest against British taxation grew into something so large that the men who took part in it could not agree on what it was, something so complex that historians ever since have been arguing about it.

I

It is this very complexity, these seeming contradictions, that actually make the Revolution something worth celebrating and worth thinking about. Perhaps John Adams was right in saying that it took place in the minds and hearts of the people, but he was not right in thinking that it was all over by 1775. It was not over even in his own mind and heart by then. The Revolution was not merely a protest against British taxation. It was not merely the movement for independence that followed that protest. It was much more. It meant different things to different men—and different things to the same men at different times. It was a revolution because it upset men and made them think as they never thought before, made them see things that they never saw before, made possible what had seemed impossible before. It was a revolution because it challenged the human imagination and because Americans responded to the challenge as they have never responded to any subsequent challenge in our history.

But before I go any further, let me explain what I mean by imagination, when I say that the Revolution challenged it. Imagination is a quality on which all thinking persons set a high value but which is not easy to define. Sometimes we call it originality, an ability to see a problem in a new way or to offer a new solution to it. I like to think of it as an awareness that something need not be the way it is, that it might be different, or in the immortal words of *Porgy and Bess,* that "it ain't necessarily so." Few of us have the imagination to pronounce those words in most situations. We tend to take things for granted. We tend to see what we expect to see, and we often see it even when it isn't there simply because we expect it must be there. We sometimes see crime where there is no criminal and peace where there is no peace. Our limited vision, our lack of imagination helps to perpetuate the world as we find it. Perhaps it is just as well that our imaginations are seldom very active, for we gain a certain stability by taking things for granted. But revolutions are made by not taking things for granted. When a whole people suddenly stop taking for granted the institutions under which they have been brought up and begin to think about how else things might be, a revolution is under way and there is no telling where it will stop.

In the American colonies the first protests against British taxation required no use of the imagination. The colonists objected to the stamp tax and the Townshend duties precisely because they were not what Americans had hitherto taken for granted—their exclusive right to tax themselves. The new taxes were innovations, produced by imaginative finance ministers in England, to whom it had occurred that the colonies might offer a fresh source of revenue to the hard-pressed British treasury. The colonists insisted that they merely wanted to keep things the way they were.

It was only as the quarrel progressed and finally came to a showdown that Americans turned to novelty, to independence; and even independence may at first have seemed to many simply a last, desperate means of averting the mother country's innovative attempts to tax them. But once embraced, the idea of independence excited the imagination, and made Americans realize that things they had taken for granted were not necessarily so. From a population of scarcely three million, the challenge of independence generated a galaxy of leaders unmatched in the previous or subsequent history of the country: Franklin, Washington, Adams, Hamilton, Jefferson, Madison, not to mention a host of lesser lights who in any other period would have stood out as giants. By almost any standard that can be devised to measure greatness, the American Revolution produced more great men in public life than all the rest of American history put together. They were great because they had imagination to respond to the challenge of the Revolution.

A few of them, Benjamin Franklin for example, might have achieved a modest renown in any country or any century, but most of them would have been unknown except for the Revolution. John Adams would have been an effective lawyer trying cases in Boston and plowing the profits into his farm in Braintree. George Washington would have been a well-to-do Virginia planter and land speculator whose only distinction would have been the introduction of new English farming methods to Virginia. Thomas Jefferson might have gained a reputation for wide learning, for brilliant conversation, and for constructing amusing gadgets at his Monticello home. Instead, these men became architects of a new nation, a nation with the potential both of dominating the world by its immense power and of liberating the world by teaching men not to take for granted the kings and aristocrats who had ruled them for so long.

The capacity of the Revolution to challenge the minds of men was a source of wonder even at the time. As David Ramsay of South Carolina looked back in 1789, it seemed to him that the Revolution "not only required, but created talents. Men whose minds were warmed with the love of liberty, and whose abilities were improved by daily exercise, and sharpened with a laudable ambition to serve their distressed country, spoke, wrote, and acted, with an energy far surpassing all expectations which could be reasonably founded on their previous acquirements."[5]

We could trace the awakening of the imagination in these men, and show the way in which each of them responded to the challenge that American independence posed, the challenge to look at every part of the world they had known and ask whether it was a good thing, whether it was needed or whether it had served its purpose and should be discarded. But if we did so, I fear we should not get beyond whichever one we started with.[6] Instead, I would like to look at three of the many ways in which the Revolution prompted Americans as a whole to examine and discard the assumptions with which they had grown up, three ways in which they thought new thoughts and built new institutions based on new ideas that would never have occurred to them but for the Revolution.

II

The first of the old ideas to be examined and discarded was the assumption that the American colonists were so diverse and so divided against one another that they would never be able to agree on anything without the superior superintending force of the mother country to hold their varying selfish interests in check. This assumption was as old as the colonies and there was a great deal of evidence to support it. The Puritans had no sooner arrived in Massachusetts than they started expelling each other into Rhode Island, which other New Englanders thenceforth regarded as a sink of iniquity. And the New England view of people outside New England was always less than charitable. John Winthrop noted of a Massachusetts man who had had the bad judgment to move to Virginia that he "was given up of God to extreme

[5] David Ramsay, *The History of the American Revolution* (Philadelphia, 1789), II, 316.

[6] I have discussed the impact of the Revolution on three of them in *The Meaning of Independence: John Adams, George Washington, Thomas Jefferson* (Charlottesville, 1976).

pride and sensuality, being usually drunken, as the custom is there."[7] New England views of Pennsylvania and New Jersey could not be much better, dominated as those colonies were by Quakers, a people for whom the seventeenth-century New Englanders thought hanging was the proper treatment. Besides, the people of Connecticut believed that the northern part of Pennsylvania rightly belonged to them, and in the eighteenth century the Connecticut government organized a township there, whose citizens ultimately engaged in war with the Pennsylvanians. The New Englanders in the Vermont region similarly quarreled with New Yorkers over land titles and developed a bad habit of hoisting New York sheriffs up flagpoles and leaving them there. The New Englanders' feelings about other colonies were returned with interest. Even after the Revolution began, George Washington, trying hard to like the Yankees among whom he had come to recruit his Continental Army and maintain the siege of Boston, found the New Englanders "exceeding dirty and nasty" and bewailed an "unaccountable kind of stupidity in the lower class of these people" as well as the fact that "such a dirty, mercenary spirit pervades the whole."[8]

Before 1765 it had seemed that the only thing that kept the colonists from flying at each other's throat was their common loyalty to the mother country and the restraining hand she exercised upon them. Toward England they showed none of the animosity that they continually vented toward one another. They celebrated the king's birthday like all good subjects and continually sang the praises of the British constitution, which had brought them liberty, prosperity, and happiness without measure, while the benighted subjects of France and Spain, both at home and in the New World, labored under the tyranny of popish superstition and absolute monarchy.

Thus whenever anyone suggested that England's colonies

[7] J. K. Hosmer, ed., *Winthrop's Journal* (New York, 1908), II, 20–21.

[8] J. C. Fitzpatrick, ed., *The Writings of George Washington from the Original Manuscript Sources, 1745–1799* (Washington, D.C., 1931–44), III, 433, 450; IV, 124.

were growing weary of their dependence and might set up for themselves, the thought was sure to be dismissed as visionary. Eventually, yes. A continent could not be expected to remain forever dependent on an island three thousand miles away. But not now, and not for a long time to come. The Americans themselves, when the contest with England began, predicted disaster if the quarrel should be carried to the point where they felt obliged to cut the ties that bound them to England. If the ties were cut, said John Dickinson of Pennsylvania, the result would be "a Multitude of Commonwealths, Crimes, and Calamities, of mutual Jealousies, Hatreds, Wars and Devastations; till at last the exhausted Provinces shall sink into Slavery under the yoke of some fortunate Conqueror."[9] Hence the ardent affirmations of loyalty that accompanied the American protests against British taxes. The colonists did not yet have the imagination to consider seriously the possibility that they might come together and form one people, form a new, independent nation.

It was in the intercolonial congresses of the Revolutionary era that the challenge of working together, thinking together, acting together began to stimulate the imagination of colonial leaders. At the Stamp Act Congress in 1765 the New Englanders were a little surprised to find that southern gentlemen were not always drunk, and the southerners were surprised to find that not all New Englanders were as mean-spirited as they had supposed. And they all surprised each other by agreeing so readily on the principles of their opposition to British taxation.

The Stamp Act Congress was an eye-opener, and the challenge it presented to the conventional view of the colonists' mutual jealousies was widened with the meeting of the First Continental Congress in 1774. Not that sectional jealousies disappeared, then or later, but the men who attended the Congress could perceive the possibility that lay before them of operating for the first time on a continental scale. It had been one of the weaknesses of British rule that it offered no oppor-

[9] Morgan, *Prologue to Revolution*, 119.

tunity for a colonist with political talent to use that talent in contributing to the direction of the great empire that demanded his loyalty. The most that a colonist could aspire to was some office within his own colony, and even there the highest office, that of governor, was usually reserved for an Englishman. At the First Continental Congress men from twelve colonies began to make policy for the whole group, which they then called the United Colonies but which shortly became the United States. They not only adopted numerous resolutions affirming American rights, but they established a policy of non-importation from Great Britain, non-exportation to Great Britain, and non-consumption of British goods. And having adopted the policy they created machinery, in the form of local committees, to enforce it everywhere. They began to act, in other words, like a national government. And the men who participated in the action, including George Washington and John Adams, gained a sense of the larger field of operation that might be opening to men who had the vision to see beyond the borders of their own particular colony. They felt what it might mean for Americans to direct their own affairs together.

Not everyone sensed the opportunity, and even after the Declaration of Independence made it a reality, the sectional jealousies that everyone had previously considered insuperable continued to be potent. After 1776 some of the men of largest vision and influence like Washington, Adams, and Franklin were drawn away from the councils of the new nation to fight the war or to represent the country abroad, seeking aid from the absolute monarchs of France and Spain, whom the colonists had so recently scorned. In their absence the members of Congress lost the boldness and the solidarity displayed in 1776. Voting became increasingly sectional, with northern and southern states arrayed against each other, and the Congress became increasingly timid and ineffective while the individual state governments grew stronger. With the coming of peace the states showed themselves to be no less self-centered and jealous of each other than the old colonial governments had been. But men of imagination, who had felt the stirrings of national pride, were unwilling to let the old prophecy be fulfilled. In Alexander Hamilton's phrase, they had learned to think continentally. It was *not* necessarily so, they had decided, that Americans could not work together and act together as one people. In what has sometimes seemed almost like a conspiracy, they met together at Annapolis and then at Philadelphia to construct a workable government for the whole country.

In creating that government they had to overcome not only local jealousies and local power structures, but a widespread belief that a strong government of continental scope was incompatible with the republican liberty that all Americans had come to cherish. After the Declaration of Independence the people of every state had adopted a republican government, and never seriously considered any other form. But republican government was supposed to be suitable only for small states. When attempted on a large scale, it would either break up into smaller parts or degenerate into tyranny. That, at least, was what the political philosophers said, and no one could point to an example from history to contradict them. Indeed, the progressive debility of the Continental Congress seemed to offer one more demonstration. If there was such a thing as a national republican government in America, it was about to fall apart. And was not the Constitutional Convention an attempt to transform it into a tyranny?

It required high daring for the men at Philadelphia to defy the beliefs that others took for granted and to brave the accusations about what they were up to. They had to overcome not only their own doubts but those of the voters as well. They had to persuade themselves that republican government was not merely possible on a large scale but actually better suited to large countries than to small. By hook or by crook they got the rest of the country to give the idea a try. And then they took charge of the new government, with Washington at the head, for long enough to demonstrate that it could work and would work.

This creation of a new nation from a crowd of quarrelsome colonies was the first great triumph of the imagination in the Revolutionary period. It was also the most obvious, and I have dwelt upon it only to point out that it *was* an achievement of the imagination, an achievement that depended on the ability to see that things need not be the way they were.

III

The second achievement of the imagination that I want to examine had its beginnings in an assumption that was even more deeply rooted in colonial consciousness than the quarrelsomeness of the colonies. This was the assumption that the abundance of land in America and the relative thinness of the population must make manufacturing an unprofitable, uneconomical, and unwise activity for Americans. Labor in America was scarcer than in Europe and accordingly more expensive. But a man, unless somehow bound by law, like a slave, could obtain land easily. And by applying his labor to the land he could live more comfortably and enjoy a much greater independence than he could by selling his labor to someone else. Rather than use his valuable labor to manufacture products whose principal value came from the labor expended on them, it was much more economical for him to grow wheat or corn or tobacco or rice, an activity in which God and the land would do most of the work. Merchants would then ship his produce off to foreign markets where labor was plentiful and cheap and would bring back in exchange the manufactures produced by the foreigners' cheap labor.

The prosperity and success of the American colonies within the British Empire seemed to be ample demonstration of the validity of this assumption. England's commercial policy forbade the colonies to develop manufactures that might compete with those of England and required the colonies to buy their manufactures from England rather than from other European countries. The colonists did not find this policy oppressive, for it directed them to do what they would have done anyhow. The requirement that they purchase manufactures only from England could have encouraged English merchants to charge higher prices than European competitors, but in fact English manufactures were probably as cheap as any, and the colonists wanted no others.

Many of those who participated in the Revolution saw in it no challenge to the assumption that manufacturing would remain uneconomical for Americans. They might wish to do their shopping in other countries as well as in England, but they would still spend their own time most profitably in agriculture. George Washington explained to Lafayette in 1786 that the United States would furnish a market in which French manufacturers would continue to sell their products for as long a time as land in America remained "cheap and plenty, that is to say, for ages to come."[10]

In this prospect Thomas Jefferson found the best insurance that the United States would remain a free country. For he believed that freedom rested on the individual who made his own living on his own land, the independent individual with no employer to coerce him. In Europe the scarcity of land and abundance of people obliged large numbers to live in cities and work for other men. The dependence of these urban workers on their employers was, he believed, the source of corruption and misery, and he rejoiced that in America the plenty of land would prevent manufacturing for the foreseeable future. "While we have land to labour then," he said, "let us never wish to see our citizens occupied at a work-bench, or twirling a distaff. . . . let our workshops remain in Europe."[11]

Although Americans, including the Founding Fathers, were slow to recognize the fact, the Revolution from its earliest stages began to wear away the assumption that it was either necessary or desirable for Americans to keep their workshops in Europe. The initial impulse came from the colonists' decision to bring pressure on Parliament by stopping the purchase of British manufactures. The merchants of the various cities did this in their non-importation agreements against the Stamp Act in 1765 and the Townshend Acts in 1767. The First Continental Congress repeated the tactic in the more

[10] Washington, *Writings*, XXVIII, 519.

[11] Thomas Jefferson, *Notes on the State of Virginia*, William Peden, ed. (Chapel Hill, 1954), 165.

drastic non-importation, non-exportation, non-consumption Association of 1774. In each of these movements the objective was to make Parliament respond to American demands, but that objective was overshadowed almost from the beginning by the means of achieving it. It became patriotic not merely to do without British manufactures but to make your own. Societies to promote spinning, weaving, and knitting were patriotic societies. After the war began, patriotism was reinforced by sheer necessity. Although France supplied much that was no longer available from England, the Americans were obliged to make things for themselves. And by the time the war was over, it had occurred to a number of people that manufacturing might not be an impossible or uneconomical activity for Americans even in peacetime, in spite of their abundance of land.

It took time, however, before most Americans could take this possibility seriously. The efforts toward manufacturing before and during the war had not derived from a belief that manufactures might be economically profitable for Americans. The advocates of home manufactures had urged Americans to make things for themselves or do without because frugality was virtuous and because it would help the Revolutionary cause. "Save your money and you will save your country" had been the slogan. And when the country was saved, when England conceded American independence and peace returned to the land, most Americans assumed that they need no longer do without the things they had formerly bought from Britain. They cast off their homespun clothes, went on a buying spree, and ran up huge bills, which they expected to pay, as of old, from the profits of trade. But they found that many of the pre-war markets for their wheat and corn and cattle were closed to them, because they were no longer part of the British Empire. American merchants sought out new markets for wheat and tobacco and rice, but before any could be found, many Americans went bankrupt and a sharp economic depression settled over the country.

The result was to make Americans think again about the role of manufactures in their lives. Manufactures had been necessary in order to achieve independence. Perhaps they were also necessary in order to maintain independence. Perhaps it was necessary to be independent economically as well as politically. Perhaps the two could not be separated. Even if labor was expensive in America, American manufactures might be worth the extra cost that the high price of American labor entailed, if a more balanced economy would make the country less dependent on the whims of the foreign market.

Many Americans reached this conclusion in the 1780s, and it was a principal factor in the move to establish a stronger national government, capable of regulating American trade with foreign countries, and capable by that regulation of encouraging American manufacturing. But this was still a step away from repudiating the assumption that manufacturing could not be done in the United States cheaply enough to compete with the manufactures of those countries where labor was abundant and cheap. Manufacturing still meant what its name implies, making by hand. And American hands were still scarce.

And yet in less than a century, while American hands were still scarce and American lands were still abundant, the United States became one of the principal manufacturing countries in the world. It required some encouragement from the new national government in the form of customs duties levied on foreign importations, but it also required the imagination of men who were willing to bet that the old assumptions were not necessarily so. By the use of labor-saving devices, they felt, it might just be possible to overcome the handicap of scarce labor in America. The initial source of those labor-saving devices was England, where Richard Arkwright's power frame for spinning thread had come into use just before the Americans broke their ties with the mother country. After the war, as it became apparent how much the spinning frame could do, a few Americans like Moses Brown and the immigrant Samuel Slater sensed the opportunity it presented in a country where labor had always been in low supply. In short order they showed that it was possible to manufacture thread profitably in

America. And quickly the old assumption was turned on its head.

The very fact that labor *was* so scarce in America made labor-saving machinery more attractive to Americans than to Europeans. Americans turned their ingenuity toward more and more ways of making things by machinery. Almost overnight the factory, with its power-driven machines, took a place by the farm as a characteristic American institution. This was not a change that had taken place in the minds and hearts of the people before the war for independence began. It was a response to challenges posed by the Revolution. The first questionings of the old assumptions about America's capacity to manufacture for itself had come with the non-importation agreements. If the Revolution had not followed, it is unlikely that Americans would soon have disputed the policy behind England's Navigation Acts. Manufacturing was tried as a way to independence. It became a way of life as independence challenged the American imagination to make the most of the country's scarcity of labor. What seemed to be an iron law of economics dissolved before the power of the human mind to think it not necessarily so.

IV

A third and final achievement of the Revolution in challenging the minds of men—final only among those I have singled out here—was probably the most far-reaching and lasting in its importance. Even more than the other two, it took on dimensions and implications that stretched beyond the political contest that prompted them all. This was a challenge directed to the old assumption that human safety and divine command alike required men to be divided into serried ranks, each subordinate to the one above it. John Winthrop had intoned the old adage to the first settlers of his colony of Massachusetts Bay while en route aboard the *Arbella*. "God Almightie," he said, "in his most holy and wise providence hath soe disposed of the Condicion of mankinde, as in all times some must be rich some poore, some highe and eminent in power and dignitie, others meane and in subjeccion."[12] Winthrop was a Puritan, but there was nothing particularly Puritan in his statement. It was a commonplace that society could not exist without an ordered hierarchy of social classes. When men did not each have a place and keep to it, society crumbled. As Shakespeare put it,

> Take but degree away, untune that string,
> And, hark, what discord follows!

And we find the idea not merely among those on top, who stood to benefit, but also among those on the bottom. A number of prospective settlers of Virginia were deterred from coming when they heard that the governor of the colony was not to be a member of the nobility but a man of no higher rank than themselves. All men, they said, would willingly obey someone clearly superior to them, but the colony might collapse if the social pyramid lacked a proper top.[13]

A hundred and fifty years later as the colonists began their contest with the mother country, they were still convinced that God and nature required society to be divided into ranks. To be sure, colonial society did not show the same fine gradations that English and European society were supposed to. The colonists in the course of their history had never seen more than one or two members of the English nobility, and even genuine knights, who stood at the bottom of the aristocratic class in England, were a rarity in the colonies. On the other hand, the lowest rank in the American social scale was lower than the lowest rank in England. Roughly 20 percent of Americans at the time of the Revolution were slaves, a status not recognized in English law. The social divisions among the other 80 percent were less sharply defined than in England,

12 Massachusetts Historical Society, *Winthrop Papers* (1930–), II, 282.
13 Susan M. Kingsbury, ed., *The Records of the Virginia Company of London* (Washington, D.C., 1906–33), III, 231.

but it was clear to the people of every colonial community that some of them belonged to what they called the poorer sort, some to the middling sort, and some to the better sort.

When Americans questioned the authority of Parliament to tax them, they had no intention of questioning this basic assumption of social structure. Indeed, the men who spoke for the colonists, the men who had been elected to the colonial representative assemblies and the continental congresses were mainly of the "better sort." In affirming their right not to be taxed by Parliament, they did not say that all men are or ought to be alike or ought to have precisely the same rights. But they did say that Americans ought to have the same rights as Englishmen. And in doing so they perhaps unconsciously began to discount the significance of social class. They did not pretend to be the equals of dukes or earls or marquesses: it was not the special privileges of the nobility that they wanted. What they wanted were the basic, irreducible rights that went with being English, the right above all of not having whatever property belonged to you taken without your consent. The better sort might have more of it to lose than the middling sort and a lot more than the poorer sort, but they could all share in outrage against the attempts of a British Parliament to take what they had. In standing together against the threat from overseas they had to join hands, and the experience tended to break some of the barriers that separated them.

As the quarrel with England deepened, they pushed a step further, to emphasize their rights not simply as Englishmen but as men, to think of what rights might belong to men as men, rights conferred by God and nature on all men. James Otis, responding in 1764 to the first attempts of Parliament to tax the colonies, affirmed that "The Colonists being men, have a right to be considered as equally entitled to all the rights of nature with the Europeans."[14] As the contest progressed, Americans continued to insist that they were the equals of

---

[14] James Otis, *The Rights of the British Colonies Asserted and Proved* (Boston, 1764), 30.

Englishmen and of anyone else. And when they came to declare independence, when they ceased appealing to England and appealed to the world, they had to phrase their appeal in terms not of the rights of Englishmen but of the rights of man.

"All men," wrote Jefferson, "are created equal." It seems unlikely that in 1776 Jefferson or anyone else quite realized how much he had said. He had not in fact said that all men *are* equal, only that they were created that way. But the affirmation was much more than a challenge to the authority of Englishmen to rule Americans. It was a challenge to the imagination to look at society in a new way, a challenge to think whether society might not do better to leave men the way God created them, namely equal, rather than piling the weight of the extravagant few on the shoulders of the many, in the hierarchy of social dignity that men had hitherto taken for granted.

The response to the challenge was immediate, and has continued to affect human relations not only in America but in the rest of the world ever since. The sudden change in American sentiment from loyalty to independence was very largely a response to this challenge. It was the king who had stood at the apex of the social pyramid, and the authority both of king and of Parliament was closely linked to the old assumptions about society. When Americans rejected king and Parliament, they went a long way toward rejecting the hierarchical social structure that went with them. And once rejected, there was no taste for returning, either to the English king or to the kind of society that needs a king. Nothing in the Declaration of Independence specifically rejected monarchy as such. The list of facts submitted to a candid world were all indictments of the "present" king of England. But in basing the Declaration on the premise that all men are created equal, Americans were in fact turning their back not merely on George III but on monarchy and, indeed, on aristocracy. In the first draft of the Articles of Confederation, entered on the journals of Congress only six days after the Declaration of Independence, it was provided that neither the United States nor any individual state should ever confer any title of nobility on anyone. And though another four and a half years passed before the Articles of Confederation, with many revisions, were ratified, this provision was never questioned. It remained in the Articles of Confederation in every draft and from them was carried into the Constitution of 1787.

It did not follow that Americans proposed to drop all social distinctions, or that they even recognized all the inequalities and inequities that lay around them, but they did begin at once to examine some of the implications of the idea that all men are created equal. Their readiness to question old institutions and their eagerness to build new ones on an egalitarian foundation are evident during the 1780s and 1790s in the espousal of reforms that often went beyond anything that has been accomplished since then. In a world that had hitherto been based on the desirability, indeed the necessity, of human inequality, they were trying to determine what should be different in a world based on human equality. Sometimes they carried their thoughts to ludicrous extremes. In Connecticut, for example, when a plague of quack doctors led the more experienced practitioners of medicine to call for a licensing of physicians, to be supervised by doctors who had studied medicine and received university degrees, the proposal met with a spirited opposition from some members of the Connecticut legislature. To require such licensing of physicians, they said, would be to establish an aristocratic corps of doctors. All men ought to be equally free to practice medicine.[15] Fortunately, this view did not prevail. But some ideas that might be equally frowned on today were widely accepted, for example, the idea that property ought to be as equally distributed as possible. When it was proposed during the depression of the 1780s, again in the Connecticut legislature, that there be a moratorium on the payment of debts, the proponents argued that it was necessary in order to maintain a general equality of

15 *New Haven Gazette and Connecticut Magazine,* June 21, 1787.

property. The opponents of the measure did not argue against the desirability of fostering such an equality but rather that a moratorium on payment of debts would not achieve it. Both sides thought equality of property a good thing.[16]

Thomas Jefferson was the most eloquent and most ingenious advocate of measures to secure a basic economic equality among free men. In Virginia he urged, though in vain, that men who had no land be given fifty acres, enough on which to support themselves and their families. Jefferson was particularly concerned to bring about an equality between generations. He secured in Virginia the abolition of primogeniture, by which the eldest son of a family might inherit all of his father's land, and the abolition of entail, by which a man might require this practice to continue through subsequent generations.

Jefferson was never able, however, to gain acceptance of his favorite scheme for securing equality of generations. That scheme was expressed in his maxim that the earth belongs to the living. It was unfair, Jefferson believed, to saddle children with the debts and decrees of their fathers. From life tables he calculated that the majority of people alive in any given year would be dead twenty years later. Therefore any existing public debt or law passed twenty years previously no longer had the consent of the people affected by it. No law, he believed, should be valid beyond twenty years without re-enactment. And no government should be allowed to borrow money without making arrangements to pay it back within twenty years. What the history of the United States might have been like if this principle of equality had ever been adopted is difficult to calculate.

In embracing it, Jefferson saw more of the implications of equality than other men of his own time or of ours. But he did not see some implications that we have since discovered in the idea of human equality. Jefferson, for example, did not show any disposition to include women in the equation. Although he was fond of their company, he was also fond of

16 *Ibid.*, June 21, 28, 1787; *New Haven Gazette* (Meigs, Bowen, and Dana), Sept. 1, 1785; *American Mercury*, April 26, 1787.

reading them little lectures about their proper place being in the home. And when his Secretary of the Treasury, Albert Gallatin, suggested to him that it might be possible for women to be elected to public office in the government, Jefferson thought this an idea for which the public was not yet ready, and added, "Nor am I."[17]

Similarly, in dealing with race and racial slavery Jefferson was not ahead of his time. Indeed, he was behind it. Many other Americans, including some of his fellow Virginians, had found it embarrassing to be fighting for their own freedom and to be affirming that men are created equal, while at the same time holding other men in slavery. Some Virginians freed their slaves, and in most northern states, where the number of slaves was small, the state governments put an end to the institution. Jefferson, too, was embarrassed by slavery, but he did not free his slaves. And though, in disputes with French philosophers, he maintained the biological concept that all men were equally the descendants of a single divinely created pair, he doubted whether the men who now peopled Africa were the equals of those who peopled Europe and America.

The fact that a man like Jefferson, the most brilliant, most imaginative of the Founding Fathers, did not grasp the full implications of the creed he bequeathed to the nation suggests how far the American Revolution had to go. The winning of independence from England was indeed, as Benjamin Rush said, only the first act. The Revolution challenged men to think, challenged their imaginations, and thus made statesmen out of provincial politicians and philosophers out of tinkerers. It denied the assumption that Americans could not work together. It denied the assumption that Americans must be farmers. And it denied the assumption that some men were born to ride booted and spurred over others. Each of these denials brought with it a challenge.

Americans responded to the challenges in the 1780s and 1790s as they have seldom responded since. The Founding

[17] P. L. Ford, ed., *The Writings of Thomas Jefferson* (New York, 1892–99), IX, 7.

Fathers of those days deserve the esteem that has been heaped upon them. They had the imagination to think that things need not be the way they were. And they had the nerve to act as their imaginations directed. But they did leave a number of things for the rest of us to do. If we are to celebrate their achievement in the bicentennial of independence, it should be, I suggest, by continuing to think that things need not be the way they are. The challenge of their history is not to restore the past, but to enliven the imagination, to look at the unwarranted assumptions of our own time and have the nerve to say once more, "It ain't necessarily so."

INDEX

COLONIAL AND REVOLUTIONARY AMERICAN HISTORY IN NORTON PAPERBACK

Eric Robson   *The American Revolution, In Its Political and Military Aspects, 1763–1783*   N382

Charles Royster   *A Revolutionary People at War: The Continental Army and American Character, 1775–1782*   95173

Darrett B. Rutman   *American Puritanism*   N842

Darrett B. Rutman   *Winthrop's Boston*   N627

Peter Shaw   *The Character of John Adams*   N856

R.C. Simmons   *The American Colonies from Settlement to Independence*   998

Abbot E. Smith   *Colonists in Bondage: White Servitude and Convict Labor in America, 1607–1776*   N592

Paul H. Smith   *Loyalists and Redcoats: A Study in British Revolutionary Policy*   N628

Julia Cherry Spruill   *Women's Life and Work in the Southern Colonies*   N662

Thad W. Tate and David L. Ammerman   *The Chesapeake in the Seventeenth Century: Essays on Anglo-American Society and Politics*   956

Robert J. Taylor   *Massachusetts: Colony to Commonwealth*   9396

Frederick B. Tolles   *Meeting House and Counting House*   N211

Arthur B. Tourtellot   *Lexington and Concord*   N194

Alden T. Vaughan   *New England Frontier: Puritans and Indians, 1620–1675*   (Rev. Ed.) 950

Wilcomb E. Washburn   *The Governor and the Rebel: A History of Bacon's Rebellion in Virginia*   N645

Gordon S. Wood   *The Creation of the American Republic, 1776–1787*   N644

Peter H. Wood   *Black Majority: Negroes in Colonial South Carolina from 1670 Through the Stono Rebellion*   N777

Hiller B. Zobel   *The Boston Massacre*   N606

Michael Zuckerman   *Peaceable Kingdoms: New England Towns in the 18th Century*   895